John Ford's *Stagecoach*

Stagecoach is one of the classics of Hollywood cinema. Made in 1939, it
revitalized the Western genre, served as a milestone of John Ford's career,
and made John Wayne a star. This volume offers a rich overview of the
film in essays by six leading film critics. Approaching *Stagecoach* from a
variety of critical perspectives, they place the film within the contexts of
authorship, genre, American history, and culture. Also examined are the
film's commentary on race, class, gender, and democracy, as well as the
film's artistry.

Barry Keith Grant is a professor of film and director of the Graduate
Program in Popular Culture at Brock University. His books include
*The Film Studies Dictionary, Voyages of Discovery: The Cinema of Frederick
Wiseman,* and *Film Genre Reader.*

THE CAMBRIDGE UNIVERSITY PRESS FILM HANDBOOKS SERIES

General Editor: Andrew Horton, *University of Oklahoma*

Each CAMBRIDGE FILM HANDBOOK is intended to focus on a single film from a variety of theoretical, critical, and contextual perspectives. This "prism" approach is designed to give students and general readers valuable background and insight into the cinematic, artistic, cultural, and sociopolitical importance of individual films by including essays by leading film scholars and critics. Furthermore, these handbooks by their very nature are meant to help the reader better grasp the nature of the critical and theoretical discourse on cinema as an art form, as a visual medium, and as a cultural product. Filmographies and select bibliographies are added to help the reader go further in his or her own exploration of the film under consideration.

VOLUMES IN THE SERIES

Buster Keaton's "Sherlock Jr." ed. by Andrew Horton, University of Oklahoma

Spike Lee's "Do the Right Thing," ed. by Mark Reid, University of Florida

Ozu's "Tokyo Story," ed. by David Desser, University of Illinois, Urbana–Champaign

"The Godfather Trilogy," ed. by Nick Browne, University of California, Los Angeles

Hitchcock's "Rear Window," ed. by John Belton

Godard's "Pierrot le Fou," ed. by David Wills, State University of New York, Albany

Buñuel's "The Discreet Charm of the Bourgeoisie," ed. by Marsha Kinder, University of Southern California

Bergman's "Persona," ed. by Lloyd Michaels, Allegheny College

"Bonnie and Clyde," ed. by Lester Friedman

John Ford's
Stagecoach

Edited by
BARRY KEITH GRANT
Brock University

CAMBRIDGE
UNIVERSITY PRESS

PUBLISHED BY THE PRESS SYNDICATE OF THE UNIVERSITY OF CAMBRIDGE
The Pitt Building, Trumpington Street, Cambridge, United Kingdom

CAMBRIDGE UNIVERSITY PRESS
The Edinburgh Building, Cambridge CB2 2RU, UK
40 West 20th Street, New York, NY 10011-4211, USA
477 Williamstown Road, Port Melbourne, VIC 3207, Australia
Ruiz de Alarcón 13, 28014 Madrid, Spain
Dock House, The Waterfront, Cape Town 8001, South Africa

http://www.cambridge.org

First published 2003

Printed in the United Kingdom at the University Press, Cambridge

Typefaces Stone Serif 9.5/13.5 pt. *and* Gill Sans   *System* $\mathrm{\LaTeX\,2_\varepsilon}$ [TB]

A catalog record for this book is available from the British Library.

Library of Congress Cataloging in Publication Data
John Ford's Stagecoach / edited by Barry Keith Grant.
    p.   cm. – (Cambridge film handbooks)
    Filmography:
    Includes bibliographical references (p.) and index.
    ISBN 0-521-79331-9 – ISBN 0-521-79743-8 (pbk.)
    1. Stagecoach (Motion picture)   I. Grant, Barry Keith, 1947–   II. Cambridge
    film handbooks series.
PN1997.S65733 J65   2002
791.43′72–dc21   2002020179

ISBN 0 521 79331 9 hardback
ISBN 0 521 79743 8 paperback

Contents

Acknowledgments and Credits   *page* ix

List of Contributors   xi

Introduction: Spokes in the Wheels   1
Barry Keith Grant

1   ***Stagecoach* and Hollywood's A-Western
    Renaissance**   21
    Thomas Schatz

2   **"Powered by a Ford"?: Dudley Nichols, Authorship,
    and Cultural Ethos in *Stagecoach***   48
    Charles J. Maland

3   **That Past, This Present:
    Historicizing John Ford, 1939**   82
    Leland Poague

4   **"A Little Bit Savage": *Stagecoach* and Racial
    Representation**   113
    J. P. Telotte

5   **"Be a Proud, Glorified Dreg": Class, Gender, and
    Frontier Democracy in *Stagecoach***   132
    Gaylyn Studlar

6   ***Stagecoach* and the Quest for Selfhood**   158
    William Rothman

Reviews of *Stagecoach*   179

Welford Beaton, *The Hollywood Spectator* (February 18,
1939)   179

Frank S. Nugent, *The New York Times* (March 3, 1939)   181

John Mosher, *The New Yorker* (March 4, 1939)   182

Filmography   185

Select Bibliography   233

Index   239

Acknowledgments and Credits

Many thanks to Andy Horton and Beatrice Rehl of Cambridge University Press for their support, encouragement, advice, and patience. Both are a pleasure to work with. I also am grateful to my colleagues in the Department of Communication, Popular Culture, and Film at Brock University, Ontario, for listening to me talk about John Ford. And of course I owe a special debt of gratitude to my family, who helped me balance work with more fuddle.

Quotations from the draft screenplay of *Stagecoach* appearing in Charles J. Maland's essay are part of the John Ford Papers in the Indiana University Library and are used courtesy of the Lilly Library, Indiana University, Bloomington, Indiana.

J. P. Telotte's "'A Little Bit Savage': *Stagecoach* and Racial Representation" is based on material previously published as "A Fate Worse Than Death: Racism, Transgression and Westerns" in *Journal of Popular Film and Television* 26: 3 (Fall 1998): 120–7. Used with permission of *Journal of Popular Film* and Heldref Publications.

Frank S. Nugent's review of *Stagecoach* is reprinted by permission of the *New York Times*.

Stills courtesy of Film Stills Archive, Museum of Modern Art; Jerry Ohlinger's Movie Material Store; and the authors' own collections.

Contributors

BARRY KEITH GRANT is a professor of communication, popular culture, and film at Brock University in Ontario, Canada. He is the author of *Voyages of Discovery: The Cinema of Frederick Wiseman* and *The Film Studies Dictionary* (with Steve Blandford and Jim Hillier) and editor of numerous volumes, including *Film Genre Reader, The Dread of Difference: Gender and the Horror Film*, and *Documenting the Documentary: Close Readings of Documentary Film and Video* (with Jeannette Sloniowski). He is currently editor of the "Genres in American Cinema" series for Cambridge University Press and the "Contemporary Film and Television" and "TV Milestones" series for Wayne State University Press.

CHARLES J. MALAND is Lindsay Young Professor of Cinema Studies in the Department of English, University of Tennessee, Knoxville. He is the author of *American Visions: The Films of Chaplin, Ford, Capra and Welles 1936–1941, Frank Capra*, and *Chaplin and American Culture*, winner of the Theatre Library Association Award in 1990 for best book in the area of recorded performance.

LELAND POAGUE is a professor of English at Iowa State University. He has written books on Frank Capra, Ernst Lubitsch, Billy Wilder, Leo McCarey, and Howard Hawks; is co-author of *Film Criticism: A Counter Theory* (with William Cadbury), and with Kathy A. Parsons of *Susan Sontag: An Annotated Bibliography 1948–1992*; and has edited or co-edited volumes on Susan Sontag and Alfred Hitchcock. His articles have appeared in such publications as *Cinema Journal, CineAction, Post Script, Film Criticism*, and *Hitchcock Annual*.

WILLIAM ROTHMAN is a professor of motion pictures and director of the graduate program in Film Studies at the University of Miami. He is the author of *Hitchcock – The Murderous Gaze*, *The "I" of the Camera*, *Documentary Film Classics*, and *Cavell's The World Viewed: A Philosophical Perspective on Film* (with Marian Keane). His essays and reviews have appeared in numerous journals, and he is editor of Cambridge University Press's "Studies in Film" series.

THOMAS SCHATZ is a professor and chair of the Radio-Television-Film Department at the University of Texas at Austin. He is the author of four books on Hollywood cinema, including *Hollywood Genres*, *The Genius of the System*, and, most recently, *Boom and Bust: American Cinema in the 1940s*. His writing on film has appeared in various publications, including *Film Comment*, *The Nation*, *Premiere*, and the *New York Times*. He teaches and consults frequently throughout the United States and overseas on American film and television, and he also has worked on many television documentaries focusing on the movie industry.

GAYLYN STUDLAR is director of the Film and Video Studies Program at the University of Michigan, Ann Arbor. She is the author of *In the Realm of Pleasure: Von Sternberg, Dietrich, and the Masochistic Aesthetic* and *The Mad Masquerade: Masculinity and Stardom in the Jazz Age* and co-editor of books on John Huston, James Cameron's *Titanic* (1997), and John Ford's Westerns. Her writing has appeared in numerous film journals and in such anthologies as *Screening the Male: Exploring Masculinities in Hollywood Cinema*.

J. P. TELOTTE is a professor of literature, communication, and culture at the Georgia Institute of Technology in Atlanta. He is the author of *Voices in the Dark: The Narrative Patterns of Film Noir*, *Replications: A Robotic History of the Science Fiction Film*, *Dreams of Darkness: Fantasy and the Films of Val Lewton*, and *Science Fiction Film* for Cambridge University Press's "Genres in American Cinema" series. The author of dozens of articles on popular film, he also edited *Beyond All Reason: The Cult Film Experience*.

Introduction
Spokes in the Wheels

THE GOLDEN COACH

A famous passage in Walker Percy's novel *The Movie-goer* testifies to the mythic power of John Ford's *Stagecoach*. As Binx Bolling, Percy's eponymous narrator, confesses:

> The fact is, I am quite happy in a movie, even a bad movie. Other people, so I have read, treasure memorable moments in their lives – the time one climbed the Parthenon at sunrise, the summer night one met a lovely girl in Central Park, and achieved with her a sweet and natural relationship, as they say in books. I, too, once met a girl in Central Park, but it is not much to remember. What I remember is the time John Wayne killed three men with a carbine as he was falling to the dusty street in *Stagecoach*, and the time the kitten found Orson Welles in *The Third Man*.[1]

But in fact Ford does not show us John Wayne as the Ringo Kid killing the three Plummer brothers. After Ringo drops to the dusty street as he fires his three bullets, the film cuts to Dallas (Claire Trevor), showing us her reaction to the gunfire that carries over on the soundtrack, her fear that one of those bullets may have injured or killed Ringo. Bolling remembers – or, more accurately, misremembers by embellishing – the second of *Stagecoach*'s two thrilling climaxes as if he actually saw it. As Ed Buscombe notes about this scene, it is "believable only because we don't actually see it."[2] Bolling's "belief" in the scene is so strong, so etched in his consciousness, that he remembers having "seen" it.

1

This climactic moment from *Stagecoach* reverberates in Bolling's mind because the film is one of most powerful and important instances of the Western myth in the history of the American cinema. Ford's handling of the conventional shootout-on-main-street scene in *Stagecoach* – here, in expressionist evening darkness rather than the more typical high-key daylight at high noon – is characteristic of the entire film. For *Stagecoach* is built upon the numerous established elements of the Western genre, many already familiar enough to have become cliché, but they are imbued with extraordinary depth and admirable artistry throughout. As André Bazin said, *Stagecoach* is "the ideal example of the maturity of a style brought to classical perfection."[3]

There is indeed a fundamental truth to the common claim that *Stagecoach* was the first "adult Western," for the film achieves a fine balance of the genre's specific visual pleasures, the action and *mise-en-scène* that audiences expect from a Western, with generic innovation and authorial expressiveness. *Stagecoach* is frequently cited as the movie responsible for reviving interest in and the production of Westerns, a genre that was dominated by formula B-pictures and singing cowboy serials during the 1930s. Released in the pivotal year of 1939, *Stagecoach* was both a solid commercial hit and a critical success, blazing the trail for the many A-Westerns that would follow for the next two decades. In the opening essay in this volume, Thomas Schatz closely examines *Stagecoach* within the context of a generic cycle that included such other important and contemporary Westerns as Cecil B. DeMille's *Union Pacific* and *Dodge City* with Errol Flynn. Schatz questions the extent to which *Stagecoach* actually influenced the production of these movies or simply anticipated them, but while the film's direct influence on these specific Westerns is debatable, it is clear that Ford's film marks the beginning of the genre's golden age.[4]

Stagecoach's influence on the genre is evident in subsequent Westerns, from Raoul Walsh's *Dark Command* (1940), which reunited Wayne and Trevor on the frontier just a year after they lit out for the territory at the end of *Stagecoach*, to the flat 1966 remake (an idea about as good as remaking Hitchcock's *Psycho*). Ford's film set the stage for all subsequent stagecoach melodramatics, as can be seen, for example, in Martin Ritt's *Hombre* (1967), which deliberately plays off some of the characters and situations in *Stagecoach*. Its influence, in fact, extends well beyond the Western, for *Stagecoach* provided a template for other kinds of action and adventure films as well. In *Raiders of the Lost Ark* (1981), director Steven Spielberg acknowledges *Stagecoach*'s profound influence on subsequent action movies by visually quoting Yakima Canutt's famous riding stunt as an Apache who jumps from his own horse to one of the stage's lead team and then, after being shot by Ringo, hangs briefly from the stagecoach's tongue before dropping under the bolting horses. (Ford maximizes the impact of the stunt by holding his camera, even though it is tracking with the coach and the pursuing Indians, on the action long enough to show Canutt getting slowly to his feet after rolling on the ground so we can see that it was actually he and not a dummy.)

Apart from Orson Welles's famous claim that he saw *Stagecoach* forty times in preparation for making *Citizen Kane* (1941),[5] *Stagecoach*'s influence on popular cinema has been so wide in part because it is an adept generic hybrid, taking elements not only from the Western but from a number of other genres as well. In addition to being a Western, the film also mobilizes elements of the melodrama, the road movie, and the disaster film, particularly those featuring a "ship of fools" format. At the time of its release, *Photoplay* called it "a *Grand Hotel* on wheels."[6] One can already see aspects of *Stagecoach* worked into the adventure film *Five Came Back*, about a group of passengers trying to survive a plane crash in the Amazon, also released in 1939.

As Schatz points out, this omnibus narrative device, which brings together a disparate group of individuals in the context of dramatic action, had already been used in Bret Harte's Western story "The Outcasts of Poker Flat" (1892) almost a half century earlier. Ford directed the screen adaptation of Harte's story in 1919 and used a similar narrative construction years later in *Wagon Master* (1950). That Ford was partial to this type of story (elements of which can also be found in *The Hurricane*, made two years before *Stagecoach*, and *The Grapes of Wrath*, made one year after) suggests how central *Stagecoach* is, not only in the context of the Western and American cinema but also for its director. The omnibus plot allows Ford to explore in the context of the Western such themes as class and social prejudice, community, and democracy and America, themes frequently found in his non-Western films as well.

Released in the same incredibly fertile year that also produced *Drums Along the Mohawk* and *Young Mr. Lincoln, Stagecoach* marked Ford's return after more than a decade to the Western, thus initiating the beginning of the director's mature period and greatest work. Ford acknowledged the importance of *Stagecoach* to his career in *My Darling Clementine* (1946), when a stagecoach travels through the center of the climactic gunfight at the OK Corral, and in the opening of *She Wore a Yellow Ribbon* (1949), which includes a shot of a stagecoach running out of control after an Indian attack in the desert. Years later, a substantial part of the elegiac poignancy of *The Man Who Shot Liberty Valance* (1962) was established by the images of the dusty old Overland coach sitting neglected on blocks inside the train station.

Stagecoach also established Ford's most recognizable authorial marker, for it was the first film he shot in Monument Valley, a remote, picturesque area in the Navajo Indian Reservation straddling the border between Arizona and Utah. Ultimately Ford would shoot a total of nine movies in Monument Valley between 1938 and 1964, working the images of its distinctive contours to the extent that, as Joseph McBride and Michael Wilmington have observed, the place transcends its geographical location to become a "state of mind . . . pointing toward Eternity."[7] Ford's use of Monument Valley is so distinctive that subsequent films containing scenes shot there cannot avoid invoking his name in most viewers' imaginations. In *Stagecoach* Ford counterpoints the epic grandeur of Monument Valley with the personal dramas inside the stage in the film's celebrated alternation between long shots of the coach wending its way through the expansive vistas of Monument Valley and more intimate two-shots and closeups of the characters riding it. For Andrew Sarris, this technique is the essence of Ford's "double vision," his unique ability to capture both the concrete immediacy of the story and its more abstract mythic implications – "both the twitches of life and the silhouette of legend," as he put it.[8]

Stagecoach also made John Wayne a star, one of the most enduring Hollywood has ever produced. Before Ford cast him in *Stagecoach* (over the objection of the producer Walter Wanger, who wanted Gary Cooper), Wayne was churning out B-Westerns for Republic, a lowly Poverty-Row studio. Appropriately, Wayne's first appearance as the

The epic journey of the stagecoach through Monument Valley. (Museum of Modern Art/Film Stills Archive)

Ringo Kid in the film, afoot in the desert, rifle in one hand and saddle in the other, is, as Buscombe notes, "one of the most stunning entrances in all of cinema."[9] Wayne's physical presence, his bearing and gait, seems perfectly to embody Ringo's charming combination of romantic innocence and unwavering toughness. Raoul Walsh earlier had tried to make a star of Wayne in *The Big Trail* (1930), but it was his performance for Ford in *Stagecoach* that elevated the actor to A-level status. Wayne's role as the Ringo Kid established his screen image as the embodiment of rugged American individualism – an image so strong that it informs Wayne's characters in the Westerns he made subsequently both with Ford as well as with other directors such as Howard Hawks (*Red River*, 1948) and Don Siegel (*The Shootist*, 1976), his last film, and even in non-Westerns like the war film *The Fighting Seabees* (1944), the McCarthy-era anti-communist tract *Big Jim McLain* (1952), and the pro-Vietnam *The Green Berets* (1968), which Wayne also directed.

MOUNTING THE STAGE

Stagecoach was Ford's first Western in thirteen years, the first since
3 Bad Men in 1926 and only his second after the epic achievement of *The Iron Horse* in 1924. But it was a film that he very much
wanted to make. Ford purchased the rights for the short story "Stage
to Lordsburg," on which *Stagecoach* is based, by the prolific Western
writer Ernest Haycox, just a few months after it was published in
Collier's magazine in April 1937. The director once suggested to Peter
Bogdanovich that the premise of *Stagecoach* was based on Guy de
Maupassant's story *"Boule de suif "*[10] (literally, "tub of lard"), but
while both narratives share a coach, a prostitute as a central character,
and a strong sense of class difference, Maupassant's story of French
refugees during the Franco-Prussian War bears little resemblance to
the plot of Ford's film.

Unlike most of the films Ford made in the previous decade, which
were studio assignments, *Stagecoach* was from the beginning a personal project for the director. Despite Ford's established reputation
(in the 1930s Ford had directed such prestige pictures as *The Lost
Patrol*, 1934; *The Informer*, 1935; and *The Hurricane*), it took him and
the producer Merian C. Cooper (whose previous credits included co-
directing *King Kong* in 1933) a year to arrange financing for the film.
For most of the decade Westerns were held in low regard by the studios. David O. Selznick, eager to work with Ford, famously dismissed
the script of *Stagecoach* as "just another Western" and refused to produce the film for his company Selznick International. Columbia and
RKO also turned it down, but eventually the project was picked up by
Walter Wanger, a respected independent producer, to be distributed
through United Artists.

The screenplay was written by the important Hollywood screenwriter Dudley Nichols, with whom Ford worked closely. In his essay
in this volume, Charles J. Maland examines the evolution of the script
and its departures from Haycox's story. Some of Ford's additions to
the script were merely pragmatic, such as adding a line spoken by
Buck, the driver (Andy Devine), explaining that he has chosen the
high road to avoid "those breech-clout Apaches," to account for an
overnight snowfall that occurred during shooting. Other changes
were more substantial, however, the most important undoubtedly
being the famous penultimate line spoken by Doc Boone ("Well,

they're saved from the blessings of civilization"), a line that adds considerable ideological ambiguity to the film's message and which for that reason has been the focus of much critical commentary. Maland demonstrates the significant influence of Nichols's liberal political views on the film without denying the considerable influence of the director, particularly in the characters of Gatewood the banker and Doc Boone, both of which have no counterparts in Haycox's story and were invented by Nichols.

Ford apparently decided to shoot *Stagecoach* in Monument Valley after being shown photographs of it by Harry Goulding, one of the first white settlers in the area and the owner of the only trading post and lodge nearby. But filming there offered a serious challenge. According to the director's grandson, Dan Ford:

> . . . in 1938 Monument Valley was an exceptionally difficult place to work. One of the least accessible points in the United States, it was a 200-mile drive over washboard dirt roads from Flagstaff, Arizona. There were no telephones, no telegraphs, and no bridges over the countless streambeds that cut across the single road. At an elevation of almost 5,000 feet, it was bitterly cold in winter and unbearably hot in summer.[11]

Although parts of the 1925 silent Western *The Vanishing American* had been shot in Monument Valley, no sound film had ever been photographed there. But Ford enjoyed shooting in Monument Valley not just because of the picturesque possibilities of the landscape. Leaving Hollywood far behind for distant location shooting may have had pragmatic advantages for the director. By all accounts he was happy to be at a far remove from studio interference; and by filming in a remote, isolated area he was able to establish the kind of close, almost familial working relationship with cast and crew that allowed him to develop his distinctive stock company. Ford also employed Navajos as extras, bit players, and laborers, a practice he would maintain for all the films he would go on to shoot in Monument Valley.

Shooting commenced on October 31, 1938, and lasted until December 23. In addition to the location photography in Monument Valley, exteriors were shot on the Western-town set at Republic and interiors at the Samuel Goldwyn Studio. Ford fended off studio

John Ford on location in Monument Valley shooting *Stagecoach*. (Museum of Modern Art/Film Stills Archive)

interference by shooting sparingly, giving the studio little to re-edit. The film came in at slightly under its less than exorbitant budget of $546,200.[12] *Stagecoach* was previewed on February 2, 1939, at the Fox Westwood Theatre in Los Angeles and given wide release exactly one month later. According to Ronald L. Davis, when the film opened at Radio City Music Hall in New York City, "it did fantastic business and received rave notices."[13] Across the country, reviewers were unanimous in their praise for *Stagecoach*. It was a substantial hit both critically and commercially, grossing more than a million dollars in its first year.[14]

In his contribution to this volume, Leland Poague examines some of the ways in which the film was promoted upon its initial release. Through his examination of contemporary newspaper advertisements, Poague provides an intriguing context for the reception of *Stagecoach* in Ford's earlier pictures, particularly his other two films released later in 1939, *Drums Along the Mohawk* and *Young Mr. Lincoln*. Poague sheds considerable light on how *Stagecoach* would have been read by audiences at the time, and among his surprising conclusions are the extent to which the film was marketed for its multi-generic qualities and the degree of awareness the promotional campaign assumed about not only the director but the film's producer as well.

The National Board of Review rated *Stagecoach* the third best film of 1939, and Ford would win the New York Film Critics Award for best director of the year. *Stagecoach* garnered two Academy Awards, one for Thomas Mitchell for Best Supporting Actor for his portrayal of the drunken Dr. Josiah Boone, and another for Richard Hageman's score, which skillfully interweaves more than a dozen standard folk and popular songs, including Ford's signature tune "Shall We Gather at the River?" Some of these songs function as musical leitmotifs associated with particular characters, as with Stephen Foster's "I Dream of Jeannie with the Light Brown Hair" for the southern lady Lucy Mallory (Louise Platt), while others are connected to the action on the screen, as with "Bury Me Not on the Lone Prairie," which is heard when the stagecoach is shown traveling through Monument Valley. Because Hageman's ability to interpolate popular music into his scores was well suited to the director's mythic folksiness, he provided the music for six more of Ford's films. *Stagecoach* also received Academy Award nominations in five other categories (Best Film, Director, Art Direction, Editing, and Cinematography) but lost, mostly to *Gone with the Wind*.

PRINTING THE LEGEND

Stagecoach tells the story of seven disparate passengers, along with the driver and the marshal riding shotgun, on a perilous journey through the American Southwest aboard a Concord stagecoach in the 1880s. Each of these characters has a personal drama. Dallas is a prostitute who is being forced out of town by conservative moralists, as is Dr. Josiah Boone, an alcoholic; Ringo is an escaped convict bent on revenge against the three men who killed his father and brother, and who falls in love with Dallas; Hatfield (John Carradine) is a former southern aristocrat who, after the Confederacy's defeat in the Civil War, has become a drifting gambler; Mrs. Lucy Mallory (Louise Platt) is a dutiful pregnant wife trying to find her husband, an officer in the cavalry; Ellsworth H. Gatewood (the blustery Berton Churchill) is a bank manager and prominent member of the town of Tonto's business community who is fleeing with embezzled funds; and Samuel Peacock, a timid whiskey salesman (the appositely named Donald Meek), is struggling with his own inclination for self-effacement. Taking these passengers on their dangerous journey from Tonto to Lordsburg is the comical driver, Buck Rickabaugh (Andy Devine), beset by his large Mexican family, and Marshal Curley Wilcox (George Bancroft), torn between his knowledge of Ringo's innate goodness and his duty as lawman.

The stagecoach must travel through territory containing hostile Apaches, forcing the passengers to cooperate and show their mettle in order to arrive at their destination safely. In her essay in this volume, Gaylyn Studlar explores the historian Frederick Jackson Turner's concept of the frontier as democratic "crucible," and how the stage's journey and the changing attitudes and relationships among the characters enact this idea dramatically. Leaving Tonto, the stagecoach stops at the Dry Fork way station (with its famous dinner sequence, discussed here from different perspectives by Maland, Studlar, and William Rothman), Apache Wells (where Mrs. Mallory's baby is born), and the burnt-out Lee's Ferry, after which comes the thrilling chase on the salt flats, followed by the stage's arrival in Lordsburg. On the journey the individuals in the group interact with one another, forming allegiances and animosities, undergoing character development or steadfastly resisting it. As Studlar explains, class barriers are broken down by the immediate demands of frontier survival. The film's characters, on the "stage," with its connotations of a theatrical space, act out the epic drama of defining a communal harmony befitting the peculiar challenges of American democracy. The fact that these otherwise very different characters, a cross-section of American types, are thrown together in the first place is indicative of the democratic promise of the frontier.

The people on the stage travel on an epic journey – physically, from civilization to the wilderness and back to civilization again, and thematically, from Old World values to New World ones (in the movie, from the Oriental saloon in Tonto to the El Dorado saloon in Lordsburg). On the journey, as virtually every commentator of the film has observed, the majestic panoramic shots of the stagecoach at the bottom of the frame, dwarfed by and moving through the

magnificent mesas of Monument Valley, suggest both Turner's notion of the sublime frontier as democratic crucible and the tenuous
vulnerability of nascent civilization in the wilderness. Civilization
ultimately triumphs, as the film imagines the establishment of a virtuous society among the microcosmic group on the stagecoach by
the completion of its journey. The corrupt and selfish Gatewood is
arrested, and class distinctions are erased as Hatfield is killed and
both Mr. Peacock and Mrs. Mallory, who earlier had moved to the
other end of the table at Dry Fork, both acknowledge Dallas ("If you
ever come to Kansas City, Kansas, I want you to come out to see us,"
the wounded Peacock says as he is carried away on a stretcher after
the stage arrives in Lordsburg). In Peter Stowell's nice distinction, the
passengers on the coach must learn to be "truly civilized, not simply
cultured."[15]

According to Janey Place, *Stagecoach* lacks a humanist complexity
that prevents it from being a great work of art largely because it relies
too heavily on generic conventions.[16] Many critics share this view,
especially when comparing *Stagecoach* with later Ford Westerns like
The Searchers (1956). But such a judgment misses both the point and
power of *Stagecoach*, for popular cinema is also artful insofar as it
works as cultural myth, particularly through the ritual repetitions of
genre; and *Stagecoach* specifically is fully aware of itself as a genre film,
right from its opening images of two riders galloping on their horses
in the desert distance and the ominous word "Geronimo" before the
opening fadeout. Yes, the film relies heavily on genre conventions:
Scenes such as the one in the saloon before the climactic showdown,
with the piano player who stops playing with dramatic abruptness
and the mirror taken off the wall and stored temporarily under the
bar, are common to the Western. And just as *Stagecoach* is replete with
narrative conventions of the Western, so the characters are types familiar to the genre. The film's casting, as Buscombe notes, "is virtually
a résumé of western film history."[17] In fact, *Stagecoach*'s reliance on
the familiar types of the genre is one the film's most interesting and
important qualities.

Perhaps Place finds the dramatic contrasts between the film's characters too schematic because, as Buscombe notes, they fall neatly
into pairs.[18] These pairs make for a series of thematic contrasts that
are variations of the essential binary opposition between nature

and culture, wilderness and civilization, that is commonly seen as being the thematic core of the Western.[19] They constitute a dense network in which each of the characters plays off some of the others in telling ways. So, for example, the timid whiskey drummer Peacock is the opposite of the pushy Gatewood, while the respectable officer's wife, Mrs. Mallory, is contrasted with the fallen woman, Dallas. Dallas, in turn, is paired with Ringo in that they are both social outcasts because, as Dallas muses, "things happen." At the same time, Ringo's code of Western justice is set against Hatfield's outmoded code of chivalry. Similarly, Gatewood and Doc Boone are both professional men, both fleeing from the clutches of Mrs. Gatewood (Brenda Fowler), the embodiment of some of those dubious "blessings of civilization." But while the banker is socially respectable but inwardly corrupt and cowardly, the disgraced doctor is inwardly noble, like Dallas and Ringo, showing his true bravery during the Indian attack and later when he takes the shotgun away from Luke Plummer (Tom Tyler) before his showdown with Ringo. Even the cavalry officer, Lt. Blanchard (Tim Holt), a relatively minor character who, as he tells Gatewood, "always follows orders," is contrasted with the more individualist marshal, Curley Wilcox, who bends the letter of the law when he allows Ringo and Dallas to escape across the border rather than take the Kid back to prison.

In *Stagecoach* Ford consistently uses the types and tropes of the Western, but he provides them with a new depth of detail. For example, at one point on their journey when the trail is dusty, Hatfield offers Lucy Mallory a drink of water. The mysterious gambler and the eastern lady are both characters common to the genre, and the canteen is an important icon, or "outer form," of the Western.[20] But Ford adds considerable complexity to the scene as Hatfield pours the drink for Mrs. Mallory from the communal canteen into a silver cup that he produces from his breast pocket. The silver cup provides some background exposition about Hatfield when, in response to Lucy's question, he denies knowledge of the "Greenfield Manor" crest emblazoned on it. Although there is an earlier clue to the gambler's identity (in Dry Fork he tells Lucy that Hatfield is "what I'm called"), but we understand the significance of both scenes only in retrospect, near the end, with Hatfield's dying words ("If you see Judge Greenfield, tell him his son . . ."). Perhaps Hatfield had to flee because of something to do with the Confederacy's defeat in the Civil War ("You mean the war for the Southern Confederacy, sir," he snaps earlier in response to Doc Boone's reminiscing about "the War of the Rebellion"). Or maybe he has had a falling out with his father, been disowned, or possibly dispossessed by carpetbaggers.... And, further, even as the business with the silver cup deepens the character of Hatfield, it also serves as a contrast to both the liquor bottles that Doc Boone swills and to the more egalitarian Western hero, Ringo, who follows by offering a drink from the canteen to "the other lady," Dallas, after Hatfield repockets the silver cup, an obvious social snub to Dallas ("Sorry, no silver cups," says Ringo to Dallas).

If the characters, in Place's words, "fit with contrived perfection into the script,"[21] that is because in *Stagecoach* Ford so perfectly achieved what Tag Gallagher calls the director's "vignette style":

> Through broad playing and multitudes of tics, somewhat in the manner of the British stage or commedia dell'arte, it characterizes instantly and narrates economically. Each shot becomes a vaudeville "turn." Cutting isolates a character within his own "atmosphere," yet juxtaposes him between contrasting shots of others and *their* atmosphere. By rapid passage through a variety of "turns" (shots or scenes)... an entertaining, kaleidoscopic suite of emotions is obtained.[22]

Although Gallagher is speaking here of *Kentucky Pride* (1925), one of Ford's silent films about horse racing, it is a most perfect description of *Stagecoach*. As Rothman notes in his essay in this volume, Gallagher assesses *Stagecoach* as an "extreme application" of Ford's vignette style. Indeed, for Rothman these characters live and breathe, have the same desires and fears as real people. Through a sensitive reading of *Stagecoach*'s editing and *mise-en-scène*, particularly the relay of gazes established by the montage, Rothman captures both the strengths and limitations of the film's female characters.

Auteurs in Hollywood cinema express their vision largely through their shaping of their generic material, and the shaping hand of director John Ford upon the story's generic elements is everywhere evident in *Stagecoach*. So, for example, the scene with the silver cup functions also as part of a network of water imagery in Ford's Westerns, connecting with *3 Godfathers* (1948), in which water is crucial for the survival of the men and the baby left in their charge, and *Fort Apache* (1948), in which Capt. Kirby York (John Wayne) praises the troopers as the ultimate embodiment of tradition and family because they would "share the last drop in their canteens." Similarly, when the baby is born, all the men gather in hushed admiration in a tight circle, a brief but true community. The baby, another element of *Stagecoach* not in Haycox's original story, is always precious for Ford, part of the nuclear family that he cherishes and the promise of the future that is crucial for maintaining civilization. Babies and children appear in numerous Ford films, perhaps most emphatically in *3 Godfathers*, in which a trio of bank robbers comes upon a baby in the desert and become spiritually reborn in their efforts to deliver it safely back to civilization. In *Stagecoach* Ford emphasizes the importance of the baby by inserting a cutaway of the helpless infant in Dallas's arms at the height of the dramatic Indian attack. The elitist characters ultimately accept Dallas because she helped with the delivery and subsequent caring of the newborn infant for its weakened mother.

With its numerous subplots, *Stagecoach* requires two climaxes to resolve all its narrative strands. The exciting pursuit of the stage by the Apaches across the dry lakebed is the first dramatic highpoint, climaxing when the cavalry comes charging to the rescue of the besieged stagecoach in the nick of time, when the group has just run out of ammunition and is about to be overtaken by the renegade Apaches. This in turn is followed by the shootout between the heroic Ringo and the scurrilous Plummer brothers, a showdown presented with enough imagination alone to surpass the climactic showdown of many another Western. The film's predominant sense of closure (despite Doc Boone's line about "the blessings of civilization") offered an upbeat message for prewar America in which evil is punished, heroic virtue triumphs, and an ideal microcosmic democratic community is forged in the process. At once an exciting action film and an ideological tonic, *Stagecoach* offered a particularly welcome mythic vision in an era of rising despots who, like Geronimo in the movie, have "jumped the reservation" by invading neighboring countries.

Yet the actual representation of Geronimo, the renegade Indian now on the warpath, and his Apache band in the film, is itself a complex question. Ford's treatment of Native Americans in his Westerns in general has been a matter of some debate – Sarris asserts that Ford's cavalry movies constitute "a dance of racial triumph and exultation," while Bogdanovich says that the director always treated Native Americans with dignity[23] – and *Stagecoach* is no exception. As J. P. Telotte points out in his essay in this volume, Ford's work encompasses both crass stereotypes and progressive images that challenge racist assumptions. On the one hand, the film presents the Apaches simply as an evil Other. In the film Ford first shows the Apaches by panning across Monument Valley to where they wait quietly in ambush, as if a natural part of the landscape. The film offers no information about them or their motives and reveals nothing of their culture. Consequently, they are like a natural threat to the people on the stage (strengthening *Stagecoach*'s connection to the disaster film), whom we are invited to view, therefore, as "innocent" people under unwarranted attack. When viewers of *Stagecoach* glimpse the burnt body of a woman at the charred ferry station, and when the Apaches attack the stage, they are likely to wonder, along with Nadine Groot in *Red River*, "Why they always want to be burning good wagons fur?" On the other hand, as Telotte argues, the film opens up this seemingly unproblematic perspective by measuring the moral value of the characters on the coach in large part by their response to the threat of the Indians. Ford lets us know at the beginning of *Stagecoach* that, as Dallas says about the intolerant and self-righteous ladies of the Law and Order League, "there are worse things than Apaches." Thus, for McBride and Wilmington, "*Stagecoach* leaves the question of American imperialism, the cavalry vs. the Indians, tantalizingly unresolved."[24]

Still, the Apaches inevitably fail in their attack on the stagecoach because civilization is destined to establish itself on the frontier. And just as certain as the nation's Manifest Destiny, Ringo's personal quest must succeed because it is synonymous with the public good, with moral justice. Curley admits to Buck that the territory definitely would be better off without the Plummers – a judgment that is shown to be entirely correct when we finally see Luke Plummer, a gruff, uncouth cowboy who guzzles his liquor, pushes dance-hall girls around, and intends on taking a shotgun to a showdown. Ringo is able to redeem his outlaw status by simultaneously fulfilling his personal quest for revenge and purging society of an obvious evil.

In so doing, he departs at the end with Dallas, and with the blessing of Doc Boone and the marshal, who bends the law when he lets Ringo go. In the end, Ringo rides out of town, but with a woman, not alone, like Shane; a horseless cowboy at the beginning, now he rides the buckboard, Western icon of family and domesticity (and doctors!). Paradoxically, Ringo seems to escape from society, yet he sets off for his ranch to foster it.

Ringo's quest for revenge, a generic convention since the time of the Beadle dime novels, is never itself questioned, as it is in later psychological Westerns like, say, Fritz Lang's *Rancho Notorious* (1952) and Anthony Mann's *The Man from Laramie* (1955). In short, Ringo is destined to triumph because he is morally right, like America itself. According to Roland Barthes, "the very principle of myth" is that "it transforms history into nature."[25] *Stagecoach* works in this manner in part by suggesting that Ringo's revenge quest is less a matter of personal than divine justice, a fated restoration of an overriding natural order (itself intimated in part by the contemplative grandeur of Monument Valley). Place notices that "There is a feeling of destiny about the gunfight, created by high camera angles and by dark shadows on the three Plummers, which seem to entrap and doom them,"[26] but she finds no thematic significance in this observation. Yet fate permeates the film and is accepted by the characters within the story as part of nature, much like the landscape. Playing poker before the showdown, Luke Plummer draws aces and eights – the "Dead Man's Hand" (a superstition that began with the hand held by Wild Bill Hickok when he was shot in Deadwood on August 2, 1876), acknowledged explicitly by another cowboy in the saloon. Luke's cards foreshadow his fate ("Cash in," he ominously says as he rises from the table), as does the black cat that crosses the path of the brothers when they walk toward their showdown with Ringo. Also, Doc Boone philosophizes about predestination when he muses on the bullet that may be waiting somewhere, sometime, for him; and, of course, the cavalry appears *deus ex machina*, as if in answer to Lucy Mallory's fervent prayers.

In the end, *Stagecoach* asserts that there is no conflict between the moral individual and the demands of society, because moral authority will naturally subsume the legal. In *Stagecoach*, then, Ford takes the advice that will be offered years later by the newspaper editor in

The Man Who Shot Liberty Valance: "When the legend becomes fact, print the legend."

THE NEXT STAGE

In their books on Ford, Andrew Sarris, John Baxter, Peter Bogdanovich, and Joseph McBride and Michael Wilmington all refer to the director as a film "poet." As classic auteurist critics, they depict Ford as a filmmaker whose personal vision transcended the political and cultural contexts in which his films were produced, except as these influences may have been hindrances to the director's intentions. Baxter prefaces his book on Ford with Walt Whitman's ecstatic proclamation that "The United States themselves are essentially the greatest poem," and then on the very first page claims about Ford that "on the level of invention at which he works, ideology is irrelevant."[27] Sarris says much the same thing about *Stagecoach*, specifically making the astonishing claim that the film "does not seem to be about anything by 1939 standards."[28] Conceptualizing Ford in this manner, as a "poet" among auteurs, seems to have discouraged serious critical analysis of his seemingly more routine genre films like *Stagecoach* and *Wagon Master*. Lindsay Anderson explicitly attacks academic Ford criticism for blocking the fundamental pleasures of Ford's films: "We can only pity the critic whose heart cannot leap at the bugle's call" (198) in the work of "one of the great poets of humanity in our time."[29]

But whatever the reason, despite its undisputed importance and the overwhelming praise it has received, *Stagecoach* has been the subject of surprisingly little critical analysis. Edward Buscombe's monograph for the British Film Institute's Film Classics series and a few scattered articles in academic journals constitute the extent of critical writing on the film. The numerous critics who have written on Ford's Westerns have preferred to concentrate their attention on the later Westerns, particularly *The Searchers* and *The Man Who Shot Liberty Valance*. In 1971, a special issue of *Action*, the magazine of the Directors' Guild of America, was devoted to the film, but it consists mostly of reminiscences by members of the cast and crew.[30] Similarly, Nick Browne's oft-cited analysis of the Dry Fork meal scene is really less about the construction of the spectator's point of view and character identification in *Stagecoach* specifically than it is about the general ability of the classic Hollywood cinema to structure point of view and identification.[31]

Until now there has been no critical work on *Stagecoach* remotely comparable to the celebrated detailed analysis of another of Ford's 1939 films, *Young Mr. Lincoln*, by the editors of *Cahiers du cinéma*. But the essays in the present book together constitute the most sustained examination of *Stagecoach* yet produced, demonstrating that, like the more obviously politicized project of *Young Mr. Lincoln*, it too is "heavily determined at every level of its existence."[32] Thomas Schatz contextualizes the film within a network of generic affiliations; Charles J. Maland argues for a collaborative view of the film's authorship, particularly the screenwriter Dudley Nichols; Leland Poague places our understanding of the film, and that of the film's contemporary audience, within the context of the period's exhibition practices and marketing strategies; Gaylyn Studlar examines the film within the context of ideological constructions of the frontier and its preoccupations with distinctions of class and gender; and J. P. Telotte considers the cultural constructions of the film's representation of race.

In the process, *Stagecoach* emerges as a complex interaction of the multiples forces of authorship, genre, history, and culture, at once a product of the American film industry and a work of cinematic art, a movie infused with the elements of genre and the personal expression of its makers. *Stagecoach* may well be, as Bazin said, "like a wheel, so perfectly made that it remains in equilibrium on its axis in any position."[33] But the essays in this book go far in turning the wheels of that coach to reveal the ideological and aesthetic spokes that shape it.

NOTES

1. Walker Percy, *The Movie-goer* (Harmondsworth, UK, and New York: Penguin, 1966), p. 12.
2. Edward Buscombe, *Stagecoach* (London: British Film Institute, 1992), p. 75.
3. André Bazin, "The Evolution of the Western," *What Is Cinema?*, Vol. 2, ed. and trans. Hugh Gray (Berkeley: University of California Press, 1971), p. 149.
4. Buscombe has questioned this received wisdom on the grounds of United Artists' relatively limited promotional abilities compared with the major

studios' and because the films' release dates are close to each other. Buscombe, *Stagecoach*, pp. 83–4.

5. "... John Ford was my teacher. My own style has nothing to do with his, but *Stagecoach* was my movie text-book. I ran it over forty times." Quoted by Peter Cowie, *The Cinema of Orson Welles* (New York: A. S. Barnes, 1965), p. 27.

6. Buscombe, *Stagecoach*, p. 82.

7. Joseph McBride and Michael Wilmington, *John Ford* (New York: Da Capo Press, 1975), pp. 36–7.

8. Andrew Sarris, *The John Ford Movie Mystery* (London: Secker & Warburg/British Film Institute, 1976), p. 85.

9. Buscombe, *Stagecoach*, p. 9. For a discussion of the mythic quality of Wayne's entrance in *Stagecoach*, see my essay "Two Rode Together: John Ford and James Fenimore Cooper," in *John Ford Made Westerns: Filming the Legend in the Sound Era*, ed. Gaylyn Studlar and Matthew Bernstein (Bloomington and Indianapolis: Indiana University Press, 2001), pp. 205–6.

10. Peter Bogdanovich, *John Ford* (Berkeley: University of California Press, 1968), p. 69.

11. Dan Ford, *Pappy* (New York: Da Capo Press, 1998), p. 125.

12. Details of the film's budget are given in Buscombe, *Stagecoach*, pp. 17–19.

13. Ronald L. Davis, *John Ford: Hollywood's Old Master* (Norman and London: University of Oklahoma Press, 1995), p. 101.

14. Tag Gallagher, *John Ford* (Berkeley: University of California Press, 1986), p. 145.

15. Peter Stowell, *John Ford* (Boston: Twayne, 1986), p. 27.

16. J. A. Place, *The Western Films of John Ford* (Secaucus, N.J.: Citadel Press, 1974), pp. 30–8.

17. Buscombe, *Stagecoach*, p. 21.

18. *Ibid.*, p. 47.

19. See Jim Kitses's influential structural analysis of the Western, *Horizons West* (Bloomington and London: Indiana University Press, 1970).

20. Edward Buscombe, "The Idea of Genre in the American Cinema," in *Film Genre Reader 2*, ed. Barry Keith Grant (Austin: University of Texas Press, 1995), pp. 11–25.

21. Place, *The Western Films of John Ford*, p. 33.

22. Gallagher, *John Ford*, p. 35.

23. Sarris, *The John Ford Movie Mystery*, p. 82; Bogdanovich, *John Ford*, p. 94.

24. McBride and Wilmington, *John Ford*, p. 56.

25. Roland Barthes, "Myth Today," in *Mythologies*, ed. and trans. Annette Lavers (New York: Hill and Wang, 1972), p. 129.

26. Place, *The Western Films of John Ford*, p. 35.

27. John Baxter, *The Cinema of John Ford* (New York and London: Zwemmer/Barnes, 1971), p. 9.

28. Sarris, *The John Ford Movie Mystery*, p. 81.

29. Lindsay Anderson, *About John Ford* (New York: McGraw-Hill, 1981), pp. 11, 198.

30. *Action* 6, no. 5 (September–October 1971).

31. Nick Browne, "The Spectator-in-the-Text: The Rhetoric of *Stagecoach*," *Film Quarterly* 29, no. 2 (Winter 1975–6): 26–38.

32. Editors of *Cahiers du cinéma*, "John Ford's *Young Mr. Lincoln*," *Cahiers du cinéma*, no. 223 (August 1970), reprinted in *Film Theory and Criticism*, ed. Gerald Mast and Marshall Cohen (New York: Oxford University Press, 1979), p. 786.

33. Bazin, "The Evolution of the Western," p. 149.

THOMAS SCHATZ

1 *Stagecoach* and Hollywood's A-Western Renaissance

"When the legend become fact," the newspaper publisher famously opines in *The Man Who Shot Liberty Valance* (1962), "print the legend." That sentiment certainly applies in the case of *Stagecoach*, which according to legend singlehandedly resuscitated the Western as a viable A-class Hollywood genre in 1939, elevating it to critical and aesthetic respectability in the process. That legend persists in many quarters, although it has been challenged for decades. More recently, in fact, critics and scholars have come to see *Stagecoach* in far more objective and complex terms with regard to changes not only in the Western at the time but also in the Hollywood film industry at large.

Among the historical facts about *Stagecoach* are these: First, the film was part of a fairly widespread resurgence of the Hollywood A-Western during the prewar era. Various estimates put the output of A-Westerns from 1939 through 1941 at about thirty, with the crop in 1939 also including *Jesse James, Dodge City, Union Pacific, The Oklahoma Kid, Frontier Marshal, Stand Up and Fight, Man of Conquest,* as well as Ford's own *Drums Along the Mohawk.*[1] Second, this A-Western resurgence had less to do with the remarkable vitality of the B-Western at the time (then in its heyday, numbering well over one hundred per annum) than with the currency of other A-class production trends, cycles, and genres, from Technicolor spectacles and "outdoor" pictures to historical costume epics, biopics, swashbucklers, and Foreign Legion films. And third, although *Stagecoach* appeared early in the A-Western renaissance, others like *Jesse James* and *Dodge City* were released at about the same time and were more successful commercially and far more influential in the short term, spawning the dual strain of outlaw biopics and historical epics that dominated the A-Western through the prewar era.

Notwithstanding these facts, however, there is still basis enough for the *Stagecoach* legend. While the film was scarcely an isolated genre phenomenon, it was altogether singular among the era's A-Westerns on several counts – particularly its canny reformulation of B-Western elements, its disdain for historic in favor of more timeless mythic appeals, its renewal of Ford's investment in the genre, and its pronounced long-term impact on the form. Moreover, *Stagecoach* was quite simply an excellent film, the one Western of the period routinely singled out by critics – then and now – as a work of exceptional narrative and cinematic quality. Remarkably, *Stagecoach* was the only Western released from 1939 through 1941 to be nominated for a Best Picture Oscar (in an era when the Academy nominated ten per year) or to be listed among the top ten films by the National Board of Review and the *New York Times*.

This essay aims to reconcile the fact and legend of *Stagecoach*, to assess the quality of the film and to situate it within the larger context of 1939 Hollywood – not only in relation to other key renaissance Westerns but also to the wider genre landscape and the rapidly changing mode of production in the halcyon prewar era. Indeed, the film epitomized classical Hollywood during its so-called golden age, and its production speaks volumes about Ford's career, the status of the Western genre, and the general state of independent production, "prestige" pictures, and the authority of top directors. Thus we begin by charting the creation of the film and the contemporary industry conditions, although the ultimate objective is to examine *Stagecoach* itself as the consummate renaissance Western – as a film in which, as André Bazin so aptly put it, "John Ford struck the ideal balance between social myth, historical reconstruction, psychological truth, and the traditional theme of the Western *mise-en-scène*."[2]

JOHN FORD'S *STAGECOACH*

Bazin's auteurist bias here is reasonable enough. In terms of Ford's own career and the general workings of the industry in the late 1930s, *Stagecoach* was altogether exceptional in its stature as a

"director's film." Ford orchestrated virtually every phase of its development and production, and his creative control proved crucial to
the film's distinctive quality and revitalization of the Western genre.
The nominal producer of *Stagecoach* was Walter Wanger, but he too
endorsed Ford's authorship of the film. Wanger publicly admitted
that he financed the film "without having a hell of a lot to do with
it," and he privately informed a United Artists marketing executive
just prior to its release, "While I am proud to be the producer of
'Stagecoach,' will you please do everything in your power to see that
the picture is known as John Ford's achievement."[3] Dudley Nichols
received sole screenwriting credit for *Stagecoach*, but he actually col-
laborated closely on the script with Ford, whom he told in a personal
note after the successful New York premiere: "If ever there was a
picture that was a director's picture, it was that one."[4] Even the
New York film critics took up the auteurist chant, with Frank Nugent
of the *New York Times* – who later would turn to screenwriting and
in fact would script several of Ford's postwar Westerns – arguing in
a February 1939 column that the cinema was a "director's medium"
and citing *Stagecoach* as a case in point.[5]

The actual development and production of *Stagecoach* support
this view. Ford at the time was under a long-term studio contract (to
20th Century–Fox) that allowed him an occasional "outside" picture
on a freelance basis, and he initially planned *Stagecoach* as an outside project. He paid Ernest Haycox $2,500 for the screen rights to
his short story "Stage to Lordsburg" after it appeared in the April 10,
1937, issue of *Collier's*[6] and then took it to the independent producers Merian C. Cooper and David Selznick. Ford earlier had signed
a two-picture deal with Cooper's Pioneer Pictures, before a merger
with Selznick International Pictures (SIP) transferred the contract to
SIP.[7] Cooper was keen on Ford's Western project, but Selznick balked
because of the uncertain market for A-Westerns as well as Ford's determination to cast John Wayne and Claire Trevor as co-stars. Both
were B-grade players without the "marquee value" that SIP required,
and Wayne carried the added stigma of having starred in *The Big Trail*
(1930), an early sound Western that along with *Cimarron* (1931) had
seriously undermined the A-Western's currency. Selznick pushed for
top stars but really had little faith in the project, insisting that SIP
"must select the story and sell it to Ford instead of him picking some

uncommercial pet of his."[8] Cooper backed Ford, however, dissolving the SIP–Pioneer partnership over the dispute; a short time later, he and Ford decided to create their own independent operation, Argosy Pictures. But the newly formed company was without funding, which left "Stage to Lordsburg" dead in the water.[9]

With his own project stalled, Ford directed *The Hurricane*, an outside picture for Sam Goldwyn, and then two routine action dramas for Fox, *Four Men and a Prayer* and *Submarine Patrol*. But he continued to pitch "Stage to Lordsburg." Darryl Zanuck at Fox passed on the project, as did top executives at Paramount and Warner Bros.[10] – not that they weren't interested in the A-Western. The recent success of Technicolor "outdoor pictures" and two rather conventional A-class Westerns from Paramount in 1936, *The Texas Rangers* and *The Plainsman*, augured the resurgence of the A-Western, and soon several studios joined the pursuit – notably Fox with *Jesse James*, Paramount with *Union Pacific*, and Warner Bros. with *Dodge City*. Rather than take on an outside project like Ford's, these studios clearly preferred to convert their established resources and house styles to the Western genre.

Consider, for instance, the development and production of *Dodge City*, which provides an especially illuminating example of such conversion because Warners, the only major studio besides MGM without a B-Western operation, actually took the lead in the prewar A-Western trend. Moreover, Warners was known for its factory-based operations and its commitment to rigid star-genre formulas, and in fact the studio looked to two other very different genre-bound stars for *Dodge City* before settling on Errol Flynn. The project was initiated (in early 1938) for resident biopic star Paul Muni as a biography of Wyatt Earp. When Muni resisted, deeming the genre beneath his dignity, Jack Warner and production chief Hal Wallis considered a Western reformulation of the studio's signature gangster genre with James Cagney as star. But the producer Robert Lord, who by now (summer 1938) had the film ready for production, insisted that Cagney was "all wrong" and began pushing for Errol Flynn. Flynn at the time was among Warners' biggest and highest-paid contract stars (at $4,500 per week), having surged to stardom in a succession of costume adventure-romances co-starring Olivia de Havilland, including *Captain Blood* (1935), *The Charge of the Light Brigade* (1936), and *Robin Hood* (1938). The last of these was a Technicolor hit and Flynn's first teaming with the director Michael Curtiz, and its success set the stage for *Dodge City* as a Flynn–de Havilland vehicle. Warner, Wallis, and Lord agreed that Flynn's swashbuckling persona was ripe for conversion to the American West while Cagney and frequent co-star Humphrey Bogart were cast in a gangster–Western hybrid, *The Oklahoma Kid*.[11]

The script for *Dodge City* was reworked to feature Flynn as Wade Hatton, a roguish but upright wagon master and trail boss of Irish origin who fought for the Confederacy before coming west. Circumstances in Dodge City induce Hatton to pin on a marshal's badge and clean up the town, winning the heart of de Havilland's independent-minded newspaper reporter in the process. The story ends with the newly wed couple heading farther west for Virginia City, another unruly town in need of law and order. *Dodge City* was shot over a forty-eight-day period from November 1938 to January 1939 on the Warner lot and on location in nearby Modesto at a cost of $910,000.[12] Released in April 1939, four weeks after *Stagecoach*, *Dodge City* was a hit, setting off a quick succession of Warner Bros. films – *Virginia City* and *Sante Fe* in 1940, *They Died with Their Boots On* in 1941 – featuring Flynn as a bona fide Westerner. With his portrayal of George Custer in the latter film, Flynn's star persona was thoroughly Americanized and the studio's transformation of a key star-genre formula was complete.

Ford, meanwhile, managed to sell "Stage to Lordsburg" to Walter Wanger, an independent producer who had a financing and distribution deal with United Artists. Wanger announced the Ford Western project in July 1938, stating publicly that it would be a million-dollar production but securing Ford's assurance that the film would cost half that – and in fact Ford already had budgeted it at $490,700.[13] Once the deal was set, Ford took *Stagecoach* through scripting and production with remarkable speed and efficiency, continuing to maintain complete control over the picture. He went to work on the script with his frequent collaborator Dudley Nichols (in their twelfth teaming as director and writer) while attending to myriad other tasks, from casting and set design to preparing for location work in Monument Valley, Arizona, then a remote and inaccessible area scarcely amenable to movie production.

Nichols and Ford hammered out the screenplay in a few short weeks, an impressive feat given its radical departure from "Stage to Lordsburg." Haycox's spare tale did supply the three plot lines – a stagecoach journey through hostile Indian country, a romance between a cowboy and a whore, and a revenge saga – and provided many of the principals as well. The stagecoach occupants include a driver and his shotgun guard, along with six passengers: the fiancée of a cavalry officer; a whiskey drummer from St. Louis; an Englishman carrying "an enormous sporting rifle"; a "solid-shouldered cattleman"; a gambler; a mysterious blond cowboy, "Malpais Bill" (en route to Lordsburg to "settle a debt" with two men named Plummer and Shamley); and "a girl known commonly throughout the Territory as Henriette" (who "runs a house in Lordsburg"). The threat of Indian attack and budding romance between Bill and Henriette supply most of the dramatic interest, with the attack finally coming just outside Lordsburg. Several passengers are killed in a furious running gun battle, but the stage does "get through" – and without the aid of nearby cavalry units. In Lordsburg, Bill escorts Henriette to her "house," reiterating his intention to marry her while rebuffing her pleas to avoid the showdown. "A man can escape nothing," he says. "I've got to do this. But I will be back." He then goes to meet Plummer and Shamley while the focus remains on Henriette, who hears four gunshots and then (in the words that end the story) sees Bill "coming toward her with a smile."[14]

While preserving Haycox's main story elements and pulp-populist tone, Nichols and Ford substantially altered the ensemble and fleshed out the overall narrative. The whore is unchanged except for her outcast status, but the cowboy becomes an escaped convict and local legend, the Ringo Kid, out to avenge the murder of his kin. The hunter with the large rifle is replaced by Doc Boone, a drunken philosopher who supplies both commentary and comic relief. The shotgun rider is replaced by Curley, a lawman on Ringo's trail who brings legal authority and a complex sense of democracy and justice to the narrative. The upstanding cattleman becomes Gatewood, the embezzling banker. The cavalry officer's fiancée becomes his pregnant wife, Lucy Mallory, whose childbirth substantially changes the story, while her connection with the gambler Hatfield, here a doomed southern gentleman, is far more complex. The whiskey drummer scarcely

changes, except that he now has the alcoholic Doc Boone to con-
tend with. The adjustments in characterization allow for a much
richer narrative, and in fact each of the three main plot lines plays
out quite a bit differently than in the original story, particularly the
cavalry rescue and the lovers' final escape to Ringo's ranch across the
border. Moreover, the film is far more concerned than is Haycox's
story with social class and community, which in many ways become
the central concerns as the narrative develops.[15]

The apparent influences on the Nichols–Ford overhaul of "Stage to
Lordsburg" were many and varied, although the dominant sources
seem to be Ford's previous films. Other influences have been identified over the years, with Ford himself propagating the notion that
the French short story *"Boule de suif,"* by Guy de Maupassant, was an
important inspiration.[16] This scarcely holds up to scrutiny, however, and in fact a more likely and obvious – albeit less impressive –
literary influence was "The Outcasts of Poker Flat," Bret Harte's
classic Western tale (first published in 1892) that Ford had adapted
in 1919 and was remade by RKO as a B-Western in 1937. The
social outcast theme only implicit in Haycox's work is central to
Harte's story (and to *Stagecoach*), and what's more, Harte's outcasts
include a gold-hearted whore, a gentleman gambler, and a crusty
philosopher-drunk – obvious models for Dallas, Hatfield, and Doc
Boone, respectively.[17]

Another model for Doc Boone was the drunken doctor in
Ford–Nichols's most recent collaboration, *The Hurricane*, also played
by Thomas Mitchell. Another film about a disparate group in desper-
ate circumstances, *The Hurricane* is influential in other areas as well.
Stagecoach was often referred to as "a *Grand Hotel* on wheels," write
Joseph McBride and Michael Wilmington, and thus "bears a family resemblance to the popular omnibus films of the 1930s (*Grand
Hotel*, 1932; *Shanghai Express*, 1932; *Lost Horizon*, 1937; *The Lady
Vanishes*, 1938; and the Ford–Nichols collaboration of 1934, *The
Lost Patrol*), in which a colorful collection of characters from different social strata are thrown together in dangerous or exotic
circumstances."[18] *The Hurricane* could be added to the list, not only
as an "omnibus film" but also, like most of those just mentioned, as
a drama of imminent disaster. *The Lost Patrol* is also pertinent here
because it involved a stranded British patrol (during the First World

Stagecoach was like a *"Grand Hotel* on wheels."* (cast publicity photo; collection of the editor)

War) under relentless Arab attack in the Mesopotamian desert who are saved in a last-minute rescue.[19] Nichols and Ford clearly borrowed this motif for *Stagecoach*, although the cavalry-to-the-rescue angle had been a Western cliché since the early silent era.[20]

Another blatantly derivative aspect of *Stagecoach* involves the interplay of casting, characterization, and B-Western convention. As Ed Buscombe has shown, "Ford's casting in *Stagecoach* is virtually a resumé of Western film." The signal example, of course, is the Ringo Kid, clearly modeled on John Wayne's B-Western persona, but other instances abound. Tim Holt, who played the cavalry officer, was the son of veteran B-Western star Jack Holt. Francis Ford, John's older brother and his mentor as a director of silent Westerns, played the proprietor of the Dry Fork station – a drinking companion for Doc whose few scripted lines were cut (by brother John during production). And Berton Churchill, who made a career of playing arrogant blowhards, was ideal for Gatewood's blustering pro-business, anti–New Deal conservative. Even more to the point,

Churchill had portrayed an embezzling banker in the 1933 B-Western *Frontier Marshal.*[21]

Ford's use of B-Western icons was a key factor in keeping the budget down, although even the top talent involved worked for less than their usual fee. Nichols earned $20,000 for his screenplay, and Ford allowed himself only $50,000 for directing – well below his norm, although Wanger did agree to add 20 percent of any net profits. The entire cast cost only $80,000, with Wayne by far the lowest paid of the principals – at $3,000, less than one-tenth of Flynn's earnings from *Dodge City*. Claire Trevor parlayed her recent success in *Dead End* (1937) into a $15,000 salary, and Thomas Mitchell earned $10,000. Another economy measure was the schedule, with Ford planning the shoot for only thirty-three working days, with three days for travel despite the remote location. He also planned to do much of the studio-based work on the Republic lot, where he could work quickly and cheaply.[22]

Ford and Nichols finished a first draft in early October, then revised as Ford completed pre-production. Principal photography commenced in late October, on location in Monument Valley. This was Ford's first use of the locale, and thus he had not yet established a routine for working at – or even getting to – the Arizona location. But production there went fairly smoothly, and after two weeks the company returned to Hollywood. By then it was apparent that the talent involved, the quality of the script, and the project's ties to Ford's earlier films had put him in a "comfort zone" that enabled him to work with remarkable ease and confidence. He liberally revised the script during production, cutting dialogue to create a more "economic" (his term) drama and to enhance Wayne's performance, but also adding bits of action or dialogue when inspiration or necessity warranted it.[23] One such instance was the final exchange between Doc and Curley about the runaway lovers' being "saved from the blessings of civilization" and their ensuing decision to have "just one" drink – a coda worked out between Ford and Mitchell on the set that adds immeasurably to the story (more on this later). Production closed with the Indian attack, the only real action sequence in the entire film, which Ford shot on a dry lake near Victorville, California, relying heavily on the seasoned Western stuntman (and his second unit director) Yakima Canutt.[24]

The picture wrapped on December 23, only four days behind the thirty-three-day shooting schedule. The one phase of production that Ford did not closely control was editing, but he deemed that unnecessary. Dorothy Spencer, an editor on *Stagecoach*, later said that Ford "cut in the camera. He got what he wanted on film, and then left it to the cutter to put it together. Unlike most other directors, he never even went to the rushes."[25] A sneak preview in early February at the Fox Westwood Theatre went extremely well, as did premieres in New York and Los Angeles later in the month. By then the film's cost exceeded Wanger's half-million-dollar ceiling – just barely at $531,374 – but with a hit on his hands he was scarcely complaining. *Stagecoach* went into widespread release in early March and was a sizable commercial hit, with net revenues of $1.1 million in 1939 alone, thus giving Ford a good deal more via his profit participation deal than he had earned in salary.[26]

THE A-WESTERN AND HOLLYWOOD'S GENRE LANDSCAPE

With the early-1939 release of *Jesse James*, *Stagecoach*, and *Dodge City*, the A-Western renaissance was underway, and in the ensuing stampede of big-budget Westerns, the narrative and thematic contours of the revitalized genre quickly took shape. It's remarkable, in fact, how rapidly the A-Western trend developed and the range of films, Western and non-Western alike, that contributed to that development. The trade and popular press fueled the trend, not only in gauging its popularity but also in providing a template of sorts for both the industry and the audience to identify and assess the trend. What passed for genre analysis in the press and trade discourse was superficial at best, however; only much later would critics and scholars really glean the contours and complexities of the A-Western renaissance.

Judging from both the trade and popular press, the A-Western stampede caught the industry unawares. *Variety* in its January 1939 survey of the industry, for instance, clearly did not detect the coming trend. One article noted that "the public appetite was ripe for more pictures of the spectacle, outdoor type," especially historical epics and biopics,[27] and another identified the only significant Western trend as "guitar strumming and vocalizing dude cowpokes" – that

is, singing cowboys.[28] This view typified the press discourse just before the A-Western stampede, although a few observers did sense the
prospect of the genre's resurgence. In late December 1938, Douglas
W. Churchill wrote a *New York Times* piece on Hollywood's "New
Series of Grand (Horse) Operas." Providing an inventory of the A-class
Westerns then in development or active production, Churchill stated:
"Most of the pictures are worthy; all provoke more than casual
interest."[29] The point is well taken, although the typical use of the
term "horse opera" suggests an obvious stigma, a guilt-by-association
with the B-Western and particularly the ubiquitous singing cowboy
films.

That stigma would vanish in the coming weeks and months with
the A-Western onslaught. January 1939 saw the release of *Jesse James*
and *Stand Up and Fight* (MGM's epic saga of the Cumberland Gap
starring Robert Taylor). February saw the New York and Los Angeles
premieres of *Stagecoach*, which went into widespread release in March
along with *The Oklahoma Kid*. In April came *Dodge City, Man of
Conquest* (Republic's "near-A" biopic of Sam Houston), and *The Return
of the Cisco Kid* (Fox's revival of the series starring Warner Baxter).
DeMille's *Union Pacific* was released in early May, and by that point
the trend clearly had reached critical mass, and the Western genre
had reestablished its cultural and industrial currency. In fact, the
press discourse already had changed noticeably after the release of
Stagecoach. A *Variety* piece in early March, "Pic Cycle on Horseback,"
noted that the output of "major budget Westerns" was greater than
anything "the picture business has witnessed in a decade." It was a
"toss up" in *Variety*'s view whether *Union Pacific* or *Jesse James* had
"revived the cycle," but "it did not take long for the other studios to
fall in line."[30] Days later in the *Times*, Frank Nugent wrote, "We've
formed the habit of taking our horse operas in class B stride. . . . But all
that has changed now. The horse opera is on its high horse" – thanks
largely, said Nugent, to *Stagecoach*, "one of the best horse operas ever
filmed."[31]

Critics were understandably dubious at the prospect of Flynn and
Cagney as Westerners. Nugent's March 1939 review of *The Oklahoma
Kid* in the *Times*, for instance, wrote that Cagney on horseback "is
almost the only thing that distinguished his film" from the usual
gangster melodrama. Still, "there's something entirely disarming

about the way he tackled horse opera, not pretending for a minute to be anything but New York's Jimmy Cagney all dressed up for a dude ranch." The following day, in a general piece on the A-Western resurgence, Nugent wrote: "Errol Flynn, in spite of his training in piracy, Robin-Hooding and being a perfect specimen, is going to look mighty strange on a bronco's back in 'Dodge City.' "[32] Nor was Nugent impressed with *Dodge City* when it was released in early April. His review praised Curtiz's direction as "flawless part by part" but criticized the film's lack of "dramatic unity" and dismissed is as "merely an exciting thriller for the kiddies." Other critics (and later historians and film scholars) would be kinder, and the public clearly was taken with the film and Flynn's performance. *Dodge City* was Warner Bros.' second biggest money-maker in 1939 at $1.5 million in revenues, on a par with *Jesse James*, and it vaulted Flynn into the exhibitors' poll of top ten box-office stars.

The A-Western surge was further fueled by a heavily publicized trend toward "location premieres," lavish world premieres of prestige pictures that highlighted their status as both historical spectacle and vintage Americana. The premieres of *Dodge City* in its namesake Kansas town and of *Union Pacific* in Omaha helped spark this trend, and in fact *Stagecoach* was among the few 1939 A-Westerns that enjoyed a more customary world premiere in New York City.[33]

As the A-Western resurgence progressed, critics began to note the distinct strains and subgenres involved, although these generally were posited in vague association with other prestige forms – principally the biopic, the costume drama, and the historical epic. Only in retrospect would critics and film scholars begin to distinguish the dominant strains and cycles that both informed and developed within the A-Western renaissance. Among the first of these were George N. Fenin and William K. Everson in *The Western* (first published in 1962), who saw the A-Western surge in 1939–40 as a distinct extension of the "renaissance" of the historical epic in the mid-1930s. For Fenin and Everson, the epic impulse continued in "the tremendous upsurge in historical Westerns" like *Dodge City* and *Union Pacific*. Even more important in their view was "the cult of the outlaw," a distinctive amalgam of historical epic, biopic, and gangster film. This strain was spurred by Henry King's "somewhat pedestrian but enormously successful" *Jesse James*, leading to the 1940 sequel, *The Return of Frank James*, and a rush of biopics portraying the James Gang, the Daltons, Billy the Kid, Belle Starr, and various other Western outlaws. While *Stagecoach* clearly displays elements of both strains, Fenin and Everson regarded the film as "overrated" and far more important "in the development of Ford than in the development of the Western itself."[34]

Fenin and Everson may have misjudged *Stagecoach*, but their view of the A-Western's dual trajectory during the prewar renaissance would shape the general reading of the genre for decades to come. Few critics and scholars have gone beyond their same level of generalization, however, with the notable exception of Richard Slotkin in his monumental *Gunfighter Nation: The Myth of the Frontier in Twentieth-Century America*. After acknowledging his debt to Fenin and Everson, Slotkin advances and substantially refines their analysis of the historical epic and outlaw Westerns, then challenges their view by noting a "third type" – a strain "promulgated in John Ford's *Stagecoach*, . . . the antithesis of both the progressive epic and the Cult of the Outlaw, since it eschews the insistent historicism of those forms for the formal austerity and poetic allegory of the W. S. Hart tradition." Slotkin suggests the terms "classical" or perhaps "neo-classical" to identify this type, "because of its knowing use and modernistic adaptation of traditional and relatively 'archaic' styles and story-structures."[35]

Whereas *Stagecoach* in Slotkin's view was shaped mainly by Western genre traditions, he views the epic and outlaw strains as exemplary forms of genre blending, cross-fertilization, and recombination. He deems the historical epic the "most imposing and important" of the "new Westerns," because it "inherited the market niche" of the historical romance and epic biopic. Two crucial historical events endlessly reworked in this epic Western strain are the Indian Wars of the 1870s and '80s and the building of the transcontinental railroad. Another key genre development in the mid-1930s involved the "Victorian Empire" film, a sort of world-scale Western in which the civilized world is threatened by marauding foreign savages. In Slotkin's view, films like *Lives of a Bengal Lancer* (1935), *The Charge of the Light Brigade* (the 1936 Flynn–de Havilland film), and Ford's *Wee Willie Winkie* (1937, with Shirley Temple as mascot to a British unit in India) are essentially Westerns in exotic masquerade, "well designed to absorb the concerns and symbols associated with the Myth of the

Frontier and the Western and to recast them in a new, more exotic and spectacular and even more timely disguise."[36]

This view is consonant with Tino Balio's study of 1930s Hollywood, *Grand Design*. Balio argues that the reformulation of the Western "costume-adventure" cycle was motivated by the failure of epic-scale Westerns in the early 1930s and later by the deepening foreign crises, especially in England. He also notes that the surge of Americanism later in the decade, along with the increasingly troubled European marketplace, induced Hollywood to return to the American West as the preferred site of its epic spectacles.[37] But it is worth noting that even as the A-Western renaissance took hold, the Victorian Empire cycle enjoyed a surge of its own in 1939 with *Gunga Din*, *Beau Geste*, *Stanley and Livingstone*, and *The Four Feathers*, with the last three of these released in the same week (in August 1939).

Meanwhile, epic Westerns in the tradition of *Dodge City*, *Union Pacific*, and Ford's *Drums Along the Mohawk* (November 1939) celebrated America's past as crucible for current events and, in the process, became increasingly political and progressive. "True to the canons of the 'historical romance,' 'costume epic,' and 'bio-pic,'" writes Slotkin, "the ideological thrust of these films is relentlessly 'progressive' in its reading of history, celebrating all persons, tendencies, and crises that yield higher rates of production, faster transportation, more advanced technology, and more civilized forms of society."[38] *Dodge City* celebrates the spread of civilization via not only commerce and technology, but even taxation and government regulation, all facilitated by Flynn's Wade Hatton in his capacity as lawman. Indeed, a crucial ideological move here is the utter subordination of the hero's rugged individualism – Hatton's past as expatriate Irishman and former Confederate soldier – to the collective good of corporate capitalism, civic order, and domesticity. Hatton's decision at film's end to "tame" Virginia City comes at the behest of civic leader Colonel Dodge on behalf of the mining interests of that community, and only after Hatton is given explicit permission by his bride (de Havilland), herself now dutifully committed to patriarchy.

While Flynn's maverick nature was channeled into pro-social action in *Dodge City* and subsequent historical epics, *Jesse James* provided something of an antithesis. "The new 'outlaw Western' addressed the dark side of progressive history which the epic evaded or subsumed," writes Slotkin, "and which had hitherto been the province of the gangster film."[39] And in much the same vein, Ed Buscombe notes: "Besides the triumphalism of conquest and empire-building, there is another tradition in the Western, the tradition that in the legend of Jesse James supports the poor sharecroppers against the banks and railroads."[40] Both underscore the fact that the outlaw strain of A-Westerns was keyed to the same historical events, conditions, and iconography as the progressive epics but formulated a systematic critique of progress and a celebration of the renegades who opposed it. Indeed, the protagonists in these films invariably turn outlaw as the direct result of some egregious personal or familial assault by corrupt local agents of powerful institutions such as the government, the railroad, and the banks. In *Jesse James* and *The Oklahoma Kid*, for instance, the hero "goes bad" because of the murder of an upstanding parent, which provides not only strong motivation but also considerable audience empathy and the prospect of redemption.

This prospect is not realized in *Jesse James* or many other outlaw biopics, because of their basis in not only historicized legend but also in the gangster genre. The historical and structural cross-fertilization between the Western and gangster genres is a complex affair – far more complex than is suggested by the routine dismissal of *The Oklahoma Kid* as simply a gangster film in Western garb. The gangster film was undergoing a surge of its own in the late 1930s, thanks in part to motifs borrowed from the Western – most notably, the hero as "good-bad man" in the William S. Hart mold. Moreover, gangster sagas like *They Made Me a Criminal* (1939) and *High Sierra* (1940) depict the hero's quest for freedom and redemption via excursions outside the urban jungle and into a revitalizing wilderness that invokes the Old West.

The complex symbiosis of gangster and Western outlaw is also evident in the prewar rise to stardom of Henry Fonda in *Jesse James* (second billed to Tyrone Power), and then in the three films that Ford directed immediately after *Stagecoach*: *Young Mr. Lincoln, Drums Along the Mohawk* (both 1939), and *The Grapes of Wrath* (1940). By the time he played the lead in *The Return of Frank James* (1940), Fonda not only was a top star but had developed a persona that effectively amalgamated the gangster and outlaw types, and the epic figure as well. Slotkin aptly notes that Fonda's portrayals of Frank James and Tom Joad coalesce into "a single heroic figure agrarian, Lincolnesque, a fugitive and an outlaw – who is finally able to articulate the social and political meaning for which the outlaw has been a metaphor."[41] Fonda's performance and emergent persona noticeably distinguish *The Return of Frank James* from its precursor, as does Fritz Lang's more somber, unsentimental direction and the story's looser ties to history and biography. As Lang himself said at the time, the Western "is not only the history of the country, it is what the saga of the Nibelungen is for the European" – that is, a foundation myth and epic revenge saga endlessly reworked, retold, and reinvented. In this sense, *The Return of Frank James* owes less perhaps to *Jesse James* than to *Stagecoach*, that earlier saga of an outlaw-hero's quest for redemption and revenge.[42]

STAGECOACH: THE RENAISSANCE WESTERN *PAR EXCELLENCE*

The ultimate accomplishment of *Stagecoach*, simply stated, is its deft synthesis of the epic-historic and outlaw-biopic strains of the renaissance Western, yet without the claims to novelty, historical validity, and critical respectability of films like *Jesse James* and *Dodge City*. On the contrary, *Stagecoach* presents itself from the outset as utterly conventional, unabashedly mythic indeed, positively antique and as audience-friendly as the pulp story that inspired it. The resulting paradox, of course, is that *Stagecoach* has come to stand as the most original, socially astute, and formally accomplished of Hollywood's new breed of A-Westerns.

   While Ford's shrewd use of genre convention is crucial to the film's appeal, it does raise interesting questions about the presumed genre literacy of the audience in 1939, given the limited play of A-Westerns at the time. The majority of first- and second-run moviegoers in 1939 – that is, those who saw movies in downtown urban theaters – were likely to be semi-literate at best in terms of Western genre convention. The singing cowboy had expanded the genre's clientele, mainly because of its appeal to women (as well as to men and boys), but still the genre's circulation was limited mainly to subsequent-run theaters in small towns and rural areas. Thus urban audiences may have seen *Stagecoach* as even more novel than the epic and outlaw A-Westerns, given the ties of the latter to other prestige cycles. That doesn't change the derivative, recombinant, and convention-bound nature of Ford's film, however. From casting and characterization to plot structure and theme, virtually nothing in *Stagecoach* is actually new, not even the use of Monument Valley. Yet Ford manages to use convention and cliché in the service of a narrative that, in the words of McBride and Wilmington, "defined Western archetypes and created a new frame of reference rich in irony and sophistication."[43] A consummate case of revitalizing a long-established but moribund form, *Stagecoach* is at once a product of other Westerns, of other Ford films, and of other genres, while also standing as an internally coherent and organic work unto itself – a far cry, finally, from the blatantly synthetic, patchwork pastiche of films like *Dodge City* and *Union Pacific*.

Using genre convention as narrative shorthand, Ford creates a story of remarkable economy, efficiency, and simplicity. The film's opening immediately establishes these qualities. Notably devoid of even a dateline after the credits, let alone the elaborate historical exposition featured in *Jesse James* and *Dodge City, Stagecoach* begins with stark understatement. Two riders in the distance, bare specks on the vast desert landscape, approach the camera. A series of dissolves takes them into a cavalry camp and a telegraph office, where a group of men receive a single coded word before the lines go dead: "Geronimo." Consider the economy and complexity of this communiqué, which situates the action in 1880s Arizona when renegade Apaches plagued the area while eluding U.S. and Mexican troops but does so without belaboring or even clarifying the point.[44] Indeed, that single word not only motivates the action but invokes the Apache warrior in terms of myth and legend as well as American history. It also presents the West not in progressive terms but as a savage wilderness whose outposts of civilization are held together tenuously by telegraph lines, military patrols, and, we soon learn, stagecoach lines.

The ensuing Tonto sequences, which introduce all of the main characters except for the Ringo Kid, are similarly efficient. A succession of genre-coded stereotypes, stock figures, and character actors fleshes out the ensemble. But these formulaic characters immediately

The stagecoach in Monument Valley: a tenuous foothold of civilization in a savage wilderness. (collection of the editor)

take on a richness and complexity – indeed, a distinct individuality – that is altogether unique among renaissance Westerns. Moreover, the themes of class conflict and social prejudice that will deepen throughout the film are clearly drawn before the stagecoach even leaves Tonto. And once it enters the vast expanse and genre dreamscape of Monument Valley, the terms of the narrative become completely clear. This entails the stark contrast between town and desert, between bustling civilization and primal wasteland, and also between the interior and exterior of the stagecoach itself – the claustrophobic microcosm of frontier society versus the spectacular and vaguely prehistoric landscape that visually overwhelms the stage (often depicted in long shot, dwarfed by the monuments and vast, open sky).

It is in this wilderness that Ford presents the Ringo Kid in an archetypal flourish – a true epiphany of star-genre iconography, punctuated by a rare (for Ford) dolly-in on Wayne as he hails the stage and cocks his rifle. Despite his belated introduction, Wayne's Ringo Kid is the dramatic epicenter of *Stagecoach*, the prime motivating force for the narrative. His escape from prison and quest for revenge spurs the action far more than Geronimo's raiding parties, although a curious parallel exists between the two renegade warriors, both escapees who are obsessively driven by vengeance.[45] Moreover, Ringo's quest propels the stagecoach out of Tonto in the first place when the lawman Curley, determined to capture Ringo, learns that the Plummer brothers are in Lordsburg and hence induces the cowardly driver Buck to press on, despite the Apache raids. Wayne's performance drives the narrative in a more immediate sense as well. His B-Western pedigree and obvious limitations as an actor become assets under the sure hand of Ford, who minimized Ringo's dialogue and elicited from Wayne a minimalist performance that is vital to the film's understated effect. Wayne's inexperience and uncertainty in an A-class role further inform his character – indeed, Ringo comes off as far younger than Dallas, although Wayne was actually two years older than Claire Trevor, and his naïve innocence counters the cynical ennui of fellow outcasts Doc and Dallas. But Wayne's callow youth is also a tight-lipped, determined killer, and in this sense Ringo is as complex a figure as any in the film.

The revenge saga provides the narrative spine of *Stagecoach*, with the "larger" ensemble drama framing that subplot while remaining somewhat distinct from it. To put it another way, Ringo is simply another passenger on the stagecoach – albeit one of the principals along with Doc, Dallas, Curley, and Gatewood. Lucy Mallory, the officer's pregnant wife, is a more secondary figure, along with Buck, Peacock the whiskey salesman, and Hatfield the gambler, although the birth of her baby is a key narrative event. The plight of the ensemble intensifies throughout, less because of the threat of Indian attack than of the social and interpersonal dynamics of the group itself. What begins as a loose amalgam of distinct individuals becomes in the course of the journey a coherent, self-contained, and self-reliant unit – all except Gatewood, the obvious antagonist in the social drama. The group steadily develops into an idealized social community, forged by a combination of necessity, travail, and democratic action. The catalyst here is the birth, which provides both a climax for the social drama and redemption for Doc and Dallas, who successfully deliver the baby and care for its mother. In the ensuing Apache attack the group's communion grows so intense that, by the time the stage reaches Lordsburg, it has become more than an idealized social

The Ringo Kid (John Wayne) first appears in an archetypal flourish. (frame enlargements)

microcosm – in fact, it has become a counterculture of sorts, acutely at odds with the other social communities encountered. But this ideal community proves fragile indeed, dissolving all too quickly upon returning to the "real world" of Lordsburg.[46]

The birth of Lucy's baby at the last desert way station marks the first of several climaxes that punctuate the last thirty minutes of the film – followed close-on by the Indian attack (and cavalry-to-the-rescue payoff), Gatewood's arrest, Ringo's gunfight with the Plummers, and the lovers' final escape to Mexico. These climaxes are themselves as conventional as the plots that require them, particularly the cavalry rescue and the final showdown. The former dates back to the dime novel and Wild West show; and in fact a major spectacle in Buffalo Bill's legendary show, which began touring in the early 1880s and continued for some three decades, dramatized an Indian attack on "the original Deadwood Coach, the Most Famous Vehicle in History" (as described and graphically depicted in advertisements for the event). Whatever its basis in historical fact, Ford's treatment of the attack flouts the edicts of verisimilitude in various ways – the violations of screen direction, for instance, and the oft-noted failure of the Apaches to simply shoot the horses. But the scene is altogether effective and credible, providing sufficient action in what is otherwise a rather weighty social drama.

Ringo's gunfight with the Plummers also involves violent action, of course, although it occurs offscreen. Here again credibility is challenged but less so, perhaps, because we do not actually see the gunfight. This removes Ringo's heroic act of vengeance to the realm of imagination and instantaneous legend, accentuated by the fact that the killings also serve to purify the town. Lordsburg desperately needs purification, of course, despite its name and its status as a safe haven for the stage. As with other Western towns in Ford's work, Lordsburg at night is a dark and desperate place. Indeed, the stage's journey from Tonto through the three desert way stations traces the steady descent of our idealized community through successively bleaker outposts of civilization and finally into Lordsburg itself, the hell-state of nascent civilization. Curley's decision to cede his authority and allow Ringo to face the Plummers alone underscores several crucial Western themes: the inadequacy of legitimate civil authorities to deal with the likes of the Plummers (although mere embezzlers like Gatewood are manageable enough); the sacred nature of Ringo's quest; and the situational ethics that require the lawman to enable the "good-bad" hero to demonstrate his goodness (along with his capacity for killing) and to escape civilization altogether.

The lovers' flight to Mexico is a final climactic reversal and a striking anomaly among renaissance Westerns. Far more than the requisite "tag scene" that closes so many classic Hollywood films, this finale is Ford and Nichols's narrative and thematic *coup de grace*. The scene resolves both the love story and Ringo's fugitive status while providing a decidedly open (and acutely ironic) ending to the film's larger conflicts. McBride and Wilmington aptly note that "*Stagecoach* leaves the question of American imperialism, the Cavalry and the Indians, tantalizingly unresolved."[47] This ambiguity is reinforced on a more intimate, personal level in Curley's absolving Ringo of his "debt to society," and also in the suggestion that Mexico is a more favorable milieu for the lovers than their homeland. For Slotkin, Dallas and Ringo "are riding out of American history, as the Western understands it," with Mexico, as it has been conjured up here, as "mythic space par excellence: outside the frame of history."[48]

This finale would seem woefully naïve except for Doc's telling rejoinder, "Well, they're saved from the blessings of civilization." Curley readily endorses the sentiment, as "frontier justice" outweighs civil authority thanks to a lawman's willingness to bend and finally break the law in pursuit of a greater good. Thus the idealized community within the stagecoach that so quickly dissolved on arrival in Lordsburg is renewed in a meager buckboard carrying Ringo and Dallas into the desert darkness. And this complex hybrid of happy ending and social critique in the closing moments of *Stagecoach* puts a perfect finishing touch on its odd amalgam of history and myth, emphatically distancing the film from the other renaissance Westerns.

CONCLUSION

To say that *Stagecoach* was at odds with other Westerns of its day would be an understatement indeed. While borrowing freely from the B-Western, Ford had taken care to ground the story in history and tradition. This set *Stagecoach* against the era's singing cowboys and series Westerns, which were curiously unstuck in time and place, openly defying historical context. But he also avoided the crude historicism of the other A-Westerns, as well as the flagrant jingoism of the epics and the revamped gangster ethos of the outlaw biopics. Ford thus created in *Stagecoach* a singular prewar Western with one foot planted in U.S. history and the other in American mythology. This symbiosis of fact and legend is the very essence of the film's enduring appeal and its tremendous influence on the regenerate A-Western form. Indeed, today *Stagecoach* looks distinctly modern in its deft amalgam of history and myth, while its A-Western counterparts seem sorely dated and heavy-handed. Back in 1939, however, the epics and outlaw biopics were better attuned to the ideological tenor of the times, which helps explain why *Jesse James* and *Dodge City* were more popular than *Stagecoach*. It explains, too, why the epic and outlaw strains would diminish considerably after their prewar surge.

Interestingly enough, Ford's own Western output would diminish even sooner. With the exception of *Drums Along the Mohawk*, the late-1939 quasi-Western epic (set during the American Revolution in upstate New York), Ford abandoned the genre altogether until after World War II – and he abandoned Hollywood as well during the war for a stint in the military, doing documentaries. Ford did enjoy a remarkably fertile prewar period after *Stagecoach*, however, largely because of his suddenly improved status at Fox, where production chief Darryl Zanuck put him in one solid project after another. In fact 1939 was arguably the greatest year in Ford's venerable career, and certainly the most productive in terms of quality filmmaking. In January while *Stagecoach* was in post-production, Zanuck assigned him to *Young Mr. Lincoln*, which began shooting in February. Once *Stagecoach* hit, projects were no longer assigned but were "offered," and in April Zanuck offered him *Drums Along the Mohawk*. Ford shot that film during the summer and closed the year with *The Grapes of Wrath*, which Zanuck screened on the Fox lot in December (about two months before its release) for a delighted John Steinbeck. All three Fox films were developed and closely supervised by Zanuck, and all were tailored for rising contract star Henry Fonda. Thus none was a "John Ford film" to anywhere the extent that *Stagecoach* had been.

Ford's wartime hiatus from the Western to make war-related documentaries corresponded in a way with Hollywood's. During the war, the A-Western surge abated and the brunt of male-action movie production focused on war films, with the rapid development of the combat film in 1942–3 owing a great deal to the Western. Indeed, the cross-fertilization of Western and war film intensified for Hollywood and for Ford throughout the 1940s, culminating in Ford's cavalry trilogy (*Fort Apache*, 1948; *She Wore a Yellow Ribbon*, 1949; *Rio Grande*, 1950). Actually, Ford's postwar return to the genre came in 1946 with *My Darling Clementine*, another Fonda vehicle for Zanuck and Fox. A mytho-historical biopic of Wyatt Earp (and the studio's third adaptation of Stuart Lake's *Wyatt Earp, Frontier Marshal*), it was also Ford's last film as a contract director. He left Fox and revived Argosy Pictures with Merian Cooper, returning to the Western with a vengeance – and very much on his own terms. *My Darling Clementine* was only Ford's second Western in the previous two decades; during the next two decades, fully half of Ford's two dozen films would be Westerns. In the process, director and genre would coalesce in a creative accord that was as intense and productive as any in Hollywood's long history.

The making of that postwar "genre auteur" began with *Stagecoach*, when Ford's stature and relative autonomy from the production machinery and executive authority of any one studio gave him the license to pursue his own singular vision, yet with the resources necessary to realize that vision. And paradoxically, Ford's autonomy in creating *Stagecoach* and his own deep roots in the Western enabled him to mine the genre in ways that other A-Western directors simply could not. Ford also was free to mine his own recent work, particularly the recent collaborations with Dudley Nichols that so crucially informed the conception and realization of *Stagecoach*. Thus the film was a watershed for Ford as well as for the Western genre, a coming of age for both filmmaker and genre and a definitive product of Hollywood's classical era.

NOTES

1. See, for instance, Edward Buscombe, ed., *The BFI Companion to the Western* (London: British Film Institute, 1988), p. 428. Buscombe, perhaps the most reliable source on the subject, puts the total number of A-Westerns produced in the five prewar years as follows: three in 1937; four in 1938; nine in 1939; thirteen in 1940; and nine in 1941.

2. André Bazin, "The Evolution of the Western," in *What Is Cinema?*, Vol. 2, ed. and trans. Hugh Gray (Berkeley: University of California Press, 1971), p. 149.

3. Wanger's public statement in the March 13, 1939, review of *Stagecoach* in *Time* magazine; quoted in Matthew Bernstein, *Walter Wanger: Hollywood Independent* (Berkeley: University of California Press, 1994), p. 129. Private statement in Wanger letter of February 9, 1939, to United Artists marketing executive Lynn Farrol; Walter Wanger Collection, Wisconsin Center for Film and Theatre Research, State Historical Society, Madison, WI.

4. Nichols's letter of March 26, 1939, to Ford in the Ford Correspondence Files in the John Ford Collection, Manuscripts Department, Lilly Library, Indiana University, Bloomington, IN. On Nichols's contribution to the screenplay, see also Charles Maland's essay in this volume.

5. Frank Nugent, "Speaking of Directors," *New York Times* (March 19, 1939).

6. Edward Buscombe, *Stagecoach* (London: British Film Institute, 1992), p. 35. Note that accounts vary regarding the amount that Ford paid Haycox for the story rights, largely because of the indication in the budget that the story property cost $7,500. But reliable sources, including Ford, himself in several interviews, put the total at $2,500 – which in fact seems appropriate, given the going rate for story properties at the time. See also Dan Ford, *Pappy: The Life of John Ford* (New York: Da Capo Press, 1998), p. 122.

7. Ronald Haver, *David O. Selznick's Hollywood* (New York: Knopf, 1980), pp. 96, 178, 183. Among the freelance directors whom Selznick was pursuing at

the time, besides Ford, were Frank Capra, William Wellman, and Alfred Hitchcock.

8. Haver, *Selznick's Hollywood*, p. 224; see also Rudy Behlmer, ed., *Memo from David O. Selznick* (New York: Viking, 1972).
9. On the founding of Argosy Pictures, see Haver, *Selznick's Hollywood*, p. 226.
10. Dan Ford, *Pappy*, pp. 101–2.
11. The information here on the development and production of *Dodge City* is culled from the Production and General Correspondence files for *Dodge City* in the Warner Bros. Collection, Doheny Library, University of Southern California, Los Angeles. On Muni as possible star, see Jack Warner memos to Hal Wallis of January 25 and February 1, 1938; on Cagney, see Warner memo to Wallis of July 7 and Robert Lord memo to Wallis of August 2; on Flynn, see letter from Flynn's agent Noll Gurney to Warner, September 1, 1938.
12. Estimated final cost as of April 14, 1939; *Dodge City* production files, Warner Bros. Collection.
13. On the film's production budget, see Ford production files in the Ford Collection, Indiana University; see also Bernstein, *Walter Wanger*, p. 147.
14. Haycox's story is reprinted in David Wheeler, ed., *No, But I Saw the Movie: The Best Short Stories Ever Made into Film* (New York: Penguin, 1989), pp. 378–91.
15. For more on social class in *Stagecoach*, see Gaylyn Studlar's essay in this volume.
16. Ford told Peter Bogdanovich that *Stagecoach* "was really '*Boul de Suif*,' and I imagine that the writer, Ernie Haycox, got his idea from there and turned it into a Western story." Bogdanovich, *John Ford* (Berkeley: University of California Press, 1978), p. 69. See also Buscombe, *Stagecoach*, pp. 36–7.
17. On the influence of Harte's "The Outcasts of Poker Flat," see Rudy Behlmer, "Bret Harte in Monument Valley: *Stagecoach*," in *Behind the Scenes: The making of America's Favorite Movies* (New York: Samuel French, 1989), pp. 104–18. See also Jon Tuska, *The Filming of the West* (Garden City, N.Y.: Doubleday, 1976), p. 375.
18. Joseph McBride and Michael Wilmington, *John Ford* (New York: Da Capo Press, 1975), p. 54. Bernstein notes in *Walter Wanger* (p. 148) that Nichols himself often compared *Stagecoach* to *Grand Hotel*.
19. Over the years, *The Lost Patrol* would be reworked in countless Westerns, war films, and even Foreign Legion films – most notably in the "last stand" films of World War II. This includes war-era Westerns like *They Died with Their Boots On* (1942) as well as war films like *Sahara* and *Bataan* (both 1943).
20. Buscombe, *Stagecoach*, p. 69. See also Buscombe, *BFI Companion*, p. 249. For an early example of a cavalry-to-the-rescue climax, see D. W. Griffith's 1913 two-reeler, *The Battle of Elderbush Gulch*.
21. Buscombe, *Stagecoach*, pp. 21–2.
22. Budget figures and production schedule here and elsewhere from the Ford Production Files in the Ford Collection, Indiana University, and also from the *Stagecoach* Production Files in the Wanger Collection.

23. Ford mentioned the film's "unusual economy of dialogue" in a conversation with Bosley Crowther, "Ford vs. *Stagecoach*," *New York Times* (January 29, 1939).

24. On the Ford–Mitchell improvisation, see Bernstein, *Walter Wanger*, p. 148. For more detailed accounts of the production, see Buscombe, *Stagecoach*; Dan Ford, *Pappy*; and Ford's own account in Bogdanovich, *John Ford*.

25. Spencer interview in *Action* (September–October 1971), quoted in Buscombe, *Stagecoach*, pp. 68–9.

26. On the preview, see Dan Ford, *Pappy*, pp. 130–1. Final cost and income figures from the *Stagecoach* Production Files in the Wanger Collection. Note that according to a United Artists Production Profits report of April 3, 1943, also in the Wanger Collection, a wartime reissue of *Stagecoach* pushed its earnings to $1.4 million.

27. Roy Chartier, "The Year in Pictures," *Variety* (January 4, 1939).

28. Jack Jungmeyer, "Film Production Trends," *Variety* (January 4, 1939).

29. Douglas W. Churchill, "Home, Home on the Range: Hollywood Takes to the Plains for Its New Series of Grand (Horse) Operas," *New York Times* (December 25, 1938).

30. "Pic Cycle on Horseback," *Variety* (March 1, 1939), p. 5.

31. Frank Nugent, "A Horse of a Different Color," *New York Times* (March 25, 1939).

32. Nugent review of *The Oklahoma Kid*, *New York Times* (March 11, 1939); Nugent, "A Horse of a Different Color."

33. Tino Balio, *Grand Design: Hollywood as a Modern Business Enterprise, 1930–1939* (New York: Scribner's, 1993), pp. 194–5; *1939 Film Daily Year Book*, pp. 802–3. The location-premiere trend peaked with the Atlanta premiere of *Gone With the Wind* in December 1939 and abruptly ended two years later with the U.S. entry into World War II.

34. George K. Fenin and William K. Everson, *The Western: From Silents to the Seventies*, rev. ed. (New York: Penguin, 1973), pp. 240–5.

35. Richard Slotkin, *Gunfighter Nation: The Myth of the Frontier in Twentieth-Century America* (New York: HarperCollins, 1992), pp. 286, 287.

36. *Ibid.*, p. 270.

37. Balio, *Grand Design*, pp. 193–4.

38. Slotkin, *Gunfighter Nation*, p. 286. Slotkin's use of the term "progressive" should not be confused with Robin Wood's distinction between "progressive" and "reactionary" horror in his oft-cited "An Introduction to the American Horror Film," in Wood and Richard Lippe, eds., *The American Nightmare: Essays on the Horror Film* (Toronto: Festival of Festivals, 1979), pp. 7–28. Whereas Wood applies the term to horror films that aggressively criticize society, Slotkin applies it to historical films that blatantly celebrate "progress."

39. *Ibid.*, p. 293.

40. Buscombe, *Stagecoach*, p. 31.

41. Slotkin, *Gunfighter Nation*, p. 303.

42. Lang is quoted in Buscombe, *BFI Companion*, p. 292.

43. McBride and Wilmington, *John Ford*, p. 53.
44. Note that the word "Geronimo" was sufficiently charged and meaningful that it served as the title of a Paramount biopic released later in 1939.
45. This parallel anticipates Wayne's Ethan Edwards and his relationship with the renegade Scar in Ford's *The Searchers* (1956).
46. See McBride and Wilmington, *John Ford*, pp. 55–6.
47. *Ibid.*, p. 56.
48. Slotkin, *Gunfighter Nation*, p. 311.

2 "Powered by a Ford"?

Dudley Nichols, Authorship, and
Cultural Ethos in *Stagecoach*

> By rights this new art form [the movies] should be controlled by
> individuals who include all functions in themselves. They should be
> film-makers. But the functions are too diversified and complex to be
> handled by the creative energy of one individual. So we break them
> down into separate crafts – writing, directing, photography, scenic
> designing, optical printing and camera effects, cutting and assem-
> bly of film, composing music, recording, mixing and re-recording,
> the making of . . . transitions; into an immense field of works which
> require the closest and most harmonious collaboration to produce
> excellent results.
>
> – Dudley Nichols, "The Writer and the Film"[1]

Upon the release of *Stagecoach* early in 1939, Frank S. Nugent con-
cluded his enthusiastic and influential *New York Times* review by writing, "This is one stagecoach that's powered by a Ford."[2] Embedded
in this comment is the widely shared assumption that director John
Ford is the unequivocal auteur of *Stagecoach*, the creative genius
who revived a genre that had been nearly comatose – at least in
A-productions – since the introduction of sound a decade earlier. It
is an assumption that many film historians and analysts have shared
in considering this landmark Western. Although it would be foolish
to deny Ford's central contributions to *Stagecoach* – he clearly was a
driving force in making the film what it was – this essay contends that
Stagecoach is powered not solely by a Ford but by other collaborators
and cultural forces as well.

In his outstanding production history of *Citizen Kane*, Robert Carringer has convincingly demonstrated that even in *Kane* – that monument to Orson Welles's auteurist brilliance – filmmaking was a *collaborative process*, which Carringer defines simply as the "sharing of the creative function by the director with others."[3] Carringer shows that without such collaborators as scriptwriter Herman Mankiewicz, cinematographer Gregg Toland, art director Perry Ferguson, and composer Bernard Herrmann, Welles could never have directed such a brilliant film. The same is true for *Stagecoach*. It is not John Ford's film alone: Important collaborators include cinematographer Gregg Toland, costumer Walter Plunkett, Yakima Canutt and his fellow stuntmen, a variety of performers, and a number of musical arrangers – not least Richard Hageman – who integrated American folk music into the score. This essay, however, focuses on the central contributions of screenwriter Dudley Nichols to the film's narrative development and ideological perspective.[4]

Besides focusing on Nichols's crucial role in *Stagecoach*, I stress that this collaborative authorship takes place amidst a larger culture in which the authors live, work, and develop a social understanding. This is as true of *Stagecoach* as of any other film: The finished film bears the imprint of what I will call the cultural ethos of Popular Front liberalism in the United States during the middle to late 1930s, what Raymond Williams would call one of the era's important "structures of feeling."[5] The imprint can be closely connected to Nichols's active political engagement in Hollywood in the period before the film went into production and while he was working on the screenplay. An examination of *Stagecoach* that emphasizes Dudley Nichols's role in the film's narrative development will help us understand better, then, the collaborative authorship of *Stagecoach* and the film's status as a key cultural document of the late 1930s.

DUDLEY NICHOLS AND POPULAR FRONT LIBERALISM IN HOLLYWOOD

Screenwriter Dudley Nichols played a key role in the making of *Stagecoach*, a role that has not been adequately explored or recognized before. In collaboration with Ford, Nichols transformed the original short story, Ernest Haycox's "Stage to Lordsburg," into several

Dudley Nichols, screenwriter of *Stagecoach*.

screenplay drafts, which then served as the blueprint for the shooting of the film. Although auteurist criticism of Ford's work often has minimized Nichols's contributions to Ford's films or disparaged his talents, evidence suggests that Nichols played a central role in shaping the film's narrative, most notably in articulating its ideological perspective. Particularly in his depiction of Gatewood and Doc Boone, two characters invented in the screenplay adaptation of the short story, Nichols infused the film with "Popular Front liberalism."

Popular Front liberalism, a specific form of American liberalism that was current in American culture between 1936 and 1939, was influenced by the 1935 legislative successes of President Franklin D. Roosevelt's "Second New Deal," which included the passage of the Wagner Act and the Social Security Act.[6] However, it was also shaped by a changed tactic in the Soviet Union, which had in the early 1930s been highly critical of the Western capitalist democracies and unwilling to cooperate with them. In 1935, concerned about Germany's growing military strength, the Soviet Union established a "Popular Front" policy, which urged communists around the globe to cooperate with liberals and other leftists in opposition to Adolf Hitler and fascism. As such historians as Richard Pells have shown, this shift in approach, as well as the outbreak of the Spanish Civil War on July 17, 1936 – which galvanized the left in its opposition to Franco – combined to generate a great deal of "ecumenical" leftist political activity in the United States, not least in Hollywood, during the late 1930s. That cooperation continued strongly until the Hitler–Stalin Non-Aggression Pact of August 1939 undermined the Popular Front and made many liberals wary of joint action with the communists.[7]

Dudley Nichols's name figured prominently in the list of engaged Popular Front liberals in Hollywood. Nichols (1895–1960) was a small-town midwesterner, born and raised in Wapakoneta, Ohio, the son of a physician and his wife. After studying engineering for a time at the University of Michigan, Nichols enlisted in the U.S. Navy when the United States entered World War I. In the Navy he became part of the North Sea Mine Laying Force, and after the armistice he volunteered for minesweeping duty and invented a method of electrical protection for minesweepers that earned him the Distinguished Service Medal in 1920. Following the war, he became a journalist, working in the 1920s for several newspapers, ultimately the *New York World*, first as courtroom reporter, later as a drama and music critic, and also for a year as a roving European correspondent. After the introduction of sound swept through the movie industry, he came to Hollywood at the bidding of a former colleague at the *World*, Winfield Sheehan, who had become an executive at Fox and invited Nichols to Hollywood to write screenplays at double his journalist's salary. After telling Sheehan that he knew nothing about screenwriting and mentioning Ford's *The Iron Horse* (1924) as one film he remembered and admired, Nichols was assigned to work with Ford when he arrived in Hollywood in June 1929.

Nichols's first screen credit was for *Men without Women* (1930), directed by Ford, and he subsequently enjoyed a long and prominent career in Hollywood. Although best known for his collaboration with Ford, he also wrote screenplays for films directed by Howard Hawks, Elia Kazan, Jean Renoir, René Clair, Leo McCarey, Fritz Lang, Anthony Mann, George Cukor, Michael Curtiz, Cecil B. DeMille, and others. He was also versatile enough to work in a variety of genres, from screwball comedies (*Bringing Up Baby*, 1938) to war films (*Air Force*, 1943), social-problem films (*Pinky*, 1949) to musicals (*Carefree*, 1938), prestige adaptations (*Mourning Becomes Electra*, 1947) to film noir (*Scarlet Street*, 1945).[8]

Despite this versatility, Nichols worked more with Ford than with any other director, particularly early in his career. Following *Men without Women*, he received screen credit for the following Ford-directed films: *Born Reckless* (1930), *Seas Beneath* (1931), *Pilgrimage* (1933; dialogue credit only), *The Lost Patrol* (1934), *Judge Priest* (1934), *The Informer* (1935), *Steamboat Round the Bend* (1935; credit shared with Lamar Trotti), *Mary of Scotland* (1936), *The Plough and the Stars* (1936), *The Hurricane* (1938), *Stagecoach* (1939), *The Long Voyage Home* (1940), and *The Fugitive* (1947). He received the Oscar for his screenplay for *The Informer* and a nomination for *The Long Voyage Home*.[9] It is clear that he learned a great deal about how movies were made through his work with the veteran Hollywood director. By the late 1930s the Nichols–Ford writer–director team was as well known as any in the Hollywood film industry, save perhaps for that of Robert Riskin and Frank Capra.[10]

Notwithstanding his success as a screenwriter, Nichols's reputation declined following his death in 1960, which was just about the time that Andrew Sarris and others were popularizing the auteur approach to film in the United States. Auteurism held that the director was or should be the central creative force in the creation of a movie, and two dimensions of the approach as it was practiced in the 1960s and 1970s worked against Nichols's reputation.[11] First, the screenwriter's contribution was minimized, unless, like Preston Sturges or Billy Wilder, the screenwriter also directed his own films.

Second, Sarris early in his career tended to downplay films that dealt explicitly with serious political issues or social problems. In part he was reacting against the social-problem films of the late 1940s and social-realist commentators like *New York Times* critic Bosley Crowther who championed them. Because Nichols was a screenwriter and often an advocate of such serious and ambitious films, his reputation didn't fare well in this new critical climate. This attitude toward Nichols's work was most prominently captured by Richard Corliss in *Talking Pictures: Screenwriters in the American Cinema, 1927–1973*.[12] After acknowledging that Nichols worked with great directors and wrote the screenplays for a number of "registered masterpieces," Corliss delivers the knockout punch: "On closer inspection, however, Nichols' world is a rigorously schematized place where Good and Evil are rarely allowed to interact within one person, and where Big Brother Dudley is forever whispering slogans of moral uplift into the ears of the mass audience he sought to liberalize but ended up insulting."[13]

While I'd grant that Nichols often sought to integrate social issues and conflicts into his screenplays, I'd like to rescue Nichols from those critics who dismiss his work because of that tendency. In fact, that tendency was quite widespread among some screenwriters whose first important work appeared during the 1930s, and it is significant that Nichols was active in industry and social politics in the years immediately before he began work on *Stagecoach*. These engagements, crucial in shaping his contributions in *Stagecoach*, revolve primarily around two sets of activities: active participation with the Screen Writers Guild (SWG) as it sought recognition from the producers and involvement with anti-fascist causes during the Popular Front era.

The SWG was formed in April 1933, partly as a response to the pay cuts instituted by the movie producers because of the economic strains engendered by the Great Depression. Nichols was one of its founding members. However, the SWG had to battle long and hard to receive recognition from the producers. Following the passage of the Wagner Act in 1935, screenwriters began to seek recognition from the studio heads. After considerable struggle, in June 1938 the screenwriters voted the SWG as their sole bargaining agent, a role the producers officially recognized in March 1939. Yet a guild shop wasn't established until May 1941, and a contract for a basic minimum wage was not signed until early in 1942.[14]

Nichols played a key role in helping the SWG survive during the difficult years between 1936 and 1938. Perhaps Nichols's most prominent and widely publicized action came in February 1936, when he won the Academy Award for his script of *The Informer* and turned down the award. In a letter to the Academy explaining his actions, Nichols wrote that as a founding member of the SWG, he was unable to accept the Oscar. He added that he resigned from the Academy when he helped found the SWG because he had come to believe that "in any major disagreement between employed talent and the studios it [the Academy] would operate against the best interests of the talent." Concluding, Nichols forcefully asserted that "a writer who accepts an Academy Award tacitly supports the Academy, and I believe it to be the duty of every screenwriter to stand with his own, and to strengthen the Guild."[15]

That spring witnessed the most intense conflict between writers and the studios in the history of the industry. The SWG board scheduled a general membership meeting for May 2, 1936, hoping to demonstrate enough unanimity among screenwriters so that the producers would be forced to bargain and grant screenwriters a number of their desired goals: cooperative agreements with the Dramatists Guild and the Authors League of America (ALA), a guild shop, minimum wage, and greater control over their creations. As the meeting approached, industry trade journals generally attacked the screenwriters, especially their desire for affiliation with the other associations of writers. *Motion Picture Herald* warned of a "writer dictatorship" if the Guild gained too much control. *The Hollywood Reporter* of April 25 suggested that in their efforts to organize, the screenwriters were trying "to kill the goose that has been hatching all those beautiful golden eggs." Nichols replied in the May 1936 issue of *Screen Guilds' Magazine* by calling the golden goose "a myth, a ghost, to haunt the timid" and urging screenwriters to combat that myth with "a laugh, a little common sense, and courage!"[16]

Although the May 2 meeting resulted in a tentative agreement to cooperate with the Dramatists Guild and ALA, it also resulted in defections by 125 screenwriters. This group, with the encouragement of the producers, formed the Screen Playwrights (SP), which in turn, according to Nancy Schwartz, "began a crusade to eliminate totally the Screen Writers Guild." The studios immediately recognized the SP and signed an agreement with the group that went into effect in April 1937.[17] Although the emergence of the SP threw the SWG into disarray, Nichols stayed committed to it. He was elected SWG president for the 1937–8 term, and in 1938–9 he continued as a board member. Thus Nichols played an important role in the SWG during its struggle for recognition, including the June 28, 1938, vote in which eligible screenwriters (in a 4:1 ratio) selected the SWG to represent them in their negotiations with the producers. In the period leading up to that vote, Nichols took out a full-page ad in *The Hollywood Reporter*. The ad urged writers to support the SWG in the election, to ally with the two other talent guilds – those of screen actors and directors – and to oppose the SP and the International Alliance of Theatrical Stage Employees (IATSE), the latter of which, Nichols charged, would institute a "boss-ruled union."[18] Despite the producers' recalcitrance following this vote, the National Labor Relations Board (NLRB) ruled in August 1938 that the June vote had indeed certified the SWG as the screenwriters' representative in negotiations. In September those negotiations began, and by March 1939 the reluctant producers finally recognized the SWG as the bargaining agent for screenwriters. Because Nichols was working on the *Stagecoach* screenplay in the summer and fall of 1938, it is no exaggeration to say that he wrote the screenplay during a period of intensely active struggle with the producers on behalf of his fellow screenwriters.

During the same period, Nichols was also becoming prominently involved in a variety of Popular Front organizations and causes. He was, for example, a member of the Hollywood Anti-Nazi League, which may have been the most well-known Popular Front organization in Hollywood between 1936 and 1939. One of his activities with the Anti-Nazi League was to co-narrate with George Jessel and Herbert Biberman in January 1937 a satirical radio review called "Four Years of Hitler." That same year he participated in the founding of the Motion Picture Artists Committee to Aid Republican Spain (John Ford was also a member). In June 1938, the same year that he was working on the *Stagecoach* screenplay, Nichols helped found the Motion Picture Democratic Committee, which emerged to support the campaign of progressive Democrat Culbert Olson, who was running for governor of California against Frank Merriam. Nichols served for a time as the organization's financial director. (Going against the tide of a Republican backlash in the 1938 congressional elections, Olson was elected that November, just as the shooting schedule of *Stagecoach* began.) That same year he joined Fritz Lang, Walter Wanger, Fredric March, and others to sponsor Films for Democracy, a group formed to "safeguard and extend American democracy."[19]

After the Nazi–Soviet Pact of August 1939, Nichols was, like many other liberals, reluctant to cooperate with communists, yet he remained politically active, particularly in support of the Allied war effort. In March 1942 he spoke publicly at a League of American Writers conference on "The Fifth Column in America," warning against those who might speak with doubt and weaken the war effort. In February 1944 he was chairman of a meeting of the Hollywood Free World Association, a liberal anti-isolationist organization, whose keynote speaker was U.S. Vice President Henry A. Wallace.[20] Through all of this, it is probably best to characterize Nichols as a liberal caught up in the enthusiasm of Popular Front activity between 1936 and 1939, directing his efforts toward support of the SWG in its struggles against the producers and toward anti-fascist activism. Pells notes that the rhetoric of the Popular Front posed capitalists and other entrenched interests against the common man – the "people" – and it is easy to see how Nichols could fit his world view into that framework. He did in his political activities, and he did in *Stagecoach*.

In thinking about Nichols's collaborative role in the creation of *Stagecoach*, it is important to consider how Nichols's social and political views compare with Ford's. Because Ford occasionally talked with Nichols when he was writing and revising screenplay drafts, and because auteurists often wish to attribute a film's social vision to the director, it is an important question. It is also a complicated one that yields no simple answer. Ford was drawn to Nichols in part because the screenwriter had Irish heritage, which was central to Ford's own sense of self. Furthermore, Ford, who grew up near the ocean in Portland, Maine, and who enlisted in the Naval Reserves in 1934, admired Nichols's experience in the U.S. Navy during and after World War I. There's also evidence, albeit somewhat conflicting, that Ford's political views moved further left in the Popular Front period than at any other time of his life. For example, in 1937 he contributed $1,000 for an ambulance for the Loyalists in Spain. He also wrote his nephew around this time that although he didn't believe communism offered the remedy the world needed, "I am a definite socialist democrat." Perhaps under the influence of Nichols, an officer of the Motion Picture Democratic Committee, Ford also let his name appear on the organization's masthead.[21]

Yet Scott Eyman convincingly argues in his recent biography that, even though Ford supported Franklin Roosevelt all four times he ran for president, "his true political religion was to be contrary, a one-man insurrection against perceived manners and mores."[22] Nor was Ford's heart ever much inflamed by Popular Front politics. Eyman suggests that his attraction to the Spanish Loyalists stemmed from his ability to generate an imaginative analogy that compared Franco's forces to British troops in Ireland and the Spanish Loyalists to the Irish Republican Army. Furthermore, when Leni Riefenstahl, Hitler's hand-picked director for *Triumph of the Will* (1935) and *Olympia* (1938), visited Hollywood in November 1938 – much to the consternation of most of the Hollywood left – Ford invited her to his house and showed her some of his movies. Upon her return to Germany, she sent him an autographed picture that Ford kept for the rest of his life.[23] Such fraternization with the enemy would have been considered taboo by most Popular Front advocates.

It is significant, too, that Ford was fond of tweaking Nichols for his leftist political views. In the 1930s Ford, Ward Bond, John Wayne, and a number of other friends who often gathered to drink at the Hollywood Athletic Club set up a mock social club that they called the "Young Men's Purity Total Abstinence and Yachting Association." A running gag of the club was to repeatedly deny Nichols membership because his liberal politics were judged "socially reprehensible" – and perhaps because he wasn't a serious enough drinker. Ford kept gag minutes of the club's meetings, and in one of his entries, he indicated that Ward Bond was being dropped from the club because of drinking *too* much and Nichols was being elected in his place. According to Ford's minutes,

> Mr. Nichols' first action on becoming a member was to put forward a motion changing the name of the Association from the YOUNG

MEN'S PURITY TOTAL ABSTINENCE AND YACHTING ASSOCIATION to
THE YOUNG WORKERS OF THE WORLD'S ANTI-CHAUVINISTIC, TOTAL
ABSTINENCE LEAGUE FOR THE PROMULGATION OF PROPAGANDA
CONTRA FASCISM. This motion was defeated. Then Brother Nichols
arose and presented each member with an autographed copy of his
brochure thesis on the "Origin, Development and Consolidation of
the Evolutionary Idea of the Proletariat," which he has recently sold
to Sam Briskin to do as a musical with the Ritz Brothers. The copies
of the pamphlet were refused by the members.[24]

Ford's use of humor here makes it pretty clear that he positioned
his own politics to the right of the views of Dudley Nichols. To the
extent that *Stagecoach* embraces the cultural ethos of Popular Front
liberalism, Nichols was more the architect than Ford.

BUILDING THE *STAGECOACH*: FROM SHORT STORY TO SCREENPLAY

The genesis of *Stagecoach* dates back to the summer of 1937, when
John Ford paid $7,500 for the rights to Ernest Haycox's story "Stage
to Lordsburg," which had appeared in the April 10, 1937, issue of
Collier's.[25] Haycox (1899–1950), a Portland, Oregon, native and a
1923 graduate of the University of Oregon, was a prolific writer of
popular Western fiction whose work appeared regularly in *Collier's*:
Between 1929 and 1939 he published more than a dozen serialized
novels and fifty short stories in the magazine.[26] Although Haycox's
works also served as the source for a number of other Western films,
including *Union Pacific* (1939), *Canyon Passage* (1947), and *Man in the
Saddle* (1951), *Stagecoach* is the most accomplished film based on his
work. Much like "The Greatest Gift," the Philip Van Doren Stern short
story that provides the kernel for a more accomplished film – Frank
Capra's *It's a Wonderful Life* (1946) – "Stage to Lordsburg" provides a
starting point for *Stagecoach* but is significantly transformed in script
and film.

Haycox's story resembles the film in several ways, not only its general handling of setting but also in some of its characters and some of
its plot development and conflicts.[27] In the most general sense, the
story's handling of time and locations is quite similar to that in the
scripts and the film. In the story the stagecoach leaves Tonto one day

with a group of passengers, makes several stops along the way, then arrives in Lordsburg at the end of the next day. The stops include an adobe relay station at noon the first day, Gap Creek (also called Gap Station) that evening, Al Schreiber's ranch the middle of the next day, and, after an Apache attack, Lordsburg at five o'clock the second afternoon. Although some of the place names are changed in the scripts and film, this journey structure is central to all versions, and except for the fact that the stagecoach arrives later in Lordsburg the second day in the scripts and film (Ringo's shootout takes place dramatically at night in the film), the narrative time is very similar in story, scripts, and film.

The story contains seven important characters who are very similar to characters in the scripts and film, although they either are given no specific names in the story or have different names in the scripts and film. Those characters include a stagecoach driver, Happy Stuart (Buck in the film); a man riding shotgun, John Strang (Curley Wilcox); the prostitute Henriette (Dallas); Malpais Bill (the Ringo Kid); an Eastern woman traveling west to meet her man (Mrs. Mallory); a gambler with a mysterious southern past (Hatfield); and a whiskey drummer (Peacock). Two other characters ride in the stagecoach but are dropped in the scripts and film: an Englishman "all length and bony corners and bearing with him an enormous sporting rifle" and a "solid-shouldered cattleman on his way to Mexico."[28] As we shall see, Nichols introduces two characters who are absolutely central to the thematic core of the narrative in the scripts and film: the banker Gatewood and Doc Boone.

Characterization is not very detailed in the story, yet of those characters who survive into the film, some are quite similar to their counterparts and some are different in key ways. As in the scripts and film, the driver Happy Stuart is cowardly in the story, the gambler has a mysterious past back East, the whiskey drummer is meek, Malpais Bill is intent on revenge (although he is not an escaped convict), and Henriette is a whore with a heart of gold. On the other hand, in a key departure, the eastern woman traveling west is not pregnant; in fact, she is not yet married. She's traveling to reach her fiancé so that she can marry. Thus the pregnancy, the childbirth, and the reactions of the characters to those situations – all crucial elements in the film – are all first inventions in the screenplay.

Finally, the story introduces, albeit sometimes in a very sketchy way, several narrative strands also taken up in the scripts and film. The constant presence of Geronimo on the warpath is central to the story, and an Apache raid provides one of its climaxes. The growing relationship between Henriette and Malpais Bill constitutes another important strand of the story and is transformed into the romance between Dallas and Ringo. Malpais Bill is portrayed as a kind person in the story (Henriette detects "something gallant, something gentle" in him[29]), and Malpais Bill is drawn closer to her after he sees her nurturing someone else (it's the ill whiskey drummer in the story and Mrs. Mallory's baby in the film).[30] The stark class difference between the eastern woman and Henriette is stressed from the start of the story, as in the Dallas–Mrs. Mallory rift in the film. As Haycox puts it, from Henriette's perspective, "The army girl was in one world and she was in another, as everyone in the coach understood."[31] The gambler is portrayed in story, script, and film as someone with something to hide, a mysterious past linked somehow to the eastern woman. As in the film, that link gradually becomes more clear as the narrative progresses. And as in the scripts and film, Malpais Bill is traveling to Lordsburg for a showdown with Plummer (but rather than also confronting Luke Plummer's two brothers, he's gunning for Plummer and a man named Shanley).

So the story provides some details that become central to the scripts and film, but some details are dropped and many are added. In some ways the transformation from story to scripts to film reinforces the notion that the short story is an ideal form for cinematic adaptation because it is briefer, sketchier, than most feature films: The short story provides the bare bones that a good screenwriter and director can flesh out, enriching the narrative and perhaps making it more complete and memorable. That certainly happened with "Stage to Lordsburg."

Nichols's collaborative contribution to *Stagecoach* appears at this stage. After writing the screenplay for Ford's *The Hurricane* in 1937 (the film was released in late December 1937), Nichols co-wrote the screenplay for Howard Hawks's *Bringing Up Baby* and received shared credits for both the story and adaptation of the musical *Carefree*, directed by Mark Sandrich. Both of these films were released in 1938. *Stagecoach* was in pre-production from the summer of 1938, when Walter Wanger finally agreed to provide financing for the film, through the end of October. Between October 10 and 23, Nichols did a revised draft as the shooting schedule was approaching.[32] (The film was shot between October 31 and December 23, 1938.)[33]

Although we don't have the first draft of the screenplay, this revised draft, as well as Nichols's handwritten revisions, probably done in the week before shooting began and into early November, is housed in the Special Collections in the Lilly Library at Indiana University.[34] It offers a good sense of how Nichols envisioned *Stagecoach* at that point and what key changes he made to the short story.

In "The Writer and the Film," an essay he wrote to help introduce *Twenty Best Film Plays* (1942), Nichols explains that his practice was to write a rough draft of a film, then take it through "two or three revisions, each nearer to the peculiar demands of cinema." He adds that "With luck the director, who must have an equal sympathy for the drama to be unfolded, will be on hand during the groundwork, contributing cinematic ideas here and there, many of which will not appear in the script but will be remembered or recorded in other notes to be used when the time appears."[35] Because Ford, who had purchased the rights to the story, typically would meet periodically with Nichols when the screenplay was being written, it's difficult to pinpoint exactly who contributed what. But the October draft script suggests that in reshaping the short story through his screenplay drafts, particularly by inventing the key characters Doc Boone and the banker Gatewood, Nichols transformed Ernest Haycox's short story into a Popular Front Western, one that drew on contemporary concerns and conflicts to energize the narrative from the point of view of a Popular Front liberal.

The inventions of Doc Boone and Gatewood made the narrative conflicts in *Stagecoach* more clearly defined and more contemporary than those evident in "Stage to Lordsburg," and I argue that Nichols's experiences with the SWG and his response to the contemporary political situation in the United States helped shape those creations. As president of the SWG in 1937–8, struggling to gain recognition from the producers, Nichols could easily perceive himself as a leader of the little people seeking some security against the movie moguls. Similarly, in 1936 President Roosevelt ran successfully for reelection, in part by going out of his way to paint business and moneyed interests in negative terms. In his 1936 State of the Union address he threw down the political gauntlet: "We have earned the hatred of entrenched greed," he told a nationwide radio audience. "They seek the restoration of their selfish power. . . . Give them their way and they will take the course of every autocracy of the past – power for themselves, enslavement for the public."[36] Similarly, in his acceptance speech at the Democratic convention on June 27, 1936, FDR criticized the "economic royalists" whose greed, he said, was slowing down economic recovery and unfairly controlling other people's lives. Although advisors like Raymond Moley urged FDR to tone down his rhetoric, he continued to make it a keystone of his campaign. At Madison Square Garden a few days before the election, the president targeted "organized money" as the culprit of the Depression: the representatives of "business and financial monopoly, speculation, reckless banking, class antagonism, war profiteering."[37] Both Nichols's SWG experiences and this political climate fed his skepticism of moneyed interests and his support for the common man.

In Nichols's October draft script the banker Gatewood – who doesn't appear in the story – is obviously designed as a representative of and spokesman for the moneyed interests that FDR opposed. Also added in the screenplay is the drunkard Doc Boone, the marginalized professional who's sympathetic to Dallas and Ringo and who acts as a foil to Gatewood. The exposition and early scenes in the screenplay set up a tension between the characters with respectability or upper-class roots – Gatewood, Mrs. Mallory, Hatfield, and the ladies of the Law and Order League (another invention in the screenplay) – and the common, unpretentious characters, especially Dallas, Ringo, and Doc Boone but also, to some extent, Curley, Buck, and Peacock. As the script develops, the birth of Lucy Mallory's baby (another invention) and the external Apache threat draw the group together, but Hatfield's death, Gatewood's arrest, and Mrs. Mallory's separation from Dallas after the arrival in Lordsburg leave the upper-class characters outside the community that has been forged by the narrative. The final scene, invented in the screenplay, in which Doc and Curley send Dallas and Ringo off on the buckboard to their life together at Ringo's ranch across the border, concludes the Popular Front Western.

A close look at the two prominent characters who were newly created in the screenplay, Gatewood and Doc Boone, gives us a vivid picture of how Nichols invented characters to develop topical cultural conflicts and to articulate the film's Popular Front liberalism.[38] Gatewood is clearly constructed to recall the "economic royalists," the representatives of "entrenched greed," whom FDR pilloried throughout the 1936 election and whom many on the left criticized in the Popular Front period. Gatewood first appears in the draft screenplay (p. 9) inside the Tonto Bank, writing a receipt for a Wells Fargo agent. He's described as "an important-looking man of affairs. His voice is smooth, cultivated, commanding respect."[39] His orientation is clear from his opening lines: "Ever since we opened this bank I've been urging the mining company to deposit its pay roll here six months in advance. It's good business." The agent replies tersely, "It's good business for you, Mr. Gatewood." And he is right. From the first, Gatewood is portrayed as a self-interested and greedy person, far more concerned about his individual rights and freedom than any sense of community. Handing the agent the receipt, Gatewood "smiles affably" and tells him, "Remember this – what is good for the banks is good for the country," lines that conjure up President Calvin Coolidge's assertion in the 1920s that "the business of America is business." Our attitude toward this banker – not, after all, the most popular occupation in the country after the bank runs and closings that spread around the country in the early 1930s – is not positive, but it is made worse at the end of the scene when we see Gatewood pull out a valise and stuff it full of money. Throughout the screenplay – even more than in the film – Gatewood constantly fusses with the valise, reminding the audience that he's absconding with his depositors' money.[40]

After Gatewood flags down the stagecoach and raises the suspicions of Curley, he gets upset when he learns that the Apaches are on the warpath. Doc Boone, in an interchange that Nichols later cut (DS, 26), says, "Calm yourself, Gatewood. I'll give you a sedative for your nerves. We're having cavalry escorts all the way." Gatewood, "inwardly bristling," according to Nichols's directions, replies: "I don't need your soothing syrup, Doctor. As a man of some standing in my community – his look says, 'which you are not' – I am concerned with the principle of safe-conduct for passengers. I shall make my complaint to the authorities in Lordsburg" (DS, 26). After briefly and contemptuously acknowledging Dallas, he tells Peacock why he wants safe travel: "Better travel means more population. More population makes more business. And business expands our great nation. Why, in fifty years prosperity will turn this wilderness into a land of milk and honey" (27). Doc Boone is skeptical: "It could do right now with a little of the milk of human kindness and the honey of hospitality."[41] In both cases Gatewood's self-interest and bluster are countered by Doc Boone's charity and kindness. Although the interchange doesn't occur in the film, the portrayals of Gatewood and Doc Boone are consistent with their characterizations in the scripts.

Later, after Ringo flags down the stagecoach and they arrive in Dry Fork, Gatewood gets upset when Lieutenant Blanchard says he and the cavalry escort must return to Tonto. Gatewood masks his self-interest in community rhetoric: "I can't go back – catches himself and blusters – It's the duty of the stage company to get us there safely" (45). Then he wrangles with the lieutenant and finally, in lines that make it to the film in slightly different form, sternly scolds him: "You're a fine officer. I'm going to report your desertion to Colonel Davenport. He's a friend of mine. I'll take it up with Washington if necessary" (46). When Lieutenant Blanchard threatens to take Gatewood into military custody, however, Gatewood shows in his response that he's more a man of talk than action: "Now you don't need to lose your temper, young man. Don't lose your temper."

Later, when the group is about to leave Dry Fork for Apache Wells, Gatewood gives a parting shot to the lieutenant, saying he'll hold him "strictly accountable" if anything happens to any of the passengers (DS, 57). After the stagecoach gets on the road again, Gatewood launches once more into his business ideology: "Just as the Army fails to protect us citizens, so the government fails to protect the business man! A man's business used to be his own affair. Today the government pokes its nose into business everywhere. Why they're talking now about having bank examiners – as if we didn't know how to run our banks! I actually had a letter, Boon [sic], from some popinjay official saying they were going to inspect my books!"[42] Directing his comments to Peacock and Hatfield, Gatewood continues with words that the National Association of Manufacturers would have applauded: "Business cannot boom in America unless the government keeps its hands off. Taxes must come down. We are staggering under a national debt of over a billion dollars. What this country really needs is a business man for President!" (DS, 62).

But Gatewood's blustery rhetoric is undermined by his actions. When Lucy Mallory is about to deliver her baby, he moans: "A sick woman on our hands – that's all we needed to make it perfect" (75). Then, after the baby is delivered, he thinks only of himself and his escape. In the evening he asks incredulously, "We can't get out of here till morning?" Then in the morning he persists: "What are we wasting time for? Sun's up. Let's make a break for it" (DS, 95). In a scene cut from the film, when Chris's Apache wife picks up his valise, "Gatewood sees her, turns, and dashes the ladleful of water hard into her face" (DS, 87). He manages to offend almost everyone with his selfish behavior and sanctimonious ideology in the course of the film, so when he (instead of Ringo) is arrested upon the arrival in Lordsburg, no one much cares but Gatewood himself. His final speech, cut from the film, recapitulates his discredited

Gatewood (Berton Churchill) is arrested upon his arrival in Lordsburg. (collection of the editor)

perspective: "This is outrageous. I'm a respectable citizen! What's the country coming to when officers of the law don't protect the American business man?" (135).

Doc Boone is the other important character invented in Nichols's screenplay, and he exhibits several striking characteristics in the draft. Two of them – his use of elevated rhetoric and his comic-relief alcoholism – are toned down somewhat in the draft script's hand-written revisions and the finished film. Throughout the draft script Nichols lets Doc parade his learning. For example, early in the film, Doc, after telling Dallas they're victims of social prejudice, says, "Take my arm, Dallas. I shall lead you to the tumbril. Ha – Countess, you look charming this morning. Robespierre is at our heels. We shall triumph over him with our gaiety. Come Countess! To the guillotine!" (12). Although the speech links Doc both to education and – aptly – to the French Revolution, it is time-consuming and – unsurprisingly, given Ford's distaste for too much speech – truncated in the film version. Several times in the draft script, Doc's more learned allusions are crossed out in Nichols's handwriting, although it is unclear whether Nichols anticipated Ford's objections or whether Ford himself requested the cuts.[43]

There is also a great deal of reference to and joking about Doc's penchant for drink in the draft screenplay, including ample horseplay between Doc and Peacock, once Doc realizes Peacock's occupation as whiskey drummer. This dimension draws on the convention of the drunken doctor, common in both Western fiction and film, but a good bit of the interplay between Doc and Peacock in the draft screenplay is cut down or eliminated by Nichols's handwritten notes, in no small part because of objections raised by Joseph Breen in the Production Code of America (PCA) office. In his first response to Wanger after a treatment was submitted, Breen warned that "there also seems to be an indication of too much display of liquor and drunkenness."[44] Ten days later, after looking at a revised script, Breen reiterated, "We again urgently recommend that you keep down the element of Doctor Boone's drinking and drunkenness to the absolute minimum necessary for plot and characterization." He went on to specify three places in the script where "gags with liquor and drinking" could be omitted, recommendations that seem to have been heeded.[45] A great deal of the Peacock–Doc Boone interplay was cut in the final film, including considerable discussion by Peacock about his former career as a temperance lecturer and his guilt about contributing to the alcoholism of people like Doc Boone.[46]

Another facet of Doc's character is more crucial to the Popular Front thrust of *Stagecoach*: Although he is judged disreputable by the Tonto respectables, Doc is presented as an altruistic, wise, and compassionate character. He appears in the draft script in a scene immediately after Gatewood stuffs money in the valise. In many ways he serves as a foil to Gatewood throughout the film – if Gatewood functions as entrenched greed and selfish individualism, Doc exhibits kindness and community spirit. In Nichols's opening description, he is "in a stage of balanced inebriation," with his clothes "untidy and a little the worse for wear." He has a Union Army overcoat over one arm (later he disagrees with the southerner Hatfield about what to call the Civil War).[47] In the opposite hand he carries "a carpetbag [perhaps an indication of his northern roots?] containing his worldly possessions." When his "benevolent but bleary eye" lights upon Dallas being herded by a "grim-jawed escort of respectable ladies," he befriends her, and in Doc Boone she sees "a kindred soul in whom some milk of human kindness may be found" (11). When Dallas asks Doc if she has to leave the town, Doc replies (in a line cut from the film): "Fight hurricanes, my child, but don't fight organized female wrath. Look – even the minion of the law [referring to a deputy sheriff escorting Dallas] quails before them" (11). Dallas's next comment – "What have I done to them? Haven't I a right to live?" – allows Doc to give his moral critique that's central in the film: "We have been struck down by a foul disease called social prejudice, my child. These excellent ladies of the Law and Order League are scouring out the dregs of the town" (12).

This first appearance sets the stage for the core of Doc's character. Nichols created him as a character marginalized by society but educated, informed, and animated by a sense of democratic egalitarianism – a sense emphasized by his allusions to the French Revolution and his reference to the Union side in the "War of the Rebellion." If Gatewood represents the hated economic royalists of the Popular Front era, Doc is the educated but marginalized professional who aligns himself with the common people (and not, incidentally, unlike the successful screenwriter who takes a leadership role in the SWG to fight the recalcitrant studio heads).

Doc's kindness is manifested a number of times. When the stage-coach stops for Ringo in the draft screenplay, Doc notes that he knew Ringo's family and asks, "Didn't I set your arm when you were knee-high? Fell off a horse or something," prompting Ringo's recognition of him. The connection links Doc Boone to the altruistic profession-als in some of Frank Capra's films of the same era: Babe Bennett's father in *Mr. Deeds Goes to Town* (1936) and Ann Norton's father in *Meet John Doe* (1941) were both altruistic doctors, too, and close rela-tives to Doc Boone. In the Popular Front cultural ethos, good profes-sionals (doctors, teachers, lawyers, and so on) did their work to help people, not simply or even primarily to make money. Doc's kind-ness extends to all the characters, not just Ringo and Dallas. When Hatfield orders him to put out his cigar, Nichols's stage directions say, "Doc doesn't like Hatfield's haughty tone, but he is a kindly soul. He addresses Lucy with dignity" (SC, 39) and apologizes for bothering her. Doc's polite response to Lucy in the stagecoach is magnified by his kindness to her when her baby is about to be born. In a key scene invented in the screenplay and included in the film, Doc springs to action when Lucy is about to deliver, drinking coffee and sobering up to show the group that he knows his job and can do it well. Doc's actions precipitate the greatest sense of community in the film: The disparate group is almost completely united by the common purpose of seeing that Lucy's baby is delivered safely.

Once the baby is born, Doc becomes matchmaker – or at least counselor – advising Dallas when she asks him whether she and Ringo have a future. He admits he's worried: "I'm afraid you're going to get hurt, Dallas...."[48] Yet he adds, "But everyone has the right to want to live.... Go ahead, if you can do it" (DS, 99). He reiterates that advice through action at the end of the film when he and Curley send Ringo and Dallas on the buckboard, in the last words of the draft screenplay, "headed for the ranch over the Border and their new life" (146). If Gatewood's actions belie his words, Doc's actions and his words are consistent. He walks his talk. He aligns himself with the common people, even if respectables want to marginalize them. Rejected himself by the elites, he shows compassion to the two other social pariahs of the film: the escaped but unjustly convicted Ringo and the orphaned woman driven to prostitution, Dallas. With

Doc Boone (Thomas Mitchell) sobers up to deliver Mrs. Mallory's baby. (collection of the editor)

his help, and the help of the law – Curley – Dallas and Ringo are allowed to start a new life together, and the film celebrates it. Without a doubt, Doc functions as the moral center of the Popular Front Western.

Thus, through his invention of Doc Boone and Gatewood, as well as a number of other narrative details created as he adapted the Haycox story into a screenplay, Dudley Nichols – the leader/advocate for the SWG and active anti-fascist when he was writing the screenplay – constructed *Stagecoach* through the lens of Popular Front liberalism. This liberalism drew its conception of American history and society from a perspective similar to that of influential progressive historians of the era like Charles Beard, V. L. Parrington, and their followers. Parrington, in particular, through his monumental three-volume study *Main Currents in American Thought*, depicted American history as a persistent conflict between capitalists and democrats, the privileged and egalitarians, powerful elites and virtuous common people.[49] And he celebrated the democrats, the egalitarians, the common man as the true heirs to the best American ideals. His synthesis of American thought from this conflict perspective had a great deal of influence, directly and indirectly, on the American left in the 1930s, not least in films like *Stagecoach*.[50]

The driving energy behind Popular Front liberalism was a dream that those on the left could cooperate to defeat those, like FDR's "economic royalists," who were driven primarily by money and over-come those, like Hitler, who were driven largely by racial prejudice and lust for power. (SWG members would surely have seen the studio heads as prime examples of "economic royalists" hurting the nation's economy and making workers suffer.) Both Nichols's screen-play and the final film fully reject Gatewood, the corrupt capitalist, and partially reject Lucy Mallory and Hatfield, the products of an outmoded aristocratic heritage of the antebellum South. Although Mrs. Mallory's desire to reunite with her husband, despite danger, is presented positively, as is the entire dynamic surrounding the birth of her baby, by the end of the film she has rejected, or at least slighted, Dallas's overtures,[51] Gatewood has been arrested, and Hatfield has been killed.

On the other hand, the source of good in the film emanates from the marginalized common people, particularly Ringo and Dallas, and those, like Doc, with the compassion, wisdom, and decency to perceive their good qualities and give them a chance. Doc and the two other Western "common people" on the stagecoach – Curley and Buck – all realize that Dallas and Ringo are basically good people to whom life has dealt some tough blows, and it is no surprise that all three befriend and support the couple. The concluding scene of both the script and the final film, in which Doc and Curley evade the letter of the law and send Ringo and Dallas across the border to a new life, is infused by the spirit of Popular Front liberalism.[52]

CODA: REALIZING THE ETHOS OF POPULAR FRONT LIBERALISM

Although Dudley Nichols's screenplay provided the essential structures for establishing this Popular Front liberalism so central to the film, other collaborators provided crucial contributions in *realizing* that perspective in the final film. The first group worthy of mention consists of the performers who turned Nichols's words into flesh, particularly Thomas Mitchell (who won an Oscar for Best Supporting Actor for his role as Doc), Claire Trevor, John Wayne, Louise Platt, Berton Churchill, and John Carradine. Second, there is cinematographer Gregg Toland, whose visual compositions were crucial in establishing the relationships between the characters. The third group comprises a collective group of arrangers who drew on American folk songs to fashion a score that supported the shifting emotional tones of the film: Richard Hageman, Frank Harling, John Leipold, Leo Shuken, and Louis Gruenberg.[53] Last but certainly not least, John Ford himself directed all these collaborators and even, contrary to his usual practice, supervised the editing after shooting was completed.[54] As the epigraph to this essay suggests, Nichols himself was well aware that the screenwriter's labor was only one step in the collaborative process of filmmaking, and a brief look at several elements from the film itself shows how these other collaborators combined to infuse the spirit of Popular Front liberalism in the finished film.

For example, in one scene invented in the screenplay, the stagecoach arrives at Dry Fork, and the group goes inside to eat a quick meal.[55] The screenplay directions note that "Dallas is uncertain whether she should sit down, knowing she is not expected to sit with 'respectable' people."[56] The framing of Toland's cinematography and the performances of the characters in two key shots break the group into respectables and social pariahs, criticizing the first and embracing the second. The two shots are the fourth and ninth in a series of ten shots, arranged as follows:

1. Medium long shot (MLS) of Ringo and Dallas. Ringo holds a chair on the near left side of the table after having invited Dallas in an earlier shot to sit down. Dallas moves toward the camera and sits down. Camera dollies in to a medium closeup (MCU) of Dallas, who looks down diffidently.
2. MCU of Mrs. Mallory staring disapprovingly at Dallas.
3. Medium shot (MS) of Dallas uneasily looking back; her eyes drop; Ringo seated beside her.
4. MLS of Gatewood glowering, a standing Hatfield looking critically at Dallas, and Mrs. Mallory with eyes down. Hatfield hands Mrs. Mallory a plate.
5. MS, same as 3, Dallas's eyes down.

6. MLS, same as 4, Hatfield says, "May I find you another seat, Mrs. Mallory? It's cooler by the window."
7. MS, same as 3 and 5, Dallas and Ringo react.
8. MLS, same as 4 and 6, Dallas stands and walks toward other end of table, followed by Hatfield, Gatewood begins to stand – match on action.
9. LS, whole table, Gatewood continues to stand and follows the others to far end of table.
10. MS, from straight across table, Ringo and Dallas, Ringo says, "Looks like I got the plague, don't it?"

The hostile reactions of the three respectables immediately brand them as intolerant and petty; Toland's balanced framing helps make those reactions clear. Similarly, his use of camera distance and the depth of the composition show how the respectables separate themselves from the social pariahs. Image, cutting, framing, and performance all blend to realize the screenplay's conception.

Doc Boone's role as a kind and compassionate social observer, so evident in the screenplay, is captured well through Thomas Mitchell's performance and Gregg Toland's camera, particularly in several closeup reaction shots.[57] For example, after Hatfield scolds him for smoking a cigar that offends Mrs. Mallory, Doc apologizes to her. The warmth and sincerity of his words are matched by his kindly facial expression. Later, Doc talks sympathetically to Dallas the morning following the birth of Mrs. Mallory's baby. Toland gives Doc another closeup immediately after Dallas has asked Doc if it would be all right for her to return Ringo's affections, given her past, and Doc has replied, "Who am I to tell you what's right and wrong?" Following this look of concern, he gives Dallas permission to go ahead with Ringo and wishes her good luck.[58] Finally, Doc reacts in another Toland closeup after proposing a toast to the other passengers just before the Apache raid begins. Doc seeks to unify the community briefly, knowing that the diverse group probably won't meet together again, given their social divisions. His look of satisfaction suggests something of the important role he played in helping to create, for even a short time, unity amidst diversity in the stagecoach community. These expressions are typical of Doc Boone's character: Thomas Mitchell's acting ability, as well as Toland's camera distance and lighting, enables Mitchell to use his face with effectiveness and nuance.

Gatewood is written in the draft screenplay as the man the audience loves to hate, and Berton Churchill's performance succeeds in making viewers dislike the banker as much as Mitchell's performance draws viewers to Doc Boone. One reaction shot of Gatewood is used twice in the film, first when the Wells Fargo agent leaves his bank, responding to Gatewood that regular deposits are good especially for the *banker*, and second when Gatewood hears his wife tell him that the Ladies of the Law and Order League are coming to their home for lunch. Throughout the film, Churchill's dour, severe expressions reinforce his fatuous, self-serving, and hypocritical commentary. His explicit business ideology, defined so clearly in the draft screenplay, is severely criticized not only by the actions outlined in the screenplay but also by Berton Churchill's performance, Gregg Toland's cinematography, and the precision of John Ford's direction and editing. Clearly the collaborators played an important role in getting Nichols's script conceptions into the finished film.

In exploring *Stagecoach* by highlighting the creative contributions of the screenwriter, I do not wish to deny the artistry and skill of John Ford, who surely was one of Hollywood's most accomplished directors. And Dudley Nichols knew as well as any screenwriter that the work he turned in was not the finished film: As he put it on one occasion, the screenplay "is not and never can be a finished product. It is a step, the first and most important step, in the process of making a film."[59] We can forgive Nichols for defending his craft in this passage. In fact, his comment not only expresses the screenwriter's desire for

The kindly-looking Doc Boone is contrasted with the stern visage of Gatewood. (frame enlargements)

recognition – so common among screenwriters who worked in the studio era – but also calls to mind Ernest Lehman's bemused recollection of how many "Hitchcock touches" he put into screenplays written for the master of suspense. Nichols acknowledged both that filmmaking was a "vast collaboration" and that to succeed, a film must be guided by "a dominant will and personality." Undoubtedly thinking in part about his work with Ford, Nichols added that "sometimes two people can work together with such sympathy and shared attitude that they can achieve a common style; and these two people must, I believe, be the writer and director."[60]

With Robert Carringer's notion of the collaborative process of Hollywood filmmaking in mind, let's give credit where credit is due. No one would dispute that this classic Western *was* in part, as Frank Nugent claimed, powered by a Ford. However, the invention of Doc Boone and Gatewood, as well as the thematic integration of Popular Front liberalism into the screenplay and finished film, makes it equally clear that *Stagecoach* was also propelled by a Nichols.

NOTES

1. John Gassner and Dudley Nichols, eds., *Twenty Best Film Plays* (New York: Crown, 1943), p. xxxi.
2. Frank Nugent, review of *Stagecoach*, *New York Times* (March 2, 1939), p. 19. Reprinted in this volume.
3. Robert L. Carringer, *The Making of* Citizen Kane (Berkeley: University of California Press, 1985), p. ix.
4. As we shall see, central to exploring Nichols's contributions to the film's narrative and ideology is an October 1938 draft screenplay with Nichols's handwritten revisions, housed in Special Collections in the Lilly Library at Indiana University. This draft screenplay stands as a crucial creative step between Ernest Haycox's short story "Stage to Lordsburg" and both the final screenplay and the completed film. Nichols's annotated draft makes it possible to identify more precisely his contributions to the evolution of *Stagecoach*.
5. On "structures of feeling," see Raymond Williams, *Marxism and Literature* (New York and Oxford: Oxford University Press, 1978), Chap. 9, especially pp. 132–5.
6. Such film historians and scholars as Jeffrey Richards, writing about some of the films directed by Frank Capra and John Ford in the later 1930s, use the term "populism" to describe the social vision of the movies. I believe that term to be too nebulous for my purposes here. In addition, because the term also refers to a specific political movement in American history, the Populist movement of the late nineteenth century, applying "populism" to these

filmmakers working during the Depression years adds the potential for more confusion. "Popular Front liberalism," as I use the term, has a much more specific historical context than the general "populism" sometimes attributed to the Capra and Ford films. It thrived from the outbreak of the Spanish Civil War until the Hitler–Stalin Pact and the consequent outbreak of World War II. See Jeffrey Richards, *Visions of Yesterday* (London: Routledge and Kegan Paul, 1973).

7. See Richard Pells, *Radical Visions and American Dreams* (New York: Harcourt, 1973), pp. 292–319. On Popular Front activity in Hollywood, see Larry Ceplair and Stephen Englund, *The Inquisition in Hollywood: Politics in the Film Community, 1930–1960* (Berkeley: University of California Press, 1983), especially Chap. 4. The Hollywood Anti-Nazi League activities and the Spanish Civil War are discussed in detail on pp. 104–17. Hollywood was politicized more than most of the country by the Spanish Civil War. David Kennedy notes that in January 1937, two-thirds of the American public had no opinion about the Spanish conflict; see *Freedom from Fear: The American People in Depression and War, 1929–1945* (New York: Oxford University Press, 1999), pp. 398–9.

8. For overviews of Nichols's life and career, see the entries on Nichols by Paul L. Jensen in *Dictionary of American Biography*, Supplement 6 (New York: Scribner's, 1980), pp. 475–7, and by Thomas Stempel in *American National Bigraphy* (New York: Oxford University Press, 1999), pp. 383–4; Richard Corliss, *Talking Pictures: Screenwriters in the American Cinema* (New York: Overlook, 1974), pp. 225–35; and Ian Hamilton, *Writers in Hollywood, 1915–1951* (New York: Harper, 1990), pp. 166–79. Andrew Sarris quotes a letter from Nichols to Lindsay Anderson about his 1929 move to Hollywood in *You Ain't Heard Nothing Yet: The American Talking Film, History and Memory, 1927–1949* (New York: Oxford University Press, 1998), p. 169.

9. Nichols also received Best Screenplay nominations for *Air Force* and *The Tin Star* (1957).

10. In his classic history of American movies, Lewis Jacobs wrote that "The close association of Capra and Riskin is, next to that of John Ford and Dudley Nichols, the foremost example of that cooperation between director and writer which is fast becoming a practice in Hollywood." A few pages later, Jacobs adds, "John Ford can be said to have found himself in his association with Dudley Nichols.... Ford alone made merely commercial box-office successes; the John Ford–Dudley Nichols combination, after a few desultory efforts, made above-the-average films." *The Rise of the American Film* (New York: Teachers College Press, 1939), pp. 476, 479.

11. In the 1960s and the early 1970s the reputations of a number of directors from the classical period who survived and were willing to talk with critics (or even to write autobiographies) – like Capra, Ford, Hitchcock, and Sirk – skyrocketed. See, for example, Capra's autobiography *The Name Above the Title* (New York: Macmillan, 1971); Peter Bogdanovich's interview book, *John Ford* (Berkeley: University of California Press, 1968); Truffaut's interview book, *Hitchcock* (New York: Simon & Schuster, 1967); and Jon Halliday, *Sirk*

on Sirk (New York: Viking Press, 1972). Robert Kapsis delineates effectively the process through which Hitchcock helped shape his reputation as an auteur during the 1960s in *Hitchcock: The Making of a Reputation* (Chicago: University of Chicago Press, 1992). Kapsis argues that the "art world" of the cinema changed in the 1960s, making it more receptive to emphasizing the achievement of the director. Concurrently, the focus on screenwriters dwindled, particularly those screenwriters whose passing prevented them from advertising themselves.

12.   This book is a kind of companion to Sarris's *The American Cinema: Directors and Directions, 1929–1968* (New York: Dutton, 1968). Corliss did for screenwriters what Sarris did for directors. Both books rank Hollywood professionals into categories and provide filmographies and overview assessments of individual directors or screenwriters. Corliss places Nichols in a lesser category, "Themes in Search of a Style," similar to Sarris's category of "Strained Seriousness." It is worth noting, too, that Sarris wrote the preface for Corliss's book.

13.   *Talking Pictures*, p. 227. More recent commentators perpetuate this assessment of Nichols. In his fine recent biography of Ford, *Print the Legend: The Life and Times of John Ford* (New York: Simon & Schuster, 1999), Scott Eyman quotes Corliss's perspective, then adds, "Nichols *was* fond of using people as symbols, the 1930s agit-prop equivalent of High Concept" (p. 205).

14.   See Nancy Lynn Schwartz, *The Hollywood Writers' Wars* (New York: Knopf, 1982), pp. 21, 129, 139, and 188; and Tino Balio, *Grand Design: Hollywood as a Modern Business Enterprise, 1930–1939* (Berkeley: University of California Press, 1993), pp. 82–5.

15.   Schwartz quotes excerpts from the letter on pp. 53–4.

16.   Schwartz, pp. 58–61. The first page of the *Motion Picture Herald* article is reproduced on p. 62.

17.   Screen Playwrights "declared itself against the idea of a closed shop, condemned the Guild for radicalism, and announced itself ready to listen to 'sane proposals' and to undertake 'sane negotiations' with the studios." It had more stringent entrance requirements for membership than the SWG, favoring experienced and higher paid screenwriters. Although the studios did sign an agreement with SP, that agreement had no mimimum wage for screenwriters, nor did it give the organization control over assigning screenwriting credits, two key concerns for the SWG. See Schwartz, *Hollywood Writers' Wars*, pp. 71–2, 99.

18.   Excerpts from the ad are quoted in Schwartz, *Hollywood Writers' Wars*, p. 125.

19.   These various activities are noted in Ceplair and Englund, *Inquisition in Hollywood*, especially pp. 107–8, 114, 116, and 132. Films for Democracy sought to raise money to support films influenced by leftist documentary filmmakers like Paul Strand. It helped support Strand's *Native Land* (1942). See Matthew Bernstein, *Walter Wanger: Hollywood Independent* (Berkeley: University of California Press, 1994), pp. 138–9.

20.   See Schwartz, *Hollywood Writers' Wars*, p. 197, Ceplair and Englund, *Inquisition in Hollywood*, pp. 209–10.

21. Letter, John Ford to Bob Ford, September 1937, John Ford Papers; Tag Gallagher, *John Ford: The Man and His Films* (Berkeley: University of California Press, 1986), p. 342.

22. Scott Eyman, *Print the Legend: The Life and Times of John Ford* (New York: Simon & Schuster, 1999), p. 135.

23. See *Ibid.*, p. 187. The photograph was inscribed "*Unter John Ford mit herzlichen grus aus Deutschland. Leni Riefenstahl*" ("For John Ford with hearty greetings from Germany").

24. See Dan Ford, *Pappy: The Life of John Ford* (New York: Prentice-Hall, 1979), pp. 112–13.

25. The story has been republished in Dudley Nichols and John Ford, *Stagecoach* (New York: Simon & Schuster, 1971), pp. 4–18. On the amount Ford paid for the story, see also p. 45n6.

26. In 2000 the University of Oregon Libraries mounted an exhibit, "Ernest Haycox and the Western in Fiction and Film," which included many of Haycox's manuscripts, publications, and photographs of him throughout his career. See the wonderfully informative Web site that accompanied the exhibit: http://libweb.uoregon.edu/speccoll/mss/haycox. According to the exhibit, Haycox's total literary output included 24 novels and more than 200 short stories.

27. See also Edward Buscombe's comparison of the story and the film in his volume in the Film Classics Series, *Stagecoach* (London: British Film Institute, 1992), pp. 33–7.

28. Haycox in Nichols, pp. 5, 8.

29. *Ibid.*, p. 8.

30. The whiskey drummer dies shortly after this in the story. He survives in the film, and the gambler dies in the Apache raid, unlike in the story, where he survives.

31. Haycox in Nichols, p. 7.

32. Eyman, *Print the Legend*, says that Ford and producer Merian C. Cooper tried to sell David O. Selznick on the project as early as the summer of 1937, but that after initially agreeing, Selznick backed out when Ford and Cooper insisted on John Wayne and Claire Trevor as leads (pp. 192–3). According to Bernstein, *Walter Wanger*, Wanger finally agreed to produce the film through United Artists in the summer of 1938 (p. 147).

33. The shooting schedule is outlined in Eyman, *Print the Legend*, p. 200.

34. Dudley Nichols, draft screenplay for *Stagecoach* (October 10–23, 1938), Manuscript Department, Lilly Library, University of Indiana, Bloomington. Hereafter referred to as "draft screenplay" or "draft script" and cited in the text as: (DS, p. ___). This revised draft was written by Nichols between October 10 and 23, 1938, in preparation for the shooting of the film, which began on October 31. It also contains handwritten emendations (including cuts, revisions, and additions) that seem to have been done between October 23 and early November. A subsequent draft, based partly on the handwritten emendations, was typed and submitted to Joseph Breen's office on November 9, and further minor revisions were submitted to his office on

November 14, after which the script was approved. I thank Kay Gibson of the Indiana University Libraries for her assistance in helping me locate this rough draft.

A final screenplay of *Stagecoach* was published in Gassner and Nichols, *Twenty Best Film Plays*, pp. 996–1038. A similar version of that script was published in the Classic Film Scripts as *Stagecoach* by Dudley Nichols and John Ford in 1971. The differences between the two published "final" scripts are itemized in the latter book, pp. 144–52. As Edward Buscombe has noted, however, even the two "final" scripts are different from the finished film and cannot be considered accurate transcriptions of the film's dialogue. The 1971 publication, for example, gives Doc Boone these lines in the final scene, as Dallas and Ringo are riding off in the buckboard: "Well, that's saved them the blessings of civilization," when the line in the film is clearly "Well, they're saved from the blessings of civilization." See Buscombe, *Stagecoach*, p. 94.

35. Nichols, "The Writer and the Film," in Gassner and Nichols, *Twenty Best Film Plays*, p. xxxii.

36. *Public Papers and Addresses of Franklin D. Roosevelt: The People Approve*, vol. 5 (New York: Random House, 1936), pp. 13, 16.

37. *Ibid.*, pp. 566–73. See also Kennedy, *Freedom from Fear*, pp. 278–85.

38. For two earlier discussions of the topicality of *Stagecoach*, see Buscombe, *Stagecoach*, pp. 28–31, who focuses on Gatewood, and Michael Coyne, *The Crowded Prairie: American National Identity in the Hollywood Western* (New York and London: I. B. Taurus, 1998), pp. 19–23. Coyne challenges Andrew Sarris's assertion that *Stagecoach* "does not seem to be about anything by 1939 standards" by arguing that the film "is most resonant as a parable of 1939 America" (p. 19). I would revise that slightly by saying that it is more a meditation on 1937–38 America from the perspective of a Popular Front liberal.

39. Nichols also indicates here that Alan Hale would play the role. Of course, Berton Churchill, who played in other Ford films (for example, the bad lawyer in *Judge Priest*), eventually got the role. This is the only instance in the screenplay where the actor indicated for the role is incorrect.

40. In *The Big Tomorrow: Hollywood and the Politics of the American Way* (Chicago: University of Chicago Press, 2000), Lary May includes an interesting graph indicating how often feature films (taken from a sample group) featured "big business villains" (including bankers) every four years from 1914 to 1958 (p. 274). The highest percentage, about 20 percent of the films in the sample, occurred in 1930, but the percentage remained quite high, around 10 percent, in 1934 and 1938, falling to almost nothing in 1942, after the United States entered World War II. The graph suggests that the negative portrayal of Gatewood, then, is relatively typical for at least one strand of American films from the 1930s.

41. Right after these cut lines, Doc turns to Dallas and says, "Courage, madame la comtessa! The canaille are stoning us as our tumbril rolls through the streets of Paris" (p. 27). This comment hearkens back to Doc's earlier lines,

as he accompanies Dallas to the stagecoach, followed by the ladies of the Law and Order League. Many of the handwritten revisions in the draft script are cut dialogue, in line with the general critical consensus that Ford liked his dialogue to be as terse as possible. And in general, as with a later line when Doc refers to Bacchus, I think the cuts of Doc's classical allusions were probably a good idea, whether they were precipitated by Nichols or Ford.

42. Gatewood's displeasure had a contemporary ring in 1939. Partly as a response to the economic crisis, FDR signed the Banking Act of 1933, which gave the Open Market Committee statutory recognition. The Committee was authorized to buy and sell U.S. government debt instruments. Then, in 1935, FDR signed legislation that put the Open Market Committee under the direct authority of the Federal Reserve Board of Governors and thus gave the Federal Reserve Board more control over modulating business cycles. Bankers in the 1930s surely began to feel the effects of government regulation of the economy in general and of banks in particular. See Kennedy, *Freedom from Fear*, pp. 242, 274.

43. After learning, in part from Ford, about how movies were made, Nichols came to share Ford's belief that a film should not rely too much on words. As he put it in one context, "The most noticeable feature of a skillful screenplay is its terseness and bareness" ("The Writer and the Film," p. xxxvi).

44. Joseph Breen to Walter Wanger, October 28, 1938. John Ford Mss., Lilly Library, Indiana University.

45. Joseph Breen to Walter Wanger, November 9, 1938. John Ford Mss., Lilly Library, Indiana University.

46. Little is *added* to Doc's role from the draft sceenplay except the brief interchange between Doc and the bartender in Tonto. The bartender was played by Ford's friend Jack Pennick, who appeared in many Ford films. In an added page with handwritten dialogue in the draft script, Doc asks Jerry for credit on one last drink, and Jerry replies, "If talk were money, Doc, you'd be the best customer I have." Ford may have requested that some lines be written for Pennick, who would then have earned more for his brief appearance in the film (see DS, 12 verso).

47. Doc Boone calls it "the War of the Rebellion," but Hatfield corrects him – to Doc's chagrin – by calling it "the War for the Southern Confederacy." These lines are used almost verbatim in an earlier Ford–Nichols collaboration, *Steamboat Round the Bend*, the 1935 Will Rogers vehicle.

48. Nichols cuts these lines and writes in a substitute, "Who am I to tell you what's right or wrong?" Then he makes a transition to the next line in the draft screenplay, "I guess everyone has the right to want to live."

49. This architectonic three-volume study of American thought from the beginnings to 1920 was published between 1927 and 1930, the third volume posthumously (Parrington was still working on the final volume at his death). All three volumes are conveniently collected in V. L. Parrington, *Main Currents in American Thought* (New York: Harcourt and Brace, 1958).

50. The consensus historian Richard Hofstadter provides a detailed analysis and critique of Parrington in *The Progressive Historians: Turner, Beard, Parrington* (New York: Random House, 1968), Chaps. 10–11. Gene Wise provides a somewhat more sympathetic look from the perspective of a New Left historian in *American Historical Explanations: A Strategy for Grounded Inquiry* (Homewood, Ill.: Dorsey Press, 1973), especially pp. 248–70. John Higham gives a concise description of Parrington's approach and achievement in *Writing American History* (Bloomington: Indiana University Press, 1970), pp. 56–9.

51. It is true that one reaction shot of Mrs. Mallory as she emerges from the stagecoach suggests that she regrets having treated Dallas so badly. However, she's unwilling to acknowledge that regret publicly to the women who greet her in Lordsburg.

52. One might add that the film depicts not only the energies but also some of the blind spots of Popular Front liberalism. Partly because Franklin Roosevelt's New Deal coalition depended on conservative southern Democrats for its majority status, civil rights was not often high on the agenda of liberals in the late 1930s. Kennedy, *Freedom from Fear*, notes that FDR, despite pleas from his wife and advisors, gave an anti-lynching bill only nominal support in the 1930s for fear of antagonizing powerful southern legislators (p. 343). One such bill was withdrawn as late as 1938. Similarly, *Stagecoach* portrays Apaches and their leader, Geronimo, simply and unequivocally as a diabolical threat; they certainly have no place in the Popular Front community. One might also explore the film's portrayal of Hispanics through the character of Chris; and of women, especially Dallas, Lucy, and Chris's wife. (For more on the film's portrayal of Native Americans and women, see the essays in this volume by J. P. Telotte and Gaylyn Studlar, respectively.) Despite its avowed sympathies for the plight of common people, Popular Front liberalism tended not to encourage a Rainbow Coalition.

53. Buscombe, *Stagecoach*, has a brief discussion on the score (pp. 47–9), which won the Oscar for Best Score of 1939. He notes that the score was farmed out to Paramount because it had to be done so quickly and that the press kit listed more than a dozen songs from the era woven into it. See also Rudy Behlmer, *America's Favorite Movies: Behind the Scenes* (New York: Ungar, 1982), p. 117. Hageman worked on six more Ford films, including *Fort Apache* (1948), *She Wore a Yellow Ribbon* (1949), and *Wagon Master* (1950).

54. Eyman, *Print the Legend*, p. 204.

55. Nick Browne offers a detailed analysis of the narration of this scene in his essay "The Spectator-in-the-Text: The Rhetoric of *Stagecoach*," *Film Quarterly* 29, no. 2 (Winter 1975–6), pp. 26–37.

56. Nichols, p. 65. The draft screenplay is missing the pages of the early part of this scene, perhaps because no revisions were made on those pages.

57. Thomas Mitchell, a veteran and successful character actor, earned $12,000 for his work on *Stagecoach*, second only to Claire Trevor's $15,000 salary. Wayne, just promoted from Monogram B westerns, earned only $3,700 on the film. (In comparison, Ford's salary was budgeted at $50,000 and Nichols was paid $20,000.) See Buscombe, *Stagecoach*, pp. 18–19.

58. The draft screenplay gives this explanation: "The old doctor looks at her with a depth of understanding. There is something regretful in his eyes, foreseeing that Dallas is on ice too thin to hold her weight. But he can't refuse this begging for life" (p. 99).
59. Nichols, "The Writer and the Film," p. xxxii.
60. *Ibid.*, p. xxxv.

3 That Past, This Present

Historicizing John Ford, 1939

Though its credit sequence features a montage of leisurely move-
ments – shots of a stagecoach and its escort moving one way; of U.S.
cavalry, then Apache warriors, the other; of the stagecoach again,
sans escort, as if returning – *Stagecoach* proper begins with riders galloping hell-bent-for-leather almost directly toward the camera, in a
long shot.[1] This shot then dissolves to an army outpost on the edge
of nowhere, hitching rails to frame left, tents and camp furniture
and a flag staff to frame right. A bugle blows. The stars and stripes
ascend the pole in the background while the riders pass back-to-
front through the frame. A more visually and dramatically central
flag raising occurs at the end of *Drums Along the Mohawk*, another
1939 John Ford film involving frontier outposts, besieged settlers,
sinister aristocrats, newborn infants, and courage tested by combat
or contest. And it concludes, almost as *Stagecoach* begins, with a display of the national banner. Few of the Revolutionary-era characters
who watch its ascent in *Drums* have ever seen the flag before; the
symbolism of its stars and stripes must literally be explained. And
individual "watchers" are picked out by Ford's camera and cutting to
witness its ascent, as if they were watching on our behalf. Claudette
Colbert's Lana Martin thinks the flag is "pretty"; a black woman,
Daisy, Mrs. McKlennar's "servant," looks up tearfully; Blue Back, a
Christian Indian, offers salute; and Henry Fonda's Gil Martin gets
a good eyeful and says it's "time to get back to work" because there's
a "heap to do from now on."

It is the work of this essay to investigate the historicity of John Ford's films and filmmaking in 1939, commonly regarded as Hollywood's and Ford's most "spectacularly prolific" year.[2] I invoke a portion of that history as prologue in order to acknowledge the necessary partiality of the enterprise. There is more to Ford than *Stagecoach*, *Young Mr. Lincoln*, and *Drums Along the Mohawk*. And there is far more to 1939 than John Ford movies. These two flag raisings also foreground the question of textuality, or intertextuality. For instance, critics have often noted the New Deal multiculturalism of the sequence in *Drums Along the Mohawk* – as if Ford were breaking his historical frame, were addressing the needs of his 1939 present by including a black and a Native American within his mythical national community.[3] That it was myth then, as it is myth now, was probably self-evident. It is hard to imagine a 1939 audience whose members did not catch some hint of irony, or naïveté, in Ford's asking them to imagine the flag being seen for the first time. It is also hard to imagine a very large 1939 audience whose members did not also assume that the black woman in question was a slave, the property of Gil and Lana, passed to them with the McKlennar farmstead upon the death of its feisty, proto-feminist mistress (Edna May Oliver).

I make the latter claim more for historical than interpretive purposes, and in order to mark the historicity of interpretation itself. Most latter-day viewers are prone to assume that Daisy is a free black. This assumption likely follows from the film's setting, in upstate New York, well above the Mason-Dixon line; yet it follows from ignorance, because "Dutch" New York, where *Drums* is set, in fact had a large population of slaves, and because slavery in many New England states was not illegal until well after the Revolution.[4] Given that the Walter D. Edmonds novel upon which *Drums Along the Mohawk* was based was in its thirty-first printing when the film was released, and that the novel's Daisy, like almost every other black character in the story, was held in bondage, it seems likely that many of the film's original viewers – those many who had read the novel, at least – would have assumed Daisy's servitude, given the absence of explicit evidence to the contrary. That Ford and his collaborators did not provide that evidence is consistent with Ford's New Deal idealism, in seeking to avoid the negative connotations of slavery, though this silence might also be taken as complicit with the racial status quo circa 1776 – or 1939.[5]

It is not the goal of this essay to claim that a "1939" reading of *Stagecoach* or *Drums Along the Mohawk* is automatically to be preferred to some ostensibly more "universal" or "formalist" analysis, or vice versa. I *do* wish, however, to second Rick Altman's claim that all film interpretation is a social process, under constant negotiation, and that the process amounts to social construction, the building of a "constellated" community via "lateral communication."[6] I have lately come to the view that *Stagecoach*, *Young Mr. Lincoln*, and *Drums Along the Mohawk* form a tightly interrelated set; part of my task here is to specify those relationships, however briefly. Setting about to "historicize" John Ford circa 1939, I decided to check my current understanding of the films against that of the films' original audience, on the assumption that differences between then and now would be telling, as the flag-raising example indicates. I hardly have direct access to that audience, to be certain; but there is precedent for thinking that some aspects of the films' original reception can be inferred from their various exhibition circumstances, understood chiefly as a matter of intertexts – those documents and films that probably functioned as "pre-texts" for members of that audience.[7]

Obviously Ford's version of *Drums Along the Mohawk* could not have served as a pre-text for the earlier *Stagecoach* until its release in November 1939. Indeed, I began my research believing that intertextual relations among *particular* films were not likely to matter as much as advertisements and news coverage of various sorts, given the view I then had of 1939 exhibition practices – of films' being released first to producer-owned or -affiliated first-run houses or "palaces," then moving out to more modern or modest neighborhood venues, with some few films, typically the most successful, being re-released after the passage of some considerable time.[8] Accordingly, I assumed that most viewers would have experienced the films sequentially – *Stagecoach* first, *Young Mr. Lincoln* second, *Drums Along the Mohawk* last – which led to the question of how much or little "John Ford" might have served as a "pre-textual" reading strategy for 1939 audiences, given the eight-month gap between *Stagecoach* and *Drums*. Was Ford an auteur for these viewers?

My initial hunch about the relative weakness of the "Ford" pre-text in the pre-auteur era seemed at least partially confirmed by the national newspapers and magazines I consulted, though Frank Nugent's reviews of all three films in the *New York Times* were em-phatically pro-Ford.[9] The *Time* review of *Stagecoach*, which got second billing to *Let Freedom Ring* (1939) as contributing (via the Western) to a trend toward "Americanism," highlights *Stagecoach* producer Walter Wanger rather than Ford; Wanger's "contempt for the Pro-duction Code" is manifested in the characters of Dallas and Ringo, one a "prostitute," the other a "desperado"; Wanger gets the por-trait photo; and Ford is mentioned only in a prepositional phrase.[10] Ford gets better treatment (for being "in peak form") in the *Variety* review of *Stagecoach* but is not mentioned by name in the *Variety* review of *Young Mr. Lincoln*, which saw the film's "production and direction" as "rather lethargic"; and Ford is mentioned only once, in passing, in *Variety*'s review of *Drums Along the Mohawk* (which "highly pleases the eye even if the story, on occasion, gets a bit slow").[11] Likewise, though all three of Ford's 1939 films received "Movie of the Week" treatment in *Life* – which amounted, in each case, to a photos-plus-legends preview of the movie – mention of Ford is min-imal by contrast with the attention paid to producers (Wanger and Zanuck) and stars (Fonda and Colbert). Ford is mentioned once in the *Stagecoach* story (as having paired with Dudley Nichols before, on *The Informer*, 1935), not at all in the storyboard presentation of *Young Mr. Lincoln*, and as an "able purveyor of raw melodrama" who nevertheless "dwells lovingly over a childbirth" in his direction of *Drums Along the Mohawk*.[12]

Once I started checking the more "local" material to which I had microfilm access, however, various aspects of this picture shifted remarkably. The exhibition data for Atlanta, Georgia, for example, quite confounded the assumption that Ford's films were ordinarily available to viewers only in order-of-initial-release sequence. Accord-ingly, I checked every 1939 day of as many local newspapers as possi-ble for the sake of tracking exhibition and promotion patterns, which effort yielded an almost literal cross-section of America, slicing south-easterly from Ames, Iowa, to St. Louis, Missouri, to Atlanta, Georgia. Also scanned for opening-run display ads and reviews were a number of other regional newspapers.

In view of the race question raised in connection with *Drums Along the Mohawk*, and of Altman's claims regarding the construction of generic and critical communities, let me say a few more words about audience, at least as regards those cities for which exhibition data were collected. With the obvious exception of *Variety*, whose ostensible reader is an industry insider, the audience invoked in all the other print venues surveyed is a "mass" audience, a "democratic" audience to the extent that everyone is ostensibly invited to consume the product on offer. Yet one social fact is well worth noting, as placing constraints upon that invitation – the fact of racially segregated theaters.

This was not an issue in Ames, Iowa. According to the 1940 U.S. Census, less than 1 percent of the state's 2.5 million people were black. In all likelihood, few blacks were represented in the census data for Ames, which tended to exclude students, given a city population of 12,555 – though the WPA guide to Iowa observes that the presence in Ames of Iowa State College gave the town "a metropolitan character and coloring."[13] Ames had four theaters in 1939. With double bills and four screens, up to fifteen films were exhibited per week; few (if any) films played more than a week, nor were there many revivals. Given the Iowa legal code, which forbade discrimination in theaters, it seems likely that filmgoing was experienced as somewhat democratic, even if minority patrons were too few to cause majority patrons much distress.[14]

Atlanta, Georgia, obviously handled its racial distress quite differently in its approximately thirty-six theaters. The daily "Amusement Calendar" listing of film times and titles in the *Atlanta Constitution* usually divided its screens into categories: Picture and Stage Shows, Downtown Theaters (these first two categories cover some ten venues, at least half of which combined films and stage acts on occasion), Neighborhood Theaters (between fifteen and twenty-four screens), and Colored Theaters (between six and eight screens).[15] Per the 1940 U.S. Census, Atlanta had a population of 302,288 and Georgia's work force was 33.48 percent black; the inference that roughly one-third of Atlanta's population was black in 1939 is confirmed by a story that ran on March 14.[16] Screens per capita favored the white population, though blacks were probably allowed to view films from balcony seating in at least some of the (probably downtown) theaters.[17]

St. Louis had by far the largest population among the three cities for which exhibition patterns were charted: 816,048 per the 1940 Census, though that number does not include the population of East St. Louis, Illinois (75,609). Per the WPA guide to Missouri, the black population of St. Louis was 11.4 percent of the total.[18] The city described in the pages of the *St. Louis Post-Dispatch* had between eighty-five and ninety-five screens, though the paper represented them differently than its Atlanta counterpart. Only the five or six downtown theaters were "listed"; the eighty-odd other venues hawked their wares chiefly through list-like, copy-crammed advertisements (St. Louis was big on double bills and giveaways) arranged mostly by reference to theater chains. Though a separate ten-venue black theater circuit existed in St. Louis and East St. Louis, these theaters apparently did not advertise in the *Post-Dispatch*.[19]

A picture of various mass media – newspapers, as in this case, but also music, cinema, sports – alternately inscribing and effacing the borders of community is at the heart of *Film/Genre*, in which Altman describes "genrefication" as a process whose moments of apparently "classical" stability are better seen as instances of precarious balance among overlapping and competing communities and interests. I will claim that the 1939 promotion and reception of *Stagecoach*, *Young Mr. Lincoln*, and *Drums Along the Mohawk* can be seen as a moment of such contestations, among producers, exhibitors, and critics; and that my own newly minted grasp of these films represents a logical extension of this process – especially to the extent that interpretation, like genrefication, involves a revaluing of the hitherto "marginal," adducing once-peripheral features as being, "in fact," central to some (more recently proposed or achieved) community.

In retrospect, a crucial site in the historical process linking then and now is the poster for *Stagecoach* – adduced as typical of the film's press-kit promotion campaign – on view in Edward Buscombe's 1992 British Film Institute (BFI) monograph on the film.[20] The uppermost part of the poster is devoted to the director – via two blocks of text and a photo of Ford (pipe in hand, posed beside a camera) – promising viewers "LUSTY EXCITEMENT AND ROARING ADVENTURE" from the "Academy Award winner" who directed *The Hurricane* (1937), *The Informer*, and *Submarine Patrol* (1938). At the center of the poster (to the left of the second block of Ford text) is a large composite portrait of the film's nine primary cast members, in costume. Immediately below that, spanning the width of the poster, is a photo-derived representation of the stagecoach, its horses at full gallop as they pull the coach from right to left. This picture is then mirrored, if inverted or reversed, in the graphic shape of the film's title, printed roughly the same size, but with its larger-type "Stage" being pulled left to right by a smaller-type "coach." Above the latter

Typical advertising poster for *Stagecoach.*

portion of the title is the phrase "WALTER WANGER presents"; below the title comes all the other cast information we'd expect, with Claire Trevor and John Wayne getting bigger billing than the rest.

There is considerable continuity of design elements between the poster reproduced by Buscombe and the display ads for *Stagecoach* I examined – even though some thirty-five *different* ads, appearing a total of forty-five times, are in question.[21] The most common elements are the film title and the graphic representation of a stagecoach (often in silhouette); the smaller the ad, the likelier these elements (alone) are present. Another common element is the emphasis on the travelers as a group. Usually this involves some version of a composite cast portrait, as a cloud of heads hovering in space, or presented separately, mug-shot or yearbook fashion. Occasionally, the copy sounds this theme: "NINE STRANGE PEOPLE!" Sometimes distinctions are made. The full-page display ad in *Life* distinguishes passengers from crew: "The Seven Oddly Assorted Strangers Who Started for Lordsburg" are shown in a poster-style box, with Wayne almost literally "on the floor." A separate, much more stylized graphic of a driver and a shotgun guard atop an invisible stagecoach is used to fill out the cast.

Other ads use gender as the pertinent difference. Thus the *St. Louis Post-Dispatch*: "HELL-BENT FOR ADVENTURE! . . . 2 women on a desperate journey with 7 strange men!" If distinctions among passengers are made graphically, it is Dallas, literally, who stands out, in six different ads, nearly always accompanied by sexually charged copy: "HER COARSE VOICE, HER INSOLENT SMILE, HER TAWDRY CLOTHES . . . Made decent people draw away!" (*Des Moines Register*); "HER CLOTHES WERE TAWDRY . . ./ HER LIPS WERE PAINTED/HER VOICE WAS COARSE . . ./ But her courage was magnificent!" (*St. Louis Post-Dispatch*). In five ads among those surveyed, Claire Trevor's Dallas is graphically paired with John Wayne's Ringo, either by the size of their portraits relative to those of other passengers on view or by placement. An ad in the *Washington Post* makes the "romance" point verbally explicit, likening the excitement generated "when the stagecoach thunders thru danger ninety miles from nowhere" to that on view "when a dance hall girl and an escaped convict look into each other's eyes!"

The sexual and/or Freudian strain of the ad campaign is palpable if understated across the whole set of ads. It is on view in the presentation of Dallas as a tart, and as erotically linked to Ringo. It

Contemporary newspaper advertisement for *Stagecoach*.

is also on view as a model of sociality, understood almost geographically as a matter of behavioral or ideological levels. Per the *Ames Daily Tribune*, the passengers are "cut off from civilization...faced with deeper and deeper danger...THEN strange things began to happen... conventions cracked and love, hate, cowardice and courage came startlingly to the surface." Similar language appears in the *New York Times*, where we are told that "emotions crack and hidden strength and failure come startlingly to the surface." This social-psychological model is also applied by the ads to individuals. A second *Ames Daily Tribune* ad tells us that "Each [character has] a hidden secret that will amaze you when it is revealed." (So can we see those Monument Valley buttes as eruptions, as of something once-upon-a-time repressed?)

It is more than occasionally claimed that *"Stagecoach* ushered in a new cycle of large-scale Westerns."[22] Not every 1939 audience would have agreed. Many of the big Westerns of 1939 preceded *Stagecoach* into the theaters here surveyed. *Stand Up and Fight, Jesse James,* and *The Oklahoma Kid* opened in advance of *Stagecoach* in Ames and St. Louis. In Atlanta the order was slightly different: *Stand Up and Fight, Jesse James, Stagecoach,* and *The Oklahoma Kid.* Moreover, many ads for those films emphatically invoked the genre as it existed *before* the release of *Stagecoach.* A display ad for *Stand Up and Fight* in the January 6 *Atlanta Constitution* declares, in no uncertain terms, that "There was 'The Covered Wagon'/ There was 'Cimarron'/ There was 'Wells Fargo'/ *And now* [...] comes" *Stand Up and Fight.* Ads in the March 15 and 16 editions of the *Ames Daily Tribune* describe *The Oklahoma Kid*, alluding to the gangster-genre legacy of stars James Cagney and Humphrey Bogart, as providing "TOMMY GUN ACTION IN THE SIX-SHOOTING WEST" and subsequently declare *The Oklahoma Kid* to be "GREATER THAN 'Cimarron.'" A display ad in the April 4 *St. Louis Post-Dispatch* is quite emphatic on the generic setting of *Dodge City* (1939): "WEST OF CHICAGO *THERE WAS NO LAW!* WEST OF DODGE CITY *THERE WAS NO GOD!"*

Stagecoach was clearly part of this trend, but by contrast with those of other films its ad campaign rather played down its genre status. The connotations of the word "stagecoach" and the associations evoked by the image of the coach do most of the genre work in the *Stagecoach* ads under examination. Only two of those ads overtly feature Monument Valley, which did not yet connote "Western." (An ad in the *Des Moines Register* refers to the "Glorious Beauty of the Southwest" as one of the film's attractions.) Some few ads, by evoking "the American frontier" (*New York Times*) or the "Raw Untamed Frontier" (*Atlanta Constitution*), echo the famous Frederick Jackson Turner thesis about the closing of the West – to the effect that the once "open" frontier had been a guarantor of political and economic democracy.[23] But the closest any of the *Stagecoach* ad copy gets to the film's westernness is in phrases that as much deny as assert the genre affiliation. Per the *St. Louis Post-Dispatch, Stagecoach* is "a *new* kind of drama about the *old* American west," while a similar phrase in the *Life* display ad nominates *Stagecoach* as "A New Kind of Picture About the American West."

By contrast with the ad campaign's reticence on the genre question, its attention to John Ford is emphatic – if sporadic. Ford is identified as the film's director in twenty of the thirty-five ads, whereas Wanger is cited as its producer in twenty-six. Ten ads, like the poster discussed by Buscombe, evoke Ford's reputation and filmography as sustaining the film's claim to attention. A Radio City Music Hall ad describes Ford as a "repeated Academy Award winner." A *St. Louis Post-Dispatch* ad avers that *Stagecoach* is "Directed by John Ford with all the power and electrifying drama of 'Hurricane' and 'The Informer.'" But six other ads expand this intertext by one title – *Submarine Patrol*, and almost always as first on the list. Most latter-day film scholars are likely to be puzzled by the inclusion of *Submarine Patrol*, if only because today it is an almost unavailable title.[24] The arrangement of the list into reverse chronology – from most to least recent – suggests an assumption about viewer memory: The older the film, the less likely it will serve promotional or intertextual purposes. So what might viewers have expected of *Stagecoach* on the basis of these particular display-ad and Ford-directed pre-texts?

If we link the purported "strangeness" of the *Stagecoach* passengers to the frontier/civilization theme also evident in the ads, we can prophesy after the fact that *The Informer* – the main character of which, Gypo Nolan (Victor McLaglen), is almost literally tortured by his estrangement from both Irish and British factions in 1922 Dublin – would prepare viewers of *Stagecoach* to attend to the way social mores and assumptions are stressed (for better, for worse) by the clash of rival cultures. Tom Connor even describes Gypo, after the latter's loudly defensive performance at the wake of Frankie McPhillip, as shouting "like an aboriginal," as if anticipating the sense in which the Irish of *The Informer* are akin to the Apaches of *Stagecoach*, in being at the mercy of an occupying army – a link then confirmed when Curley casts Ringo as an Apache, at the Apache Wells stage stop, in telling him not to stray too far from the reservation. *The Informer* also anticipates *Stagecoach* in its linkage of an outlaw character (Gypo, Ringo) with a prostitute (Katie, Dallas), thus bringing both eroticism and gender under the heading of "strangeness," thereby defamiliarizing standing definitions of "society" or "the social." These associations are made ironic one notch further when we note that Gypo's desperate decision to inform on Frankie is sparked by the hope of escaping – *to* America, with Katie, while the happiness we imagine for Dallas and Ringo is possible only upon their escaping – *from* America.

If the colonialist theme of *Stagecoach* is not pre-textually cued by its linkage to *The Informer*, it is hard to imagine a viewer of *The Hurricane* failing to make that connection upon seeing *Stagecoach* (or vice versa). These two films have almost identical endings – an Edenic "natural" couple or family escaping "the blessings of civilization" under the watchful and forgiving eyes of people who, quite literally, represent "the law" of the culture in question (French Polynesia in one, territorial New Mexico in the other). Indeed, the law officer in both cases decides to suspend the law for the benefit of some larger purpose – "justice" and "happiness" in *The Hurricane*, something its participants call would "marriage" in *Stagecoach*.[25] In both cases, a hard-drinking physician played by Thomas Mitchell is a primary figure in the ideological debate that precedes the law's suspension, when he is not busy delivering babies. More intriguingly, the race question, evoked indirectly in *Stagecoach* – in Buck's running complaints about his Mexican in-laws, in the warfare between Geronimo and the U.S. Army, and in the Civil War background repeatedly invoked in the exchanges between Doc Boone (Thomas Mitchell) and Hatfield (John Carradine) – is emphatically explicit in *The Hurricane*. Terangi is imprisoned for striking the wrong white man, though everyone knows he struck in self-defense, and he breaks out of jail, like Ringo in *Stagecoach*, to return to Manacura and his family.

The pre-textual pertinence of *Submarine Patrol* to *Stagecoach* is obviously harder to describe, given the film's unavailability. A December 24, 1938, display ad in the *Ames Daily Tribune* gives us a hint: "Landlubber weaklings... they'd never even seen a ship! Then orders came to sail their tiny craft... one of the heroic 'Splinter Fleet'... into a raging hell... and trial by danger made them MEN!" An ad in the October 18, 1939, *Atlanta Constitution* adduces the film's timeliness after the German invasion of Poland as explaining why viewers might want to have another look: "See Today's Headlines Re-enacted on The Screen!" (Theaters in St. Louis and Atlanta brought back any number of classic war movies as major-power hostilities became more likely, among them *All Quiet on the Western Front*, 1930; *Hell's Angels*, 1930; and *The Road to Glory*, 1936.) Clearly, citing *Submarine Patrol*, *The Hurricane*, and *The Informer* in the display ads for *Stagecoach* has the effect of splitting the audience of the latter, between those who have and those who have not seen (some of) the other movies. It attests to the historical difference of viewing conditions in 1939 and the present that *Submarine Patrol* is *not* generally viewable now, though I was surprised at the extent to which, by contrast with Ford's official "1939" movies, it was viewable and probably viewed at the time.

The first hint that multiple Ford films might have been screened in 1939 proximity in a given city came in the *Ames Daily Tribune*. Though *Stagecoach* played Ames for only five days in March, on three of those days *Wee Willie Winkie* (1937) was playing elsewhere in town. Other Ford films to play Ames in 1939, never for more than a week, included *Four Men and a Prayer* (1938) in January, *The Hurricane* and *Young Mr. Lincoln* in July, and *Drums Along the Mohawk* in November. The bill of Ford fare was different in Atlanta, as was the exhibition pattern, in that most of the films appeared across the year, often on multiple screens (numbers following titles for Atlanta and St. Louis indicate "screen days," i.e., days multiplied by screens, rather than total numbers of screenings): *Four Men and a Prayer* (January; two) *Submarine Patrol* (February–April, July, October–December; thirty-five), *Stagecoach* (March, May–September; fifty-four), *The Lost Patrol* (May, August–December; twenty-two), *Young Mr. Lincoln* (August–December; forty-one), *Judge Priest* (September; two), and *Drums Along the Mohawk* (November; nine).

The most striking figures regarding "John Ford – 1939" are derived from the pages of the *St. Louis Post-Dispatch*. Though released in November 1938, *Submarine Patrol* almost outdid *Stagecoach* as measured by St. Louis "screen days," playing at least one day in every month from February through May, and September though November, for a total of 225 screen days, while *Stagecoach* played in March, and in May through November, for a total of 234. The other Ford films to play St. Louis were *The Hurricane* (June through September; 32), *Young Mr. Lincoln* (June through November; 213), *The Lost Patrol* (October; 2), *Four Men and a Prayer* (November; 3), and *Drums Along the Mohawk* (November and December; 38). On 79 days of the year, astonishingly, at least two Ford films, sometimes three, were playing simultaneously in St. Louis. By contrast, there were only 14 such "multiple Ford" days in Atlanta.

Part of the story here involves what I see as differing interests between producers and critics, and possibly between producers and exhibitors as well. A difference among *producers* is evident in the display-ad pre-texts that promoted *Young Mr. Lincoln* and *Drums Along the Mohawk* – by contrast to those promoting *Stagecoach*. Partly this involves the fact that *Stagecoach* was released through United Artists, while *Young Mr. Lincoln* and *Drums Along the Mohawk* were both produced and distributed by 20th Century–Fox; the ad campaigns were mounted by competing publicity departments. Fox or its contracting exhibitors ran somewhat fewer display ads in the venues surveyed – thirty ads, forty-two placements for *Young Mr. Lincoln*; twenty-seven ads, forty-one placements for *Drums Along the Mohawk* – compared with thirty-five ads and forty-five placements for *Stagecoach*. Moreover, both of the Fox ad campaigns were, in more or less obvious ways, muddled or conflicted, a conflict partly explicable, in each case, by reference to intertextuality.

The most constant features of the *Young Mr. Lincoln* ad campaign were a block-type rendition of the film's title, usually stacked as "YOUNG/MR. LINCOLN"; *some* representation of Henry Fonda's Lincoln, sometimes alone (in five ads, though one of these, repeated thrice, featured a silhouette profile), sometimes with Mary Weaver's Mary Todd (in seven ads), more often in various "montage" configurations with other photos and graphics (several of these feature multiple Lincolns, though often one is oversized in comparison with the other figures); and a motto, which appears (with slight variations) in eleven of the thirty ads: "The Story of Abraham Lincoln that has *never* been told!"

Yet *some* aspects of that story *are* presumed to be familiar – Abe's stovepipe hat, his head-penny profile, which Fonda's makeup clearly mimes, his "lightning wit." An ad in the *Washington Post*, indeed, implores us to "See..." Lincoln "fight the famous 'moonlight murder' case." So the Lincoln depicted in the display ads tends to be, shall we say, multiple or split: a courageous attorney and an awkward lover ("This, too, is Lincoln"), a "young" man and a figure from legend, a personage both known and unknown, both history and "NOT HISTORY."[26] Quite apart from its nascent genre status as a biopic, *Young Mr. Lincoln* was only one among several Lincoln stories in high-profile circulation at the time, including Sherwood Anderson's *Abe Lincoln in Illinois* and Carl Sandburg's *Abraham Lincoln*, the last four volumes of which (*The War Years*) appeared that December, though their publication had long been anticipated. Clearly, the Fox publicity department was anxious to cash in on the trend, while maintaining the distinctiveness of *Young Mr. Lincoln* relative to the other texts, most emphatically its distinction as a 20th Century–Fox and/or Darryl F. Zanuck production. Of the thirty display ads for *Young Mr. Lincoln* in our sample, eleven carry some version of the production/producer credit.

Of the twenty-seven different display ads examined for *Drums Along the Mohawk*, eight ran more than once. The single most elaborate ad appeared with only minor variations in three major dailies: the *Baltimore Evening Sun*, the *St. Louis Post-Dispatch*, and the *Atlanta Constitution*. Allowing for variously sized ads, and partly because of repetition, the campaign to promote *Drums* was the least distinctive of the three, for being the most predictable. Nearly every ad, including many non–display ads, touted Technicolor as a selling point. Of the twenty-seven ads, twenty-two (plus most of the repeats) featured a "couple" shot or depiction of Henry Fonda and Claudette Colbert, usually aligned with the film's title. In the larger ads, the title is stacked ("DRUMS/ ALONG THE/ MOHAWK") and given three-dimensional depth, like the "20th/ CENTURY/ FOX" logo itself, to the point where the title becomes a fort, when colonialist defenders are depicted on top, with attacking Iroquois below; or a promontory, when Iroquois braves are depicted as running across it, toward the reader. ("Drums," we might note, is a similarly ambiguous reference; we *hear* drums associated with Indians, but the only drums we *see* belong to colonial military formations.) The Walter Edmonds novel is cited or alluded to in twelve different ads. And three ads feature some version of the following hook line: "When torch and tomahawk spread their terror . . . and a pioneer woman's courage had to be as great as her love!"

The "frontier" theme is picked up in the larger ad, mentioned previously, which describes the "young lovers" as venturing "into the valley where the savage Iroquois lurked," the Iroquois graphically depicted in many ads as cartoonish spear-carrying warriors. All of which might pass muster as promoting *Stagecoach*, to judge by most critical descriptions of the latter, but viewers familiar with the Edmonds novel might well wonder where all the Tory vs. American (or "Dutch" vs. American) politics of the book had gone. Likewise, viewers of the film might reasonably have been disappointed if they had gone expecting "treachery, massacre, torture" (as the same ad promises). Indeed, by contrast with the racial and sexual atrocities committed on all sides in the Edmonds novel, Ford's picture of frontier warfare is curiously civilized – crops and houses burnt, yes, even Joe Boleo (Francis Ford) threatened with immolation. But the assaults on the German Flats fort are conducted and depicted as well-disciplined military operations jointly launched by British loyalists and (treaty-honoring?) Indian allies.[27] Arguably the most brutal moment in the film comes when the German Flats defenders fire chain shot point blank into an assaulting column of Iroquois and British regulars; even the Americans are appalled by the carnage. Set against this the courtesy with which even drunken (and multilingual) Iroquois accede to Mrs. McKlennar's cantankerous wishes regarding her marital bed, the question of who is more or less civilized becomes far more complicated in the film than its ad campaign would seem to allow, despite the repeated evocation of the source novel.

If less various or coherent than the ads promoting *Stagecoach*, the ad campaigns employed to sell *Young Mr. Lincoln* and *Drums Along the Mohawk* in the venues studied were equally consistent in one crucial respect – they gave short Hollywood shrift to John Ford. Though the *Stagecoach* ad campaign gave Walter Wanger better billing than Ford, citing him twenty-six (out of thirty-five) times as the film's producer, Ford is cited as director twenty times, and nine of those include references to other Ford films, as we have seen. By contrast, the ad campaign for *Young Mr. Lincoln* lists Ford only seven times (though twice the film is described as "Brilliantly directed by John Ford"), while Zanuck is cited ten times. The Fox ad campaign for *Drums Along the Mohawk* is of a piece with that of *Young Mr. Lincoln*, with Zanuck receiving eleven mentions to Ford's four.

The evidence seems to confirm Altman's claim that the major studios generally sought to downplay genre, which was nonproprietary and shared across the industry, and to emphasize studio-specific cycles or features, typically stars, producers, then (and only then) directors, with obvious exceptions like Frank Capra and Ernst Lubitsch. For what the studios were selling, finally, was themselves. In 1939, John Ford was evidently not as crucially a company man as Darryl Zanuck, and Fox treated him accordingly in its ad campaigns. By contrast, what United Artists had to sell, to judge by its name and history, was "artistry." Though that capacity was often attributed to independent producers – people like Wanger, or Sam Goldwyn, who produced *The Hurricane* – it also seems probable that the treatment accorded to Ford by the ad campaign for *Stagecoach* was likelier to happen at United Artists than elsewhere.

I have not sufficient space here to elaborate fully the claim that *Stagecoach, Young Mr. Lincoln*, and *Drums Along the Mohawk* constitute a set of films so closely linked as to make those links crucial to any future understanding of the movies. That such links *can* be crucial is obvious beyond doubt in the way even Ford's *The Man Who Shot Liberty Valance* (1962) doubles back on *Stagecoach* – via props, casting, and theme. Such "positive" intertextual links are numerous across the films of Ford's 1939 trilogy, as my opening remarks about the narrative parallels between *Stagecoach* and *Drums Along the Mohawk* attest. Other connections between the two films include scenes in which an "eastern" character (Mr. Peacock, of Kansas City, Kansas, in *Stagecoach*; Lana Martin, lately of Albany, New York, in *Drums*) is confronted by a "savage" (Yakima, the station-keeper's Apache wife; Blue Back) and recoils in horror from the sight or thought of otherness. Both *Stagecoach* and *Drums* include instances of childbirth, more alluded to (by calls for hot water) than directly depicted, though the newborn's cry in each case is linked to the world of nature via juxtaposition – to the sound of a coyote in one, the image of a calf in the other. Once the baby is ready for introduction, on both occasions, we hear an awe-struck male declare (more or less) "I'll be doggone" – Buck, as Dallas holds the Mallory infant; Gil Martin, as he holds Gil Jr. Both films, moreover, place the fact of childbirth in close proximity to the fact or threat of death. In *Stagecoach*, the scene with Dallas holding the baby immediately precedes, and clearly prompts, the scene in which Ringo effectively proposes to Dallas ("I still got a ranch across the border..."). But that proposal is itself preceded by Ringo's report that his father and brother were murdered by the Plummers, which is matched by Dallas's recall of the "massacre on Superstition Mountain" that left her an orphan. The equivalent scene in *Drums*, by contrast, immediately *precedes* the birth sequence and depicts the aftermath of the Battle of Oriskany – in Gil's exhausted account of close and bloody combat (which includes his astonished revelation that for Ward Bond's Adam Hartman, killing and carnage amounted to "having a good time") and also in the unsuccessful attempt to save General Herkimer by amputating his leg.

The ties that bind *Young Mr. Lincoln* to *Stagecoach* and *Drums* are more subtle but nonetheless revealing. Peter Stowell, for instance, has written at some length on the role of "fences" in all three films, as marking "the metaphoric line of demarcation between civilization and wilderness," which line Ford's frontier characters must "pass beyond if they are to find themselves."[28] To the obvious extent that *Stagecoach* ends near where *Drums* begins, on the image of a wagon crossing to the "other" side, this construal is obviously helpful. What also happens along these fences, in all three films, is something we'd likely call courtship, a creation rather than substitution of allegiances. Ringo's proposal to Dallas takes place across a fence, which Curley subsequently nominates as a boundary in telling Ringo to "stick close to the reservation." Once in Lordsburg, Ringo and Dallas walk along the streets to her "home" in the red-light district, their itinerary marked by sidewalks, porch rails, hitching posts, and rail fences – at the end of which journey Ringo renews his proposal, now fully mindful of Dallas's past, and from her side of the rail. Likewise, Ann Rutledge interrupts Abe's riverside study of Blackstone's *Commentaries*, hailing him across a fence that separates Abe's "legal" space from the river bank. Abe crosses to her side, the "natural" side if you will, and they walk together along the bank. No explicit proposal is repeated, much less uttered – yet Abe says (an almost matrimonial) "I do," in regard to liking Ann's red hair, and Ann expresses a "heart set" hope that they will go to college/seminary together. That these two "courtship" scenes ought to be linked is confirmed, to my mind, by a gesture each man makes – Ringo taking and subsequently carrying Dallas's purse, Abe taking and subsequently carrying Ann's flower basket. The comparable scene in *Drums* comes after the Loyalist attack on the Deerfield settlement – when Lana and Gil

Ringo and Dallas (Claire Trevor) by the fences in the red-light district of Lordsburg. (Collection of the editor)

visit their burnt-out cabin. We first see the cabin at night, and little fencing is visible; subsequent views are more emphatic in showing how split-rail fencing links portions of the farmstead to one another and to the common byway. Ironically, when Gil and Lana return, there's more fence than cabin left standing, and it is in the ruins of the cabin that Lana proposes that they start over again by going to work for Mrs. McKlennar – to the chagrin of Gil, who now voices Lana's earlier objections to frontier life.

One other similarity is worth adducing for allowing me to propose a "negative" or "retroactive" analysis of comparable passages, along lines suggested by Altman in his discussion of "differential commutation."[29] Ford's films are renowned for their "celebration" scenes, often in the form of dances celebrating specific communal occasions. The most obvious instance in the 1939 trilogy is the Halloween sequence in *Drums*, which celebrates a bountiful harvest and the wedding of John Weaver and Mary Reall. In the midst of this festivity, Gil Martin quietly drifts away, going upstairs to gaze at his sleeping son. Lana follows, unseen by Gil, and is prompted by the sight of her husband and son to pray that their lives "go on like this forever." A similar scene appears in *Young Mr. Lincoln*. After Abe recalls the members of the Springfield mob bent on lynching Matt and Adam Clay for murder to their better New Testament senses, he receives (as if in reward) an invitation from Mary Todd to attend a party thrown by her Springfield sister. He attends, he dances (in the "worst" way), and then he retreats – at Mary's suggestion – to the mansion porch, where he gazes so intently at the river that Mary Todd literally retreats into the background, as witness to his devotion. Of course, the mood is different, in part because the upper-crust company of Springfield society makes Lincoln uncomfortably self-conscious. But the juxtaposition of family continuity (the Clays, the Martins) and something like death (the river-as-Ann, the departed souls remembered on All Hallows' Eve) is strikingly similar nonetheless. If we ask where a similar scene occurs in *Stagecoach*, the most immediate answer might be nowhere – no dance, no departing dancers, no pensive reflection nor expression of hope. But if we read these phrases in something like reverse order, we might conclude that the family catastrophes recounted by Ringo and Dallas are akin to Abe's recollection of Ann, that Ringo's description of his Mexican ranch is the hopeful vision, and that the departing dancers are, indeed, Dallas and Ringo, who exit the adobe for the station yard. Hence the communal celebration in *Stagecoach* occurs when Dallas, a "dance hall girl" (as ads and reviews describe her), shows Mrs. Mallory's daughter to her companions. The hopeful glow on Dallas's face when declaring "It's a girl" thus matches Lana's hushed prayer for perpetual good fortune.

In suggesting that borders can be negotiated as well as crossed, that meaningful relations can exist along the periphery as well as at the center of community, I am invoking Gilberto Perez's description of Ford's narrational style as "relaxed, digressive, episodic, prone to dwelling on character and situation in disregard of action." Ford's style is anti-linear, anti-hierarchical, even "feminine," on this account, and a fit medium for the social allegories of the films, in which civilization typically "undergoes a breakdown of classes and snobberies and a renewal of the democratic spirit."[30] The gender implications of this renewal as they pertain to Ford's 1939 films are more than hinted at in the exchanges of gender and class positions already discussed – though far more could be said (as, for instance, about granting voting rights to women at Dry Forks!).[31]

For brevity's sake, I will attend to only one more feature of Ford's 1939 trilogy – arguably the most interesting, for being least obvious and accordingly most forceful by way of reconfiguring one's view of the films: Ford's view of "the law." The puzzlement that prompts the inquiry is why Curley insists on taking Ringo (and everyone else) to Lordsburg at all – if the point of riding shotgun (as it is typically inferred from the remarks of Buck and Curley's deputies) is to capture Ringo *before* he gets there, thus to protect him from the butcher-like Luke Plummer and his brothers, who evidently run the town. Ringo in custody, they could just as easily return to Tonto, or return Ringo to the penitentiary, which seems closer to Tonto than to Lordsburg to judge by Ringo's progress. Indeed, in response to Buck's suggestion that Curley let Ringo shoot it out with Luke Plummer, Curley is emphatic about wanting to see Ringo back in the pen ("I aim to get him there all in one piece") on the premise that either Luke or his "just as ornery" brothers would prevail in a fight. Other dialogue makes it clear that Ringo's brother and father were murdered by or at the behest of the Plummers, and that Ringo himself was falsely convicted of killing the Plummers' foreman on the basis of their testimony – facts that nearly everyone in the territory (save Doc, who asks after Ringo's brother) seems well aware of.

As Richard Slotkin points out in *Gunfighter Nation*, there is more than one kind of justice in *Stagecoach:* "Lordsburg justice is just good enough to punish Banker Gatewood, but it cannot provide the more positive sort of justice required by Ringo and Dallas."[32] I do not have the sense that Curley intended to endanger every passenger for the sake of righting legal wrongs done to Ringo – Curley begins the journey thinking they'll have cavalry escort for the whole trip – but he remains open to the possibility that justice is better served by letting fate or vengeance take its course, a prospect effectively confirmed when Ringo proves his courage and marksmanship during the chase-and-rescue sequence. Of course, this too is an ideologically risky prospect. How is letting Ringo shoot it out with the Plummer brothers any different from letting a mob lynch Matt and Adam Clay?

The answer is that Ringo already had his trial, and justice clearly failed. What did that trial look like? Just like the trial, I want to say, in

Young Mr. Lincoln – a trial in which the law itself, in the person of Scrub White, in the person of J. Palmer Cass, in the persons of John Felder and Stephen Douglas, each an officer of the law or the court at one point or another, is as much on trial as the accused defendants. Apart from something like a miracle, the Clay brothers would have been convicted and hanged, and on the basis of perjured testimony from the actual murderer. That miracle is effectively earned, moreover, by Abe's express willingness to distinguish one law, the morality of asking Mrs. Clay to choose between her sons, from another, which claims the right to force her testimony: "I may not know so much of law, Mr. Felder, but I know what's right and what's wrong." It is hardly a mistake, then, that among the Independence Day festivities is something called (very explicitly, via a painted signboard program) a "Pie Judging Contest," right alongside a "Rail Splitting Contest." It's not the baking but the judging that's at issue. And no less at issue in *Stagecoach* than in *Young Mr. Lincoln*, even if we have to wait until the second film in the 1939 trilogy to complete that part of the picture. Indeed, in both films the male hero earns his success by pledging faith in a woman, a woman about whom he (now) knows "everything," and the token of that faith, in both instances, is something he keeps under his hat – three folkloric bullets in Ringo's case, an almanac in young Mr. Lincoln's.[33]

Nothing less than the fate of the Union, as figured in the unity of the Clay family, seems at stake in *Young Mr. Lincoln*, especially to the extent that we see the Clay brothers as stand-ins for African Americans, rural youths nearly lynched for killing a white man – Scrub White, to be exact! (I hear confirmation of this proposition in the banjo-accompanied "spiritual" that the family intones together in the Springfield jail cell of Matt and Adam; the national press made much of the appearance of Marian Anderson singing spirituals at the film's Springfield premier.[34]) *Drums Along the Mohawk*, by virtue of its Revolutionary War subject matter, requires less allegory to justify a similar attribution of "national" significance. I take the intertextual links of Ford's 1939 trilogy as indicating that something equally momentous is at stake in *Stagecoach*. Yet exactly what is hard to specify – and largely because of Ford's own fairly complex treatment of "history." Though *Stagecoach* is the first film of the set, it is simultaneously the "earliest" and the "latest." While its historical period is roughly one hundred years later than *Drums*, *Stagecoach* neverthe-less takes place in what is arguably the least civilized of the three settings, as if temporal and social progress cannot be equated.

Moreover, each of the three films features instances of historical "frame breaking" – Gatewood's Hooverite paean to *laissez-faire* capi-talism, the "Lincoln Memorial" shots that punctuate the courtroom scenes and the conclusion of *Young Mr. Lincoln*, the flag-raising scene in *Drums* – which indicate quite clearly that Ford's invocations of his-tory are always metaphorically addressed to a contemporary moment and audience. (Hence the standard view of *Stagecoach* as premonitory of World War II.) This eternal Emersonian presentness, while not ex-actly ignoring or collapsing history, has the effect of compressing it – bringing "that past" into "this present," thereby lending the present some of the exigence, the urgency, and the hopefulness of the past, when that past was "now." Conversely, such compression also at-tributes to the offscreen present some of the hindsight clarity with which the present ordinarily imbues the historical past. The flag car-ried aloft in *Drums* is the same flag we barely notice at the beginning of *Stagecoach*, is the flag that Ringo and Dallas effectively leave be-hind at film's end, its promise compromised by the film noir darkness of Lordsburg, a darkness that subsequently shadows the flag's appar-ently more hopeful ascension in *Drums*. In thus attributing to Ford a self-critical modernist practice, I find myself again in agreement with Perez, who claims that Turner's frontier thesis is too often seen as agrarian, as urging nostalgia, when it should be seen, as Ford sees it, dialectically or aesthetically, as forward looking: "Turner's – and Ford's – conception of the frontier parallels the idea of the avant-garde in the arts: the notion that art gains its vitality and its point through the continual venture into new territory."[35]

If I now compare my contemporary understanding of Ford's 1939 trilogy, at least in its abbreviated, display-ad form, with those "pre-textual" construals promoted by the publicity departments of United Artists and 20th Century–Fox, I am struck as much by the similar-ities as by the differences, though it was difference I was seeking. There is an obvious continuity of *terms*, especially those pertaining to the "frontier" thesis, which is writ large, shall we say, across the display ads for *Stagecoach* and *Drums Along the Mohawk*. Strikingly, the frontier as a geographical location is *not* invoked in the promotion of *Young Mr. Lincoln*; the frontier in that case is the past, or history, a border between the known and unknown. The topic of "the law" is only slightly less apparent in the display ads. Ringo is depicted as an outlaw, with "a price on his head," Dallas as an outcast. Lincoln is repeatedly depicted as a lawyer, an attorney for the falsely accused. Here the odd case out is *Drums Along the Mohawk*, where a political revolution – an emphatic conflict of laws and their enforcement – is barely alluded to in the ads, though it does play an explicit role in the film.

Another similarity is on view in the relationship between exhibition and reception circumstances. I began my research under the impression that circumstances then and now would yield remarkably different understandings of the films – especially to the extent that 1960s-style auteur criticism is taken as enforcing such a difference. I want to say now that the difference a director makes was a difference in dispute in 1939. The 20th Century–Fox studio, we might say, was considerably less auteurist than United Artists, though the studio did credit Ford on occasion. Indeed, 20th Century–Fox promoted *Drums* as if it were *Stagecoach*, as if the studio were trying to distinguish it from *Gone with the Wind* (1939), comparison with which might have activated the "race" subtext clearly on view in Edmonds's novel. Fox effectively used the "frontier" thesis, with its emphasis on marauding savages, as a cover story, thus avoiding the slavery question.

I speculate that exhibitors, too, kept an eye on the director credits when deciding which films to book for revival runs.[36] To the extent that revivals competed with newly released films for screen space, exhibitors may have been at odds with producers. I base this speculation, obviously enough, on the surprising number of Ford films on exhibit in 1939 in St. Louis and Atlanta. That Ford's films were so frequently on exhibit, however, provides a positive if qualified answer to the question of whether directors' names could serve generic or intertextual purposes in 1939. A strong Yes in St. Louis; a weak Maybe in Ames – to the extent that only a dedicated movie fan in the latter venue would likely have noticed the many similarities I have enumerated.

Then again, such dedicated movie fans *did* exist. We still call them film critics. One especially important to Ford was *New York Times* reviewer Frank Nugent, who eventually went on to write eight scripts with the director, among them *Wagon Master* (1950), *The Quiet Man* (1952), and *The Searchers* (1956). Reviewers in less prestigious venues had less opportunity, evidently, to express opinion, or to court Ford's. Most reviews that appeared in the *Ames Daily Tribune* and the *Atlanta Constitution*, for example, clearly smacked of "press kit." The Lee Rogers review of *Stagecoach* in the *Atlanta Constitution* opines the familiar wisdom – "On the stage is as strange an assortment of passengers as ever breathed the same tobacco smoke" – as prologue to an explication of the cast list, which constitutes the bulk of the review.[37] In this sense, we can see a considerable part of the local or regional press as taking a producer-centered view of the business.

According to David Bordwell, the 1960s transposition of auteurism from France to Britain and America, where it became a strategy for re-reading "Classical Hollywood" via "Art Film" interpretive protocols, had the effect of genrefying at least some Hollywood film directors.[38] Altman's picture of genre – in which marginal or adjectival features (visual style in film noir, say) are reconfigured as central, as definitive, thus necessarily implying that once-central features should play lesser roles – makes it easier to see how this process works. Altman's urging that we always remain aware of the potential harm this process can do, by way of marginalizing some films, some filmmakers, some film viewers, is a point well taken. In the present context, I want to say that the negative equation of Ford with conservative "Americanism" sometimes expresses a desire to put films like *Stagecoach* on the cultural margin, as embodying a regressive tendency we should repudiate or go beyond. Then again, Ford is always seeking that margin himself, and very often for the sake of asking what our center should look like, how we can move it progressively forward.

For the sake of reanimating that debate, then, I conclude by praising a marginal figure in film history, one Colvin McPherson, the "Motion Picture Critic" of the *St. Louis Post-Dispatch*. I do so despite the fact that McPherson does not attend very sympathetically to the Native American perspective. His November 12 column praises the Technicolor of *Drums Along the Mohawk*, for instance, because "Copper-skinned savages look much more frightening in natural hue." Perhaps I hope to mark some difference here between us, between then and now. And yet McPherson is also explicitly alive to the question of history – in observing, for instance, how the "savagery" on view in the film, as in the novel, is military and political, a matter of "burning the crops that could go to feed Washington's army."[39] And he is also achingly alive to the possibility of film style, to exactly those features Perez points to in declaring Ford's style both "modern" and "feminine." Thus in his review of *Stagecoach* McPherson describes how "Ford ever and again allows his cameras to survey the horizons serenely, while the musical score keeps up the spirit of the journey and the horses plunge ahead through the desert." And, unlike most of his peers, he senses how much the Lordsburg part of the story matters, though his remarks are rushed and casual: "The picture goes on for a little while afterward, to clear up matters for Wayne and Miss Trevor, and ends with one of its awe-inspiring panoramas, a fine job all the way along."[40] In Altman's terms, McPherson is building a community here, of interpretation and appreciation, one I am glad to be a part of. Though it is unlikely he saw himself as in explicit conflict with the studio system, he certainly takes a more active view of criticism than many of his peers, and I can think of at least one big Hollywood producer for whom such praise of Ford would have been anathema, given his refusal to produce *Stagecoach* in the first place – that is, *if* David O. Selznick ever found time to read out-of-town newspapers while overseeing the production of another world-historical 1939 movie: *Gone with the Wind*.

Grateful acknowledgment is due the Department of English of Iowa State University for providing research time and assistance for this project. I am also indebted to Albert Farr, who helped collect the display ad data, and to Susan Poague, Kris Fresonke, Barry Keith Grant, Jane Davis, and Susan Yager for their timely and thoughtful editorial advice.

NOTES

1. My title refers to Douglas Pye's "Genre and History: *Fort Apache* and *Liberty Valance*," published initially in *Movie* 25 (Winter 1977/78), pp. 1–11, and, subsequently, revised to answer my rejoinder, "All I Can See Is the Flags: *Fort Apache* and the Visibility of History," *Cinema Journal* 27, no. 2 (Winter 1988), pp. 8–26, as "Genre and History: *Fort Apache* and *The Man Who Shot Liberty Valance*," in Ian Cameron and Douglas Pye, eds., *The Book of Westerns* (New York: Continuum, 1996), pp. 111–22. I understand the present essay as continuing that conversation.

2. Peter Stowell, *John Ford* (Boston: Twayne, 1982), p. 15.
3. In addition to Stowell's Chapter 3 ("The Myth of the American Frontier: *Stagecoach, Young Mr. Lincoln* and *Drums Along the Mohawk*," pp. 14–53), see Janey Place, *The Western Films of John Ford* (Secaucus, N.J.: Citadel Press, 1974), pp. 42–57; John E. O'Connor, "A Reaffirmation of American Ideals: *Drums Along the Mohawk* (1939)," in John E. O'Connor and Martin A. Jackson, eds., *American History/American Film: Interpreting the Hollywood Image* (New York: Ungar, 1979), pp. 97–119; and Robin Wood, *"Drums Along the Mohawk,"* *CineAction* 8 (Spring 1987), pp. 58–64, reprinted in *The Book of Westerns*, pp. 174–80.
4. My information comes from the entry on the "United States" (especially its section on "The North," by Jean R. Soderlund, in Seymour Drescher and Stanley L. Engerman, eds., *A Historical Guide to World Slavery* (New York: Oxford University Press, 1998), pp. 395–405.
5. Though Edmonds depicts slavery in colonial New York as an established practice, he does so with considerable (liberal) irony, much of it at Lana's expense. His last chapter, for example, features a passage in which a post-Revolutionary Lana expresses bitterness at Congressional delay in settling Gil's claims to "militia pay and the indemnity for the first burning of their farm" because, "If he had had that pay, he could have bought the black girl Klock offered to sell him" (*Drums Along the Mohawk* [Boston: Little, Brown, 1937], p. 583). Ford's equivalent irony attends on the fact that Gil and Lana leave the fort *without* Daisy, though that irony depends upon their taking her for a slave in the first place.
6. See Rick Altman, *Film/Genre* (London: British Film Institute, 1999), especially Chap. 9, "What Roles Do Genres Play in the Viewing Process?" On "constellated communities" and "lateral communication," see pp. 161–2.
7. See Altman, who relies heavily on posters and display ads, but also Janet Staiger, *Interpreting Films: Studies in the Historical Reception of American Cinema* (Princeton, N.J.: Princeton University Press, 1992).
8. My view of 1930s exhibition practices follows from a lifetime of reading, often film history texts for which the "vertical integration" sought by the Hollywood "majors" and its subsequent disintegration after the *U.S. vs. Paramount* decision of 1948 became primary explanatory tools for describing the rise and fall of the "studio system." That I am not alone in holding this view is attested to in the latest (sixth) edition of Gerald Mast and Bruce F. Kawin's *A Short History of the Movies* (Boston: Allyn and Bacon, 2000) where we find the following passage: "There used to be very few ways to see an old movie – not just a 1930s or 1940s movie, but any movie that was no longer playing in theatres. Films were released, played for a few weeks or months, then faded into memory" (p. 562).
9. The titles of Nugent's *New York Times* reviews are worth citing in full, for being absent from the reviews as reprinted in *The New York Times Film Reviews*. In order, they are "A Ford-Powered 'Stagecoach' Opens at Music Hall; Mickey Rooney Plays Huck Finn at the Capital" (March 3, p. 21, reprinted in this volume), "Twentieth Century–Fox's 'Young Mr. Lincoln' is a Human and

Humorous Film of the Prairie Years" (June 3, p. 11), and "John Ford's Film of 'Drums Along the Mohawk' Opens at the Roxy – 'One Hour to Live' at the Rialto" (November 4, p. 11).

10. "New Westerns," *Time* (March 13, 1939), pp. 30, 32.

11. I cite from *Variety Film Reviews 1907–1980* (New York: Garland, 1983), which is organized only by review dates, not page numbers; see February 8, June 7, and November 8, 1939.

12. See "Movie of the Week: *Stagecoach*: Wanger Films the Log of Perilous Overland-Stage Journey in 1885," *Life* (February 27, 1939), pp. 31–2, 34–5; "Movie of the Week: *Young Mr. Lincoln*: Henry Fonda Plays the Title Role," *Life* (June 12, 1939), pp. 72, 74–7; and "Movie of the Week: *Drums Along the Mohawk*: Claudette Colbert Stars in Frontier Drama of the Revolution," *Life* (November 13, 1939), pp. 74–7.

13. *The WPA Guide to 1930s Iowa* (1938; Ames: Iowa State University Press, 1986), p. 169. Originally entitled *Iowa: A Guide to the Hawkeye State*, this volume, like its Missouri and Georgia counterparts cited below, was "Compiled and Written by the Federal Writers' Project of the Works Progress Administration."

14. See Douglas Gomery, *Shared Pleasures: A History of Movie Presentation in the United States* (Madison: University of Wisconsin Press, 1992), p. 159.

15. The terms for the first two categories tended to shift; the neighborhood vs. colored distinction was stable.

16. See Ralph McGill, "Negro's Place in Atlanta's Life Told Rotarians by Noted Leader," *Atlanta Constitution* (March 14, 1939), pp. 1, 7.

17. See Gomery, *Shared Pleasures*, p. 163.

18. *Missouri: A Guide to the "Show Me" State* (New York: Duell, Sloan and Pearce, 1941), p. 298.

19. See "Picketed Negro Movie House to be Reopened," *St. Louis Post-Dispatch* (June 14, 1939), p. 4C; and "4 Negro Movie Operators at Neighborhood Theatres," *St. Louis Post-Dispatch* (July 6, 1939), p. 3A. Only two of the ten theaters are mentioned by name in these stories – the Criterion and the Strand – and neither appears in the newspaper's listings.

20. Edward Buscombe, *Stagecoach* (London: British Film Institute, 1992), p. 77.

21. A "display ad" is not as easy to define as it might at first seem. Partly it depends on context and size: Does the ad stand out from those around it? Partly it depends on style: Are the design elements provided by the newspaper or the studio? Thus, for instance, ads for *Young Mr. Lincoln* and *Drums Along the Mohawk* in the *New York Times* were limited to small "house"-style listings identical in size to nearly all the other movie ads in the paper and hence do not qualify, in my view, as "display" ads. By contrast, Radio City Music Hall ads for *Stagecoach*, though in a house style, were much larger, and are discussed above. Readers can track down the display ads in question by reference to the following list of newspapers; the dates in parentheses (always in this order: *Stagecoach*, *Young Mr. Lincoln*, and *Drums Along the Mohawk*) indicate when the first ad of a given engagement appears: *Ames Daily Tribune* (April 8, July 1, November 21), *Atlanta Constitution* (February 26, August 1,

November 11), *Baltimore Evening Sun* (March 15, May 30, November 2), *Des Moines Register* (April 3, June 29, November 7), *New York Times* (March 1), *St. Louis Post-Dispatch* (March 22, May 4, May 28, November 8), *Washington Post* (April 25, June 14, November 30). The *Life* ad appeared in the February 13 issue. References to ads for other films are by date within the text. The numbers for ads and "screen days" are as exact as could be determined. Some days or pages of some papers were missing, and I assumed that films advertised were actually films exhibited.

22. Rudy Behlmer, "Bret Harte in Monument Valley: *Stagecoach* (1939)" in *America's Favorite Movies: Behind the Scenes* (New York: Ungar, 1982), p. 118. Behlmer, it bears noting, reprints another poster, which replaces Berton Churchill's Gatewood with Francis Ford's Billy Pickett in the cast photo. On the generic typicality of *Stagecoach*, see Michael Coyne, *The Crowded Prairie: American National Identity in the Hollywood Western* (New York and London: I. B. Taurus, 1997) and Garry Wills, *John Wayne's America: The Politics of Celebrity* (New York: Simon & Schuster, 1997).

23. Frederick Jackson Turner's "The Significance of the Frontier in American History" was first published in the *Annual Report of the American Historical Association for the Year 1893* (Washington, D.C., 1894) and has been widely reprinted. Stowell, *John Ford*, makes extensive use of Turner in his chapter comparing Ford's 1939 movies.

24. As far as I am aware, the only copy of *Submarine Patrol* available for viewing is held in the Film and Television Archive at UCLA.

25. Actually, the word Dallas and Ringo both use is the verb "to marry"; I use "marriage" by way of evoking Stanley Cavell's *Pursuits of Happiness: The Hollywood Comedy of Remarriage* (Cambridge, Mass.: Harvard University Press, 1981), thus to mark the fact that Ringo and Dallas do not, at least in our sight, solicit the validation of a marriage ceremony, which the contemporaneous remarriage comedies suggest is not validation enough.

26. Echoes of the Lacanian *Cahiers du cinéma* analysis of *Young Mr. Lincoln* are hard to miss in the paragraph this note elaborates; compare how the *Cahiers* editors describe the "subject" of the film as "the *reformulation* of the historical figure of Lincoln on the level of the myth and the eternal." "John Ford's *Young Mr. Lincoln*," in Bill Nichols, ed., *Movies and Methods* (Berkeley: University of California Press, 1976), pp. 501–2.

27. On the "Covenant Chain" relation between the League of Six Nations and the British Crown, see James Wilson, *The Earth Shall Weep: A History of Native America* (New York: Atlantic Monthly Press, 1998), especially Chap. 5, "New York and the 'Ohio Country,'" pp. 98–131.

28. Stowell, *John Ford*, p. 19.

29. Altman, *Film/Genre*, pp. 174–8.

30. Gilberto Perez, "American Tragedy," in *The Material Ghost: Films and Their Medium* (Baltimore: Johns Hopkins University Press, 1998), pp. 239, 240.

31. On the link between the Western and women's suffrage, see Lee Clark Mitchell, *Westerns: Making the Man in Fiction and Film* (Chicago: University of Chicago Press, 1996), pp. 94–119.

32. Richard Slotkin, "The Western Is American History, 1939–1941," in *Gunfighter Nation: The Myth of the Frontier in Twentieth-Century America* (New York: Harper Perennial, 1993), p. 310.

33. My construal of the courtroom sequence (and much else) in *Young Mr. Lincoln* is indebted to Ron Abrahamson and Rick Thomson, "*Young Mr. Lincoln* Reconsidered: An Essay on the Theory and Practice of Criticism," *Cine-Tracts* 2, no. 1 (Fall 1978), pp. 42–62. See also William Cadbury and Leland Poague, *Film Criticism: A Counter Theory* (Ames: Iowa State University Press, 1982), especially Chap. 1, "Beardsley's Aesthetics and Film Criticism," pp. 3–37.

34. See Walter Winchell's "On Broadway" column in the June 7, 1939, *St. Louis Post-Dispatch*: "The out-of-town showing of *Young Mr. Lincoln* netted less wordage to the film than to Marian Anderson, who guest soloed" (p. 2D). I imagine Winchell was thinking about Bosley Crowther's "Mr. Lincoln's Gala Night: Twentieth Century–Fox Haunts a Ghost at Midnight in Springfield, Ill.," *New York Times* (June 4, 1939), sec. 9, p. 3, where he reports that Anderson's performance was "broadcast over a national hookup."

Anderson's May 30 performance in Springfield was almost literally shadowed by her earlier and far more famous performance of April 9, 1939, at the Lincoln Memorial, having been denied access to the DAR-controlled Constitution Hall. Newsreel footage of the earlier concert shows the Memorial's statue of Lincoln looking right over Anderson's shoulder, toward the camera, in the very "frame breaking" pose Ford has Fonda assume in *Young Mr. Lincoln*'s courtroom sequences. Moreover, she sang very similar programs on both occasions. See Rosalyn M. Story, *And So I Sing: African American Divas of Opera and Concert* (New York: Amistad, 1993), esp. Chap. 3, "Marian Anderson: The Voice of a Century," pp. 37–58; "*Young Mr. Lincoln* Has Its Premiere," *New York Times* (May 31, 1939), p. 26; and *Treasures from American Film Archives: 50 Preserved Films* (San Francisco: National Film Preservation Foundation, 2000).

It is also worth noting that the legacy of racially motivated lynching was so strong during this period that the Georgia version of the WPA Guide, *Georgia: A Guide to Its Towns and Countryside* (Athens: University of Georgia Press, 1940), could speak almost boastfully, in its chapter on "The Negro," of the good works of "The Association of Southern Women for the Prevention of Lynching" (p. 86).

35. Perez, "American Tragedy," p. 243.

36. Though the practice of "block booking" dominates discussion of exhibition patterns during the classical era, the practice is typically described as applying to first-run films, hence my speculation that exhibitors had some leeway in regard to revival runs. If not, they still had choices to make about which "blocks" to book, which studios to deal with, and Ford did fare well during the period in question, despite the variety of his studio affiliations. On late-1930s exhibition practices, see Giuliana Muscio, *Hollywood's New Deal* (Philadelphia: Temple University Press, 1997).

37. Lee Rogers, "*Stagecoach* Assembles Strange Travelers in Loew's Drama," *Atlanta Constitution* (March 5, 1939), p. 6.

38. David Bordwell, "The Art Cinema as a Mode of Film Practice," *Film Criticism* 4, no. 1 (Fall 1979), pp. 56–64.
39. Colvin McPherson, "The Screen in Review," *St. Louis Post-Dispatch* (November 12, 1939), p. 6G.
40. Colvin McPherson, "The Screen in Review," *St. Louis Post-Dispatch* (March 26, 1939), p. 6G.

4 "A Little Bit Savage"
Stagecoach and Racial Representation

The first image of an Apache Indian in John Ford's *Stagecoach* (1939) follows a reaction shot and shout from the whiskey salesman Peacock, as he spots Yakima, the station-keeper Chris's wife. She is, he warns everyone else, "a savage!" and Chris replies jokingly – betraying some obvious pleasure in the thought – that "she is a little bit savage, I think." He also allows that she is indeed "one of Geronimo's people," and so for him a kind of security, since having an Apache wife means the "Apaches don't bother me." More than just a brief bit of comic relief or a measure of how finely these people have had to calculate their relationships – for both pleasure and safety – at this far edge of "civilization," this scene illustrates how quickly and superficially determinations about others are made here. And especially subject to this sort of quick judgment are the Indians, whom, the film emphasizes, most of the whites know only by reputation or general appearance – thus the film's opening in which a soldier mistakes a Comanche cavalry scout for a renegade Apache. This play of racial representation and judgment or misjudgment echoes a number of other instances of problematic or troubled racial representation in Ford's films, while it also points toward his larger concern with the nature of civilization, particularly its fear of the other, its hardly repressed sense that even "a little bit savage," even a slight taint, usually seems far too much for American tastes.

Of course, Ford's films have always presented a very complicated situation for the study of racial representation. For like many another filmmaker earlier in the twentieth century, Ford would at times use black actors in comically stereotyped, even demeaning roles, as in the case of the black comedian Stepin Fetchit, who appeared in such works as *Judge Priest* (1934), *Steamboat Round the Bend* (1935), and *The Sun Shines Bright* (1952). For convenient narrative purposes, Ford at times depicted Indians in pejorative or comic ways, as in the case of the drunken Indian Charlie in *My Darling Clementine* (1946) and the squaw Look in *The Searchers* (1956). He would, particularly in his later films, freely employ members of his stock company to "stand in" for a variety of ethnic types. Thus both Mike Mazurki and the black actor Woody Strode play Chinese bandits in *Seven Women* (1966); Strode, another black actor, Noble Johnson, the Latino Ricardo Montalban, and the Jewish Sal Mineo, among many other cultural types, portray American Indians in *Two Rode Together* (1961), *She Wore a Yellow Ribbon* (1949), and *Cheyenne Autumn* (1964); and in *The Last Hurrah* (1958) he cast the archetypal Spanish lover Ricardo Cortez as a Jewish lawyer.[1] And yet, in balance, we should note that Ford would also give dignity and historical relevance to both blacks and American Indians, most notably in films such as *Sergeant Rutledge* (1960), which again starred Woody Strode; in *She Wore a Yellow Ribbon*, in which he used his old acquaintance Chief Big Tree in the position of the wise Indian elder who wants to stop war; and especially *Cheyenne Autumn*, which placed the Indian in a heroic and sympathetic context unusual for American films of that day. Moreover, Ford freely employed real Indians, particularly the Navajo of Monument Valley, as extras in most of his Westerns. If his films at various times seem callous or condescending in their ethnic portrayals, especially of Indians, then, they also and just as often seem to interrogate those identities in ways that are unusual for the American film industry and that reveal much about American culture and its traditions, about the real makeup of American civilization.

Stagecoach, as I have already implied, offers an especially telling example of how Ford's play with racial representation and judgment opens up these larger concerns. It is, of course, considered one of his masterworks, as well as one of the great films in American cinematic history. Its enthusiastic critical reception and box-office success helped to reestablish the Western as an important film genre – even a suitable vehicle for adult themes, as his postwar films would especially demonstrate. And, thanks to its pioneering use of Monument

Valley as a setting, it helped to determine for audiences throughout the world the *look* of the cinematic West, as an archetypal stage on which the drama of American culture could be played out. It is, moreover, a film that announces, and in a forthright way that no other Western of its day did, that a key dimension of this drama is one of racial conflict and violence, here keyed to the cultural construction of the other.

While that construction lays its foundations from the opening of the film, the key scene in the architecture of prejudice and cultural tensions that it explores occurs late in *Stagecoach*, and it is one that borrows from a familiar American stock of xenophobic texts. For throughout the American cinema we can find an oft-recurring scene in which a white woman – or in some cases, a child – is about to be killed by a loved one. It is clearly a terrible act, this violation of the innocent, this transgression of trust and blood ties, and one that seems to call into question the very nature of love. Yet it is also, these narratives repeatedly affirm, practically necessary, ultimately even a gauge of the depths of the potential killer's feelings for the victim. For this scene usually happens in the context of racial conflict and responds to what seems a far more terrible transgression, the unspeakably savage violence anticipated from the other. In the face of such dire circumstances, of what is typically known as "a fate worse than death," the victim's only salvation from this racist's nightmare seems death itself, mercifully and lovingly delivered by someone near and dear. Yet as this description should begin to suggest, and as Michel Foucault's discussion of such liminal situations can help us see, transgression is never simple, easy to sort out in terms of victim and victimizer, good and evil. As he offers, "transgression incessantly crosses and recrosses a line which closes behind it . . . and thus it is made to return once more right to the horizon of the uncrossable," so that in the act of transgression all "certainties . . . are immediately upset."[2] And those certainties of which he speaks include not just the borders of the world in which we live but also the commonly repressed boundaries of cultural and racial identity. This "upset" of certainties, I suggest, reflects tellingly on the racist nature of the attitude implicit in this recurring scene, especially as Western films have interpreted it and as *Stagecoach* especially employs it.

Hatfield about to shoot Lucy Mallory (Louise Platt) to spare her a fate worse than death. (Frame enlargement)

As typically used in popular genres, this scene certainly has links to the early American frontier experience, as well as to the literature chronicling that experience. One of its most noteworthy formulations, for example, occurs in James Fenimore Cooper's *The Last of the Mohicans* (1826) with Cora, who would rather die than be taken as a squaw. It has deeper roots, though, in those captivity narratives popular in the early colonial and frontier eras, tales that, as James D. Hart explains, typically "described the narrator's capture, the cruel march into the wilderness, the brutalities he suffered while living among the Indians, and his eventual escape."[3] These oft-reprinted stories, exemplified by Mary Rowlandson's *The Sovereignty and Goodness of God...a Narrative of the Captivity and Restauration of Mrs. Mary Rowlandson* (1682) and John Williams's *The Redeemed Captive* (1707), find much of their appeal in their detailed accounts of the "Indian" lives of those who had somehow managed to survive that "fate worse than death." In the process, they describe a variety of boundary crossings or transgressions, and especially, as Michelle Burnham observes, many "otherwise unimaginable" female violations, while also opening onto the possibilities for women of a life outside the dominant white culture and its customs.[4] She suggests that these captivity narratives typically played up the sort of margins to which Foucault refers, for in their harrowing accounts they both confirmed the savagery of the Indian other and offered intriguing glimpses of what life might be like *as part of* that other. Consequently, they often seemed both to confirm the dominant racial and cultural identity of the audience and to offer what Burnham terms a "loophole,"[5] a possible alternative to that cultural construction, a potential for survival and for living with that "savage" influence.

While the captivity narrative, with its often implicit interrogation of feminine cultural repression, has inspired few film adaptations, we do not have to look far to find noteworthy varieties of its dark extension, of that "fate worse than death" scene, in a broad spectrum of American cinema.[6] An early paradigm appears in D. W. Griffith's *The Birth of a Nation* (1915), in which renegade blacks in the post–Civil War South besiege a cabin of whites, intent on murder and "worse." As an old white man struggles to hold a door shut against the attackers, he also readies a rifle butt to crush the skull of – and thereby "save" – a white girl in his charge. A later variation on this scene occurs in *The Sand Pebbles* (1966), as the American sailor Jake Holman shoots his favorite coolie rather than see him tortured by rebellious Chinese. More recently, it shows up in *Starship Troopers* (1997), wherein alien insects become a kind of ultimate and horrific racial other, their onslaught prompting just such a "loving" murder of a fellow trooper. But this scene seems to surface most often in our Westerns, especially those that foreground the white man/red man animosity, such as Cecil B. DeMille's *Union Pacific* (1939) and Ford's *Stagecoach* and *The Searchers*. Because they structure this scene in such a strikingly similar manner, *Union Pacific* and *Stagecoach* afford a revealing comparison. In DeMille's film, while on a journey a group of whites is isolated and attacked by an Indian war party; and with their ammunition nearly gone and the Indians upon them, one of the white men prepares to shoot a young woman as she prays. While *The Searchers* offers no single comparable scene, the characters discuss such a situation, and the narrative trajectory seems determined by a similar underlying attitude, as we see when Ethan Edwards swears to kill his niece Debbie, who has been made into the squaw of the Apache chief Scar. But what I want to focus on here are the remarkable near-mirror-image scenes in *Union Pacific* and *Stagecoach* as they suggest different attitudes toward this racially overdetermined situation and exploit the different potentials in this liminal scene. For the former film employs that scene to reaffirm certain cultural and racial assumptions, while the latter develops the "loophole" potential in such scenes, using it to cap its broader interrogation of those very certainties – and in the process to set the stage for the more complex or "adult" version of the Western that would later emerge.

While this archetypal scene usually occurs in a racially charged context, I do not want to minimize the extent to which it is fundamentally about violence and our fears of it, particularly because the Western so often seems to be about violence. Jane Tompkins points up this characteristic of the Western when she notes that "death is everywhere in this genre."[7] In this particular scene, violence practically overflows generic boundaries, for it marks a threshold in the narrative, the point at which a typically melodramatic story threatens to cross into the generic realm of horror. Ethan Edwards's comment in *The Searchers*, after finding the body of one of his nieces, that "As long as you live, don't ever ask" what had been done to her, speaks volumes in support of this conflation of violence and fear. And while political fashion today might gloss it over, we should acknowledge that such a response is not simply based in wild imaginings. As Richard Slotkin in his study of frontier violence notes, "the western tribes had no taboo against" torture and rape and, in fact, made rape "part of their celebrations of triumph, along with the torturing and sexual mutilation of male captives."[8] In such cases, something horrific, something totally beyond the normal pale, stakes a claim on the everyday world, and, as is so often the case in the horror genre, seems to necessitate an equally horrific, purgative response. In effect, that horrific event, or even *the very thought* of such an event, might bring out the monster in us. Indeed, the extremity of the reaction to the impending violation – for example, the skull crushing of the little loved one in *The Birth of a Nation* – is supposed to measure out for us, to gauge metonymically the very enormity of the violence expected from the other.

And yet this scene, as our Westerns play it out, is also always about much more than violence and our fears of it – or, to be more precise, it is about an inevitable nexus that becomes visible only at this liminal position. After all, while Edwards's niece Debbie is not killed, but rather taken by the Indians and forced to become one of them, Ethan remains ready to *kill her*, to become a killer himself in order to erase the *effects* of that racial transgression. Such a response, in which he becomes the very thing he hates – in fact, literally scalping the scalper Scar – should bring the concern with transgression itself into sharp focus. In that crossing of borders *The Searchers* emphasizes a point implicit in the other scenes we shall discuss: the nature of the boundaries by which we live. Thus Slotkin explains that, for the early settlers their fears of the Indians and the violence with which they were linked ultimately projected something more, "their fear of allowing themselves to adjust to and merge with the environment" of the frontier world, a world embodied in the "wild" Indians whom they both feared and sought to establish power over.[9] The Indian transgression, consequently, inevitably evokes the specter of another set of possible transgressions, those in which we become something wild or other ourselves, and thus prompts a reaction against the other, a racist recoil.

Before comparing *Union Pacific* and *Stagecoach* in light of this dynamic of transgression and racial fear, we should first note several similarities that might cast their different developments of the "fate worse than death" in a more revealing light. Remarkably, these two films with near-mirroring scenes premiered within approximately a month of each other.[10] Both were nominated for a number of Academy Awards, with *Stagecoach* winning two. Together, thanks in part to their critical and commercial success, they marked a transition in the Western film genre, demonstrating that a formula that had, for a decade, functioned mainly in the B-film category was also suitable for big-budget, major-studio productions. Furthermore, both *Union Pacific* and *Stagecoach* were adapted from stories by Ernest Haycox, and the plot of DeMille's film even echoes several scenes in an earlier Western epic by Ford, *The Iron Horse* (1924). However, these remarkable lines of kinship and coincidence cannot mask a significant divergence that comes into focus in their treatments of the racial dimensions of that "fate worse than death" scenario.

As Michel Foucault explains, the act of transgression, despite its often horrific implications, can also have a revealing function. For the transgressive act, he says, always "displays the flash of its passage" by which we might trace out "its origin."[11] Thus in the scenes we have noted, the point of transgression, or what he terms the "horizon of the uncrossable," may highlight the very traces of the racial tensions on which such narratives turn. On its surface, a film like *Union Pacific* would seem to have little concern with such racial tensions. It is, after all, a sprawling Western in the DeMille epic vein about what we have historically termed America's "Manifest Destiny," about a kind of cultural fate – and privilege – of extending the nation's boundaries from coast to coast, particularly through the spanning of the continent by the railroad in the late 1860s. The film's ability to overlook or minimize American culture's own transgressions in fulfilling that destiny suggests the extent to which it seeks to appropriate – and prop up – the "certainties" of American cultural history. And given both the national and international insecurities at the time these films appeared, that effort certainly has reason. While *Stagecoach* similarly centers on a difficult and threat-filled overland journey, it announces from the start a different stance, as we see the town of Tonto's Law and Order League evict two unwanted citizens, the drunk Doc Boone and the prostitute Dallas; as Doc explains matter-of-factly to Dallas, "It seems we are the victims of a foul disease known as social prejudice." And indeed, various sorts of transgression through "social prejudice" form the real focus of this film, as the microcosm of American culture constituted by the stagecoach occupants repeatedly reveals its own transgressive attitudes, even as all unite to stave off the potential transgressions of Geronimo and his band who have "jumped the reservation," stepped beyond their white-determined boundaries. If in its alliance for a cause and stirring defense of the stagecoach, Ford's film too betrays traces of the era's international tensions, of the way American culture was already beginning to "circle the wagons" against obvious foreign menaces, it also manages, as we shall later see, to turn them to a more reflective end of cultural self-examination.

In the case of *Union Pacific*, as I have suggested, a nationalist agenda of a sort familiar to the Western takes center stage and, in the process, casts that singular scene in a telling light. From its opening medley of martial and folk music, iconic images of the railroad and buffalo, and a historical title card outlining the narrative's context, a single thrust becomes obvious. As the title card notes, the film's story is that of a "nation, young, tough, prodigal and invincible," one for whom the

Doc Boone (Thomas Mitchell) and Dallas (Claire Trevor) are run out of Tonto by the Law and Order League. (Museum of Modern Art/Film Stills Archive)

West is its "Empire" and a transcontinental railroad the key to that Empire's creation. Opposed to this national destiny are both "the hidden hand that tries to stop progress" – that is, the profiteers who back an opposing railroad and try to sabotage the Union Pacific – and such "natural" barriers as the geography, the weather, and the Indians. While the problems of weather and topography figure in several scenes, the capitalist rivalry and Indian menace become the chief transgressions on which this narrative turns, and the main concerns of its protagonist, the railroad troubleshooter Jeff Butler, proclaimed to be the only representative of "the law" in this frontier world.[12]

Butler early on establishes his desire to make peace with the Indians. He initially reports to General Dodge, head of the Union Pacific project, of a successful meeting with a local chief who promises that "the Indians will lay off the railroad if the whites will lay off the Indians." However, this effort at negotiation never develops any further; it seems intended simply to make the point of white good will. The narrative thereafter treats the Indians less as a people with whom one might negotiate than as part of the Western landscape. In fact, as *Union Pacific* depicts them, the Indians seem a rather strange people, hardly the sort that *could* be bargained with. Thus shortly after Butler reports on his efforts at peace making, a train passenger is warned to shut her window because, she learns, at night Indians like to fire at the lighted images. That passing warning strikes both playful and potentially violent notes, while also foreshadowing a later scene in which a passenger shoots a young Indian racing along-side the train on horseback. At this point that playful dimension quickly dissolves into a sense of his people as terribly vengeful and savage. As Butler explains, the man who shot that Indian has effec-tively "killed a dozen white men" and "scalped and tortured women and children" – all the expected reprisal of the local Indian tribes. To amplify this complex character, a later scene shows the Indians working strategically, planning how to topple a water tower onto the tracks to derail a train and then burning a trestle to block other trains from bringing help. Yet after the Indians stop the train, the cunning and strategy vanish, as they again become almost childish figures. In a sequence not uncommon to films of this era, DeMille depicts the Indians in near-comic fashion, as one attacks a piano, another unreels bolts of material that he ties to his horse's tail, others are frightened by a wooden cigar-store Indian, one impales a derby on his rifle, and another puzzles over a corset that he eventually places over his horse's neck. And intercut with such images are violent ones in which the Indians shoot the survivors of the train wreck. In short, *Union Pacific* essentially presents the Indians as savages – less noble than childish and violently willful – who are never really humanized. They are simply one of the more complex, curious, and ultimately dangerous obstacles impeding what one character terms "this mighty enterprise" of nation building.

The film takes the full measure of this danger in its own "fate worse than death" scene, wherein Jeff Butler, his friend Dick Allen, and their mutual love, Molly Monahan, are trapped in that train wreck and besieged by the Indians. With their ammunition running out, Molly raises the specter of the "fate worse than death" situation as she turns to Jeff, whom she loves, and asks, "You won't let 'em take me alive, will you, Jeff?" More a plea than a question, her remark sim-ply articulates what all three feel is necessary at this point, as Dick Allen's seconding "Maybe you'd better do the honors all around" makes clear. Just as important as this sense of necessity is the context of cultural sanction or acceptance – a level of "certainty" – in which the film situates this self-destructive recourse. For as the highly religious Molly fingers her crucifix, she kneels and offers to "say a bit of a prayer for the three of us" while Jeff prepares to shoot her. That her prayers are interrupted by a train whistle and the three are saved by a trainload of soldiers, that a kind of divine providence intervenes at the very last moment, hardly diminishes the sense of cultural necessity and acceptance this scene has carefully built up and religiously sanctified. It simply – and in much the same way Griffith did with his cross-cut rescue scene in *The Birth of a Nation* – offers the audience an element of gratification or reward for confronting this most painful reality, for imagining and acknowledging the only correct response to the transgression of this racial other.

With this scene *Union Pacific* definitively links its story of Manifest Destiny, of the epic American adventure, with another one of cultural and racial integrity. For the Indians represent both an obstacle to national destiny and a deadly cultural antagonism, a constant potential for transgression that, the film implies, could hardly be understood, much less integrated into a functional society. And in this respect, the Indians prove radically different from even the capitalist opposition to the railroad, led by the Chicago financier Barrow. For he is ultimately forced to aid the project and ends up driving the golden spike that links the eastern and western lines. White America's ability to meet the violent transgressions of the other, in this case the Indians, with its own measure of violence, even when necessarily a self-inflicted one, becomes a telling measure of cultural strength and determination – qualities apparently needed to achieve that destiny, envisioned at the narrative's end by a reenactment of the famous joining of the rails at Promontory Point, Utah. The sense of necessity that transgression reveals "in the flash of its passage," though, is significant, for it points up the extent to which a film like *Union Pacific* envisions violence as unavoidable and even justified by the very nature of the obstacles, especially the racial obstacle of the other, that America faced in its westward march.

While appearing at the same time, *Stagecoach* offers a rather different take on that pattern of transgressions, largely because of the context in which Ford places his white/Indian confrontation. As we have already noted, the film quickly strikes a note of intolerance, with Doc and Dallas being run out of Tonto. But that scene gains added resonance in the context of the prologue, wherein we learn that a raiding party of Apaches, under Geronimo's leadership, has jumped the reservation and thus challenged another sort of effort at cultural power and "purity." Dallas's remark directed at the ladies of the Law and Order League, that "there are worse things than Apaches," points up the parallel, while also suggesting the kinship here between violence and the seemingly bloodless acts of cultural purification these ladies are undertaking, the far more subtle and everyday acts of cultural violence that attended the "civilizing" of this frontier.

Yet even before it strikes this note, *Stagecoach* offers us a register of various reactions to that news of Geronimo's escape. This start is significant because, far more so than in *Union Pacific*, the Indians then vanish from most of the narrative, so that we can gauge their presence only through the attitudes of the whites, through the "certainties" that attach to their very existence. As we have already observed, and as Ford points up here and in other films, those attitudes have some justification in frontier experience. Yet as Andrew Sinclair notes, Ford also tried to suggest how much the Indians were "creations of pioneer terror and imagination,"[13] emblems of all that the whites found frightening about this new land, as well as of the sort of racial baggage they brought to it. In fact, this note of "imagination" or attitude is the key link connecting the Indians to the other elements of *Stagecoach*'s narrative. For like the Indians, practically all the stagecoach passengers are subject to a certain level of imagination; they are judged – or expect to be judged – according to particular cultural attitudes, those "certainties" about the world and others that, without reflection, we culturally embrace. We have already noted how Doc Boone and Dallas have become the victims of "social prejudice," the ladies of Tonto having determined that "their kind" is not suitable for the town. In this same vein Lucy Mallory is warned that she should not ride the stagecoach with "that kind of woman" or eat with her; she also learns that Hatfield is a notorious gambler with a reputation for shooting people in the back; Ringo is introduced not as a "good cowhand," as he styles himself, but as an escaped murderer, the Ringo Kid; and Curley, the marshal, is suspected of wanting to capture Ringo just to collect the substantial reward, not, as he later reveals, to save Ringo from being killed by the Plummer brothers, who had previously shot Ringo's father and brother and framed him for murder. These judgments based on reputation or cultural certainty hardly differ from those made upon the largely absent Indians, as we see when Doc mockingly tells the banker Gatewood that, with Geronimo on the loose, they can all expect to be "massacred at one fell swoop," or, as we earlier noted, when Peacock fearfully reacts to Yakima, only to have the station-keeper Chris note the benefit of being married to one of Geronimo's people. That latter scene is a small reminder that the Indians too have their rules of kinship and that people, whether white or Indian, should not be so quickly judged on the basis of reputation or cultural expectation.

The Indians as creations of pioneer terror and imagination. (Collection of the editor)

While the "fate worse than death" scene in *Stagecoach* soon afterward resurrects the specter of those cultural certainties about the Indians, it also broadens our vantage once more to implicate white as well as Indian culture. It does so, as the Indians attack the stagecoach just before it reaches its destination, Lordsburg, by bringing into focus the character of Hatfield and his own prejudices. More than just the self-proclaimed protector of Mrs. Mallory, he also becomes her potential executioner, as he prepares to put his last bullet into her brain in order to "save" her from the Indians. That action, though, should hardly be surprising, because he is someone who is already reeling from the Civil War and its impact on his southern homeland. Unable to cope with that particular transgression and its effects (here too what could be described as a racially charged violence), he has fled Virginia, denied his heritage, and changed his name.[14] Faced with the potential violation of a fellow southerner, Mrs. Mallory – "a great lady" and "an angel in this wilderness," as he variously styles her – Hatfield responds in the sort of paradoxical way we might expect, trying to maintain that pure image by destroying it, to save it from violence by unleashing his own violence upon it.

And yet, while the structure of this scene, complete with the intercutting of a praying Mrs. Mallory, the image of Hatfield's gun approaching her head, and the attacking Indians, clearly parallels what we see in *Union Pacific*,[15] *Stagecoach* offers us a key difference – a "loophole," if you will. Here we find no unanimity, no agreement within this microcosm of western culture on a better way out, no moral support or sanction for a death preferable to the suspected Indian fate. Ringo, for example, while offering similar attentions to Dallas, makes no effort to spare her a "fate worse than death," even though, as we later learn, he has retained three bullets to kill the Plummers. That response to transgression is Hatfield's alone, definitively placing him, like the banker Gatewood, outside the group, outside the society that has formed in the course of this stagecoach trip, and linking him, almost in spite of himself, to that broader cultural "imagination" that informs and makes possible what Doc initially termed the "disease" of "social prejudice." His effort at a "saving" murder, providentially stopped at the last moment by an Indian shot, is simply another sort of prejudice, a desperate effort, based on his sense of "certainty" about the Indians, at escaping from what must seem to him a hopelessly tainted world.

While *Stagecoach* too offers us a cavalry rescue at the last moment, even one announced by a distant blowing of a bugle that echoes *Union Pacific*'s rescue heralded by the distant train whistle, this intervention in the fate worse than death, a counter to transgression, does not quite make things right. Social prejudice of various sorts – of race, class, gender – we gather, will continue even in the ironically named *Lords*burg. Transgressions of different types will remain, for on arrival Ringo will return to handcuffs, tagged as a murderer; Dallas, unable to mix with the likes of Mrs. Mallory in civilization, will go to the town's red-light district; Doc will once again make for the saloon and a drink. The only variation from this cultural trajectory is the surprising coda Ford offers us, one that we might do well to see as a parallel to and telling variation on the "fate worse than death" scene. As Curley and Doc arrange for Ringo to escape with Dallas, they announce, "Well, at least they're saved from the blessings of civilization."[16] This being saved at the crucial moment from the "fate" of civilization and its own deadening transgressions against the individual – saved not by death but by life and freedom – affords a very different perspective on the sort of easy salvations a film like *Union Pacific* offers. For here cultural "certainties" are not only, as Foucault says, "immediately upset," but they remain unstable, revealed as an often flawed base on which we continue to construct cultural and racial identities.

In his study of the construction of the oriental in western consciousness, Edward Said notes that the white man's sense of the racial other is usually grounded less in fact or even a sense of place than it is built around "a set of references, a congeries of characteristics,"[17] a pattern of what we have termed "creations of ... imagination." Those creations out of our cultural imagination have provided the Western, throughout its long history, with a wealth of character types, images, settings, and situations, many of which trace a pattern of racial transgression that has been a largely silent discourse in the official history of America's westward expansion. What these transgressive elements point up is an abiding sense of our culture's limits, demarcations, boundaries – in effect, the very marks of difference or otherness out of which it has tried under a variety of pressures to construct a kind of meaning. Within that constructed cultural meaning, though, we might see how transgression and racism intersect, each becoming the shadow existence, as well as the shadow justification, of the other – and ultimately a key boundary on which the genre depends.

In the paired "fate worse than death" scenes discussed here, we can particularly see how Ford, if not DeMille, seems to have recognized this connection. For DeMille, like so many other makers of Westerns, such scenes were simply part of the pool of generic conventions and a given of American cultural history that he set about celebrating. *Union Pacific's* development of this scene suggests what Sumiko Higashi has described as a "commodity fetishism involving both producer and spectator in a process of reification."[18] For Ford, though, this scene proved something more: not just a way to reify cultural and racial identities, but a site for exploring, as many of Ford's films did, the problematic nature of those identities. Thus works as different as *The Hurricane* (1937), *The Searchers, Sergeant Rutledge, Two Rode Together, Donovan's Reef* (1963), *Cheyenne Autumn*, and *Seven Women* consistently unveil the racial other as our alter ego, as they explore the sort of imagined character white society has typically – and similarly – constructed for Polynesian, black, Indian, and Chinese cultures, as well as the various social transgressions these groups have suffered at the hands of a dominant society. Through that pattern of transgressions, these films consistently cast the white culture in precisely the same mold as the members of that culture do the racial other, and in the process set in relief what Said terms the "configurations of power"[19] on which notions of cultural and racial superiority have historically depended.

We can see the intended effect of such revelation in another scene from Ford's most celebrated Western, *The Searchers*, a film toward which *Stagecoach* clearly looks. Here, after trying to kill his niece Debbie who, because of the renegade chief Scar, has been tainted by miscegenation, Ethan Edwards and his nephew Martin are attacked by Scar's band. When they drive the Indians off, Martin, who is himself part Indian, pulls an arrow from Ethan's shoulder and announces that he will "have to cut the poison out" of the wound. It is a telling line, one that works in the best Fordian tradition, for it marks a pause in the narrative and seemingly does little to advance the plot; yet it quite simply makes literal a shift that is occurring in Ethan's character (and indeed a painful one, as the closeup of his reaction to the cutting makes clear) – a turn from his near-manic hatred of the Apaches to the acceptance he demonstrates at the film's conclusion. In the final sequence, with Scar defeated and Debbie again at his mercy, Ethan does not shoot her but instead raises his niece in his arms, as he did when she was a little girl, and announces a new direction *for both of them*, telling her, "Let's go home." The "poison," the racial hatred and inability to accept the taint of the other, has to some small extent been "cut out," if only after great pain and loss – and too, only after Ethan has demonstrated that he is little different from that racial other on which he has focused so much hatred. More than "a little bit savage" himself, Ethan has had to reach precisely the sort of accommodation with his own nature that American culture, in its 1950s struggle with integration, was with no less difficulty, pain, or violence just beginning to undertake.

With the Western genre and its emphasis on violence, this mirror-imaging has not always been so readily visible. As Jane Tompkins offers, in practically every Western narrative we can find a "ritualization of the moment of death."[20] It is a way, she says, in which the genre sets about "controlling its violence," even cloaking its nature, by rendering it meaningful.[21] That effect is, of course, one of the keys to the genre's popularity, if also one that sometimes obscures its other concerns. While hardly the only instance of such a "moment" in the films discussed here, the "fate worse than death" scene stands out as an instance of this "ritualization" process, a moment when violent transgression registers a range of meanings – especially those of an ultimate love and an ultimate savagery that appear inherent in and markers of the opposed cultures involved in the genre's dynamic. Of course, a society still unstable because of the Depression and already glimpsing clouds of war on the horizon practically required that violence be given a meaningful context, as both *Union Pacific* and *Stagecoach* did, that some level of what Foucault terms cultural "certainty" be reasserted. In this respect, both films served their generic function, offering audiences a formula to help them see their cultural situations in a more purposeful light. But by looking more closely at such liminal places in the narratives, ones where the violence seems to spill over, to become excessive for the ritual, to reflect back upon the self, in those "fate worse than death" scenes, we can also begin to glimpse an element of *un*certainty, as well as a trace of the racial tension always implicit in their genre. It is the point at which the ritual seems in danger of failing precisely because the *function* of the violence has become so problematic, so clearly connected to a racist construction that it calls into question the moral architecture of our own world. It is at this moment when transgression, "in the flash of its passage," suddenly might illuminate our cultural fate and, as *Stagecoach* clearly suggests, prompt us to reassess and perhaps alter its trajectory.

NOTES

1. Ricardo Cortez was of Austrian origin and named Jacob Krantz, but upon coming to Hollywood he was groomed as competition for Rudolph Valentino and repeatedly starred in Valentino-like vehicles as a Latin lover. Perhaps we might see Ford's casting him in a part that played against that stereotyped, synthetic role, then, as something of a reflexive or self-conscious turn, or at least an inside joke at the expense of Hollywood's predilection for constructed identities and typecasting.

2. Michel Foucault, *Language, Counter-Memory, Practice: Selected Essays and Interviews*, ed. Donald F. Bouchard (Ithaca, N.Y.: Cornell University Press, 1977), p. 34.

3. James D. Hart, *The Popular Book: A History of America's Literary Taste* (Berkeley: University of California Press, 1963), p. 40.

4. Michelle Burnham, *Captivity and Sentiment: Cultural Exchange in American Literature, 1682–1861* (Hanover, N.H.: University Press of New England, 1997), p. 5.

5. *Ibid.*, p. 51.

6. Among the films that do focus in various degrees on the captivity story we should note *Run of the Arrow* (1956), *Trooper Hook* (1957), Ford's *Two Rode Together*, *A Man Called Horse* (1970), *Little Big Man* (1970) and *Dances with Wolves* (1990). However, even these films generally subordinate the issue of female captivity – and thus its ability to interrogate female cultural roles – to issues of racial/cultural conflict. Certainly, the "fate worse than death" scene, in which we typically find a male wielding the power of life and death over a female, raises its own set of gender-related questions, but those issues, I suggest, deserve their own detailed consideration. For such a discussion, see the following essay by Gaylyn Studlar.

7. Jane Tompkins, *West of Everything: The Inner Life of Westerns* (London and New York: Oxford University Press, 1992), p. 24.

8. Richard Slotkin, *Regeneration Through Violence: The Mythology of the American Frontier, 1800–1860* (Middletown, Conn.: Wesleyan University Press, 1973), p. 357.

9. *Ibid.*, p. 125.

10. *Stagecoach* premiered on March 2, 1939, while *Union Pacific* appeared a little more than a month later, on April 28.
11. Foucault, *Language, Counter-Memory, Practice*, p. 33.
12. Butler is commissioned by General Dodge, in charge of the Union Pacific project, to represent the law; as Dodge tells Butler, "You're the law and it's up to you to smash anything that threatens to delay us." That embodiment of law in a single individual, while hardly a rarity for the Western, seems strangely underscored here. By attributing this level of authority to Butler, by placing him effectively beyond all questioning, the narrative can more neatly establish the point of transgression. All that strikes at him and all that he, in turn, strikes against represent the transgressive forces here.
13. Andrew Sinclair, *John Ford* (New York: Dial Press, 1979), p. 35.
14. As we learn in his dying utterance, Hatfield is the son of Judge Greenfield of Greenfield Manor. In abandoning that fallen southern world for the wild frontier, he has effectively hidden his life – his "green" potential, if you will – under a hat.
15. Perhaps more important than the simple parallel of events is the very structure of the scene that seems tightly patterned on D. W. Griffith's earlier depiction of a similar circumstance in his Western *The Battle of Elderbush Gulch* (1913). It reminds us of the extent to which Griffith's sensibility reflected – and itself helped mold – a strong cultural attitude, as well as of the way in which Ford was able to divorce technical skill from a flawed ideology.
16. This coda, we should note, does not appear in the original script for *Stagecoach*. See the "final" screenplay version printed in John Gassner and Dudley Nichols, eds., *Twenty Best Film Plays* (New York: Crown, 1943).
17. Edward Said, *Orientalism* (New York: Random House, 1978), p. 177.
18. Sumiko Higashi, *Cecil B. DeMille and American Culture: The Silent Era* (Berkeley: University of California Press, 1994), p. 220.
19. Said, *Orientalism*, p. 5.
20. Tompkins, *West of Everything*, p. 24.
21. *Ibid.*, p. 25.

5 "Be a Proud, Glorified Dreg"

Class, Gender, and Frontier Democracy in *Stagecoach*

We're the victims of a foul disease called social prejudice.... These ladies of the Law and Order League are scouring out the dregs of the town.... Come, be a proud, glorified dreg like me.

– Doc Boone (Thomas Mitchell) to Dallas (Claire Trevor) in *Stagecoach*

No grave social problem could exist while the wilderness at the edge of civilizations [*sic*] opened wide its portals to all who were oppressed, to all who with strong arms and stout heart desired to hew out a home and a career for themselves. Here was an opportunity for social development continually to begin over again, wherever society gave signs of breaking into classes.[1]

– Frederick Jackson Turner

A commonplace observation states that Hollywood films of the studio era repressed class consciousness and were loath to acknowledge, much less seriously address, this fundamental category of social difference. Nevertheless, it seems obvious that at certain historical moments and in specific generic formulations and authorial assertions, Hollywood classical texts, as conservative as they generally may have been, did not maintain a steady state of oblivion to the inequality imposed by economic and social differences or to the class implications of gender. As I will argue in this essay, the intertwined inscription of class and gender in John Ford's *Stagecoach* presents us with a particularly revealing exception to this "rule" of inscribing class in classical Hollywood. I will argue that Ford's film pays a great deal of attention to matters of class/economic inequality and to the existence of an American social caste system and goes so far as to inflect that inscription with an awareness of the power relations of gender difference. Additionally, I will argue that the conceptual contradictions and textual complexities of Ford's film in relation to class and gender can be illuminated through a linked consideration of three key contextual frames: (1) *Stagecoach*'s status as a textual product of the economic crisis of the Great Depression; (2) influential notions of the broad social function of the West to U.S. development, such as the historical scholarship of Frederick Jackson Turner; and (3) the ideological contradictions inherent in representing class in early literary fictions of the American frontier experience. My primary textual examples will be drawn from the beginning scenes of the film, especially those set in the town of Tonto, which serve to introduce characters and class issues, and from the final sequence of the film set in Lordsburg, where the stagecoach passengers end their journey and the consequences of class differences are brought to narrative resolution.

Stagecoach's plot of people under attack certainly lends itself to a metaphorical/allegorical reading of Americans under economic threat in the Great Depression. The film is unusually preoccupied with the down and out, the geographically and domestically dislocated, and can be read as a kind of allegorical narrative focusing on the crisis of the Depression and displaced people at the margins of society. Seen in this light, *Stagecoach* is logically linked to Ford's *The Grapes of Wrath* (1940) in its championing of the common citizen who is "under attack." Such a contextualizing interpretation goes against the grain of Robin Wood's remark that Ford's penchant for setting films in the past indicated of the director, "nowhere does he show either the inclination or the ability to confront the realities of contemporary American life in his work."[2] I do not wish to suggest that the film's "Popular Front" attitude toward class difference reflects a kind of mirror-image influence of political and economic conditions in the United States; nevertheless, the heightened sense of class consciousness and economic instability of the Great Depression provides some clues to the overdetermination of Ford's treatment of class. The thematic and visual darkness of *Stagecoach* (especially evident in the final sequence in Lordsburg) may now impress us with how much the film seems reflective of the mood of the period in

The stage under attack as a metaphor of Americans under economic threat during the Great Depression. (Courtesy of the Academy of Motion Picture Arts and Sciences)

which it was made. From this perspective, the film becomes reflective of the Great Depression's nightmare scenario of social displacement with all that implies in creating acute fear of class instability in the United States and of downward movement in class. It should not escape attention that the film's narrative focuses on characters who experience literal eviction and homelessness and ends with sending the main protagonists to a foreign land as the only possibility of freedom and happiness beyond an unjust law and an oppressive social system. All these elements combine to make *Stagecoach*'s approach to class seem like very potent stuff in the context of 1939 and the Great Depression.

However, my primary interest is in how the film speaks to longstanding social contradictions inscribed in depictions (both fiction and nonfiction) of the frontier. In this respect, *Stagecoach* is squarely located within longstanding debates regarding the social function of the frontier in U.S. democracy and development. In the mythical West envisioned by Thomas Jefferson and, later, the historian

Frederick Jackson Turner, free land provided yeoman farmers with an opportunity for equality, in democratic political participation if not literally in ownership. In the shared elements of their conceptions of the West, rough egalitarianism dominated frontier society, and indifference to class divisions was the norm.[3] They argue that in such a setting true Americans would be forged out of the crucible of the agrarian pioneer experience, and divisions of ethnicity, class, gender, regionality, and, occasionally, race would be overcome. By way of contrast, the East was linked to anti-egalitarian tendencies dominated by Old World hierarchies based on inherited wealth. Class divisions that held sway in the East would be reinstituted in frontier society when it moved from stages associated with primitivism into a similarly advanced stage of civilization associated with urbanity and an industrial economy.

In these contradictory terms, Turner saw the process of settling an ever-shifting frontier as key to the development of the United States, one that would retain the perfect social values of an agrarian-based democracy at the frontier, where land or access to its resources could be distributed equally. Turner's idealistic notion of frontier democracy invokes the growing nation state as feminine but the yeoman pioneer as masculine:

> ...ever as society on her eastern border grew to resemble the Old World in its social forms and its industry, ever, as it began to lose faith in the ideal of democracy, she opened new provinces, and dowered new democracies in her most distant domains with her material treasures and with the ennobling influence that the fierce love of freedom, the strength that came from hewing out a home, making a school and a church, and creating a higher future for his family, furnished to the pioneer.[4]

The opening scene of *Stagecoach* seems compliant with Turner's influential accounting of the function of the West in U.S. development. It establishes the "wild and woolly" western landscape, the open and primitive frontier of myth, where traditional class boundaries are irrelevant to the heroic male action required for success and survival. One of the Mittens of Monument Valley looms in the background as two riders race their horses across the empty prairie. A military encampment is in the foreground, and a soldier intercepts the approaching horsemen and gallops offscreen (foreground) with them. In the next, brief scene in a military telegraph station, the men present their news to send over the wire: Apache warriors have jumped the reservation and are on the warpath. The reception of a telegraph message from Lordsburg is cut short; the only word coming through the line is "Geronimo!"

The Apache uprising forms the pretext for throwing passengers of many backgrounds and classes together on the Overland stage from Tonto to Lordsburg. The passengers undertake a journey in which the problematics of class become as inescapable a source of apprehension as Geronimo and his band of "savages." Their journey becomes a crossing of boundaries into confrontation with dangerous otherness on two levels: with racial otherness and with class otherness.

In the following scene, the stage arrives in the bustling town of Tonto to discharge passengers and take on new ones. Here all the main characters will be introduced and class divisions established. Even the Ringo Kid (John Wayne), who later appears on the road, is introduced in absentia, in a discussion between the stagecoach driver, Buck (Andy Devine), and the marshal, Curley (George Bancroft). *Stagecoach* relies on established generic norms in constructing character motivation and familiar types: the drunken doctor, the outlaw framed for a crime he did not commit, the prostitute with the heart of gold, the larcenous capitalist, the whiskey drummer, the southern lady, the gambler with the mysterious past, as well as established Western plot devices.[5] However, these familiar character types and narrative points are framed within a storyline and through specific textual inscriptions that call into question the idea of the frontier American West as a utopian space where class differences are ignored or irrelevant.

Considered in this light, the opening scene of the film is interesting by what it omits: None of the major characters is introduced, nor do they ever come to actively occupy or independently transverse this free space outside of the confined, claustrophobic space of the stagecoach. Their activities are physically delimited, even at stage stops, where interior space dominates. As a result, the space in which the characters actually "exist" creates an enforced social intimacy across class lines, which is contrary to expectations for a Western. This sense of enforced intimacy is increased by the choice of camera setups, which consistently emphasize eye-line matches and framed one-, two-, and three-shots. As Joan Dagle has remarked of the film: "A sense of separateness and conflict is thus constantly constructed inside a very intimate and communal space, capturing the ambivalent nature of this 'community.'"[6] The main narrative function of the journey is not as a mechanism for geographic discovery, but as a mechanism for assertions of social class. In the generalized process of travel, both the displaced eastern elite and the frontier working-class passengers are led to question their assumptions about class-bound social norms rather than about the land through which they travel. Thus, the American West is not offered in *Stagecoach* as a utopian escape from class but as a site of class-structured problems.

Stagecoach, like the frontier theory of Frederick Jackson Turner, reveals an internal struggle between the myth of the western frontier as a utopian realization of a classless, egalitarian democracy and the expectation that society's progress depends upon the adoption of the characteristics of an orderly civilization. As Henry Nash Smith notes, if one clings to this theory of civilization with fixed series of social stages, then the west could be only primitive and unrefined; to progress, this society was compelled to reject the primitive depravity and coarse, unbridled individualism associated with the frontier. Yet, when it lost these defining elements, the primitive wilderness became a "garden" indistinguishable from the east. It could no longer be the basis for a characteristic Western literature.[7] The notion that the frontier went through social stages on its way to civilization conflicted with the utopian, democratic possibilities of the frontier based on agrarian ideals of a classless society.[8]

The opening scene of *Stagecoach* sets up one primitive danger of the frontier embodied in Native American resistance to whites. The arrival of the stagecoach in Tonto is the first sign of a different stage of frontier development, one that contains a danger in the move from egalitarian primitivism into a civilized state that reinscribes class divisions.[9] The stagecoach will go on to move through a frontier landscape linking the towns of Tonto and Lordsburg. In Turnerian terms, these three settings represent different "stages of civilization," with Tonto representing the most civilized stage of development; Lordsburg, an earlier, more primitive stage as a "wide open" frontier town where almost any behavior is tolerated; and, at the most primitive stage, the open mesas and flats inhabited by "savages," a few homesteaders, and the patrolling army.

While the opening scene of *Stagecoach* succinctly establishes the dangers of the frontier at its most primitive (i.e., "savage"), the scene set in Tonto provides a telling depiction of Turner's theory of the frontier and articulates an ambivalence toward economic progress accompanied by the reestablishing of class stratification in western frontier society. On the soundtrack, a jaunty version of "A Trail to Mexico" provides upbeat musical accompaniment to a dolly shot that reveals the main street of a commercially thriving town.[10] The street is filled with livestock and people, and in the background, a church steeple rises. After quickly unloading a mining company payroll, Buck, the ill-dressed and porcine driver, opens the stagecoach door to let out his passengers, including Lucy Mallory (Louise Platt), a well-dressed young woman of clipped speech and curt manner. She travels alone to meet her husband, an army officer assigned to duty in the area.[11]

Lucy's presence becomes the first indicator that Tonto represents what Turner would label the most advanced stage of frontier civilization, one in which the proprieties and restrictions of class as a social caste system will come to be aligned in *Stagecoach* with the feminine. Helping Lucy out of the coach, Buck awkwardly attempts to correct his language to adhere to proper Victorian norms: "You folks might as well get out and stretch your legs – urrrr, your limbs, ma'am." On her way to the hotel dining room for a cup of tea, Lucy Mallory encounters friends, Captain and Mrs. Whitney, with whom she shares refined manners and formal greetings. Lucy and her friends draw the attention of an elegantly attired man who looks at Lucy with curiosity. He sweeps off his hat as she and her friends walk past him in silence, in what can be read only as their social slighting of the stranger. Nevertheless, Lucy's curiosity is also strong: She stares at him through the window of the hotel dining room, and interrupts her friend's conversation:

Lucy Mallory: "Who is that gentleman?"
Captain Whitney: "Hardly a gentleman, Mrs. Mallory."
Mrs. Whitney: "I should think not. He's a notorious gambler."

Lucy looks back through the window at "Mr. Hatfield" (John Carradine) as he turns and walks away. When she is again ensconced on the stagecoach, Lucy looks out the window at him as he sits at a poker game in the saloon, and he briefly returns her gaze. Lucy's and Hatfield's gazes establish the importance of the exchange of looks between characters in *Stagecoach*. The dialectic of gazes will be crucial to establishing not only the sexually tinged, class-idealizing relationship between Hatfield and Lucy Mallory but also the attraction of the main romantic couple, Dallas and Ringo. The optics of looking also figure importantly throughout the film in tracing the change of feeling and sentiment accompanying a host of other pairings and triangulations (Ringo/Buck/Curley, Doc/Hatfield, Gatewood/Dallas, Peacock/Doc/Dallas) that are implicated in class affiliations, as well as differences and divisions.

Hatfield is refined in his manners and civilized in appearance, but, as Mrs. Whitney suggests, Lucy misrecognizes him as a "gentleman." He is a prodigal son of the aristocratic Old South, a moral (if not a criminal) fugitive, who has changed his name and obscured his privileged origins. When Hatfield castigates Doc for smoking "in the presence of a lady," Doc Boone retorts by implying that so-called gentlemen like Hatfield are not above shooting men in the back. In one sense, by representing Hatfield as a gambler with a violent past, the film affirms the safety valve function promulgated in theories of western development, including Turner's frontier hypothesis. But Hatfield's situation does not illustrate the West conceptualized as Jefferson's or Turner's democratic ideal, where the accessibility of free land provides the safety valve for ambitious and honest workers, but the remote western frontier lacking law and order. This primitive state of civilization allows the frontier to be a safety valve for draining off the criminal outsiders (or "dregs") of eastern society, who, like Hatfield, relocate by choice or by force.[12]

The sequence in Tonto also sets the pattern in *Stagecoach* for social movement between classes. In *Stagecoach*, this movement is clearly dystopic. This social order seems to allow moves only down the class ladder, never up. Hatfield's status as a fallen aristocrat (and Confederate Civil War veteran) is mirrored in Doc Boone's status as a fallen professional (and Civil War veteran of the Union), thus pairing them as ambiguously classed males who embody class identity as an ongoing problematic. Even the banker Gatewood, whose wife is an especially vocal member of the Law and Order League, loses his credentials as a proper middle-class businessman when his theft of a mining payroll is revealed to the authorities, and he is carted off to jail by the marshal of Lordsburg and a boisterous crowd of onlookers.

Although he is a "notorious gambler" and not a "gentleman," Hatfield has little tolerance for those of the underclass (the prostitute, the alcoholic) although Dallas and Doc, no doubt, have frequented the same frontier haunts as he. Hatfield puts his status as a criminal outsider in temporary abeyance when he voluntarily joins the stagecoach passengers. He has one stated goal, a chivalrous one appropriate for a gentleman: to protect "this lady," Lucy Mallory. During the course of the film, Hatfield's exile from Virginia plantation life is paralleled by the self-exile of Lucy, another former Virginia aristocrat who has a newly assumed identity. She is now an army wife "determined" to reach a husband whose posting to the frontier suggests his lack of value to the military.[13] In spite of Lucy's apparent fall from aristocratic circumstances, she rejects the egalitarian West represented in Dallas's altruistic attempts to provide the expectant mother with some degree of physical comfort and emotional support. When Lucy Mallory learns her husband is wounded, it is Dallas who literally steps up to offer her sympathy and her help (which is rejected). Later, Doc will deliver Lucy's baby, and Dallas will care for Lucy and the baby with selfless devotion (even to rejecting a plan to leave with Ringo). Nevertheless, Mrs. Mallory's courage, resiliency, and stubborn persistence in traveling to join her husband are admirable. More than once, she votes to continue the journey to Lordsburg, in spite of the threat of Apaches. It is her toughness that impresses, not her compassion or her tolerance of class differences.

Given the mix of Lucy's admirable and censorable qualities, Hatfield's idealistic view of her as "an angel in a jungle" and "a great gentle woman" affirms his nostalgia for an idealized past marked by the film as characteristically southern in its refinement and gentility (its "femininity"), but also in its anti-democratic and anti-egalitarian aspects (its "masculine," patriarchal imprint). Consequently, to have eastern intolerance of lower classes in *Stagecoach* primarily represented by a pairing of displaced southern aristocrats seems significant with regard to the film's construction of class and gender.[14] Historically, many southerners emigrated west after the Civil War, but Southern plantation society, dependent on paternal inheritance,

Dallas helps care for Lucy Mallory (Louise Platt) and her baby. (Courtesy of the Academy of Motion Picture Arts and Sciences)

was the symbolic opposite of the mythic west. In the antebellum South the most coveted class credential was staying put on inherited land. This served as an economic and social countermodel to the Jeffersonian view of a democracy peopled by yeoman farmers willing to settle new territory. In contrast to the latter, southern agrarianism was dependent on the most extreme of hierarchical division – between master and slave. The plantation-based economic structure of southern society also had great political importance in debates regarding the frontier (and whether it should be pro-slavery or free). As displaced Confederates, Hatfield and Lucy Mallory are overdetermined figures representing both the necessity of the frontier (as an all-purpose safety valve for the defeated Confederacy, for criminals, for land-hungry working-class folk) and the rejection of the fabled class-indifferent society of the frontier by hierarchy-bound, anti-democratic WASP elites.

Through most of the film, Hatfield will assert Lucy's hierarchical class difference (as well as his own, by proxy) at the expense of other passengers. However, in the primitive public transportation of the stagecoach and the crude public spaces attached to it, there will be no exclusionary space for this upper class (neither a first-class tearoom in Tonto, nor separately classed compartments on the coach, nor separate sleeping accommodations at way stations). Also, in spite of the democratic tenor set by the marshal (who calls for a vote whenever they must decide how and when to proceed on their journey), these two southern elites will attempt to assert their social standards. In doing so, they stigmatize those passengers, of explicitly western origin, who are most overtly linked to the criminal underclass: Dallas, the prostitute, and the escaped convict, the Ringo Kid, who was sent "to the pen" for murder at age sixteen. The famous stage-stop dining table scene where Hatfield relocates Mrs. Mallory to a "cooler" place by the window (and far away from Dallas) is one such assertion of the right of self-identified aristocrats, even ones in economically reduced circumstances, to a more exclusive society of their own kind.

Through these various strategies, the scene in Tonto establishes on several levels the association between class hierarchy and femininity. Just as Lucy Mallory is introduced as the representative of mainstream WASP sensibilities and cultured eastern femininity, the prostitute Dallas is introduced as the *ostensible* opposite. She is the frontier prostitute (who lacks even a last name), first glimpsed as she is marched out of town by the WASP "ladies" of the Law and Order League and the local marshal.[15] No inversion of gender-determined social exchange or gender-linked social duties occurs in *Stagecoach*. In the film, women function as traditional patriarchal tokens of exchange between men and as symbols of the private, the domestic, the familial, the sexual.

Nevertheless, the film does suggest that at the frontier, women's relationships to patriarchy are symbolic and illusory. Hatfield's idealization of Lucy Mallory gives her symbolic value as a woman who must be protected, who deserves protection. As a result, Mrs. Mallory, as the "respectable" woman, obviously has a more privileged relationship to patriarchal power than Dallas, who, as a fallen woman, has neither husband nor father nor brother to protect her. She has been reduced to the public status of a cheap, temporary sexual commodity (as opposed to a middle-class wife as an expensive, permanent one).[16] As she is marched out of town, a closeup focuses on Dallas as she reacts to an argument in the street; at this very moment, we hear the words "now my dear lady." Dallas is thus "introduced" with these words displaced to her from their actual addressee. Of course, the displacement is entirely apt, for the question of whether Dallas deserves to be regarded and treated as a "lady" will underscore the entire stagecoach journey to Lordsburg.

Dallas knows the man who utters these words, and she rushes forward on the sidewalk to obtain help from Doctor Josiah Boone (Thomas Mitchell). Doc is in economic straits, thrown out on the street for nonpayment of rent. Dallas asks him: "Doc, doc . . . can they make me leave town when I don't want to?." . . . Haven't I any right to live? What have I done?" To Dallas, expulsion from the community leaves her without any rights. This is a moral and social judgment rendered by the representatives of the WASP mainstream, the ladies of the Law and Order League, who are, in Dallas's own words, "worse than Apaches." Their judgment is enforced by the law, yet it is not enough to expel Dallas; the League also must warn others against being contaminated by her. After Dallas is seated on the coach, Mrs. Gatewood, the leader of the League, suggests to Nancy Whitney that she not let Lucy "travel with that creature." Dallas and Doc are both social outcasts, but it is Dallas who is targeted in what was historically a common occurrence of the late 1800s, "respectable" women organizing to cleanse frontier society of prostitutes.[17]

This raises the question of whether Doc's expulsion from Tonto was planned or merely a result of his coincidental pairing with Dallas at this moment. The fact that Dallas at once recognizes and, indeed, is on friendly relations with Doc suggests any number of unsavory social possibilities: Is he a former customer (of her sexual wares)? Has he treated her (for some dangerous sexually transmitted disease)? Doc's education and profession should put him in an elevated social and economic class, but his obvious failures (anticipating both the alcoholism and professional incompetence of Doc Holliday in *My Darling Clementine*, 1946) functionally place him in much lower social conditions. Doc is an habitué of the same class as Dallas by choice (if alcoholism is a choice). He is a self-proclaimed "dreg," but a "proud, glorified dreg."

Doc and Dallas are regarded by civilization's defenders as lower-class degenerates who need to be swept from town. "Two of a kind," sneers one of the League ladies, "just two of a kind," and, indeed, the film will link Dallas, the orphan who has fallen into prostitution, and Doc, the fallen professional, throughout the narrative. Doc takes on an avuncular, almost paternal role to Dallas. It is he who will encourage her to take her chance and help Ringo escape before they arrive in Lordsburg. Doc tells her that in Lordsburg, Ringo will "know all about you," for the end of the journey promises nothing more than a renewal of her life as a prostitute.

Dallas is beaten down, shamed as a sexual embarrassment to her gender. Dallas's marginalized position as a prostitute might be used to suggest female rebellion or unruliness (as occurs, in some degree, with the character of Chihuahua [Linda Darnell] in *My Darling Clementine*), but her only moment of defiance is when two men whistle as she inadvertently reveals an expanse of stockinged leg as she climbs into the coach. Dallas offers a cynical smirk to them in a kind of exaggerated performance of "whorishness," drawing attention to her leg.

Doc is marginalized as an embarrassment to his class, but, in spite of his drunkenness, he retains his erudition and uses it as a comic weapon to wield against his oppressors. He denounces his hatchet-faced landlady with an ironically applied classical allusion ("Is this the face that launched a thousand ships...and burned the topless towers of Ilium?" He moves (rhetorically) into an impromptu performance in which he and Dallas become French aristocrats going to the guillotine. As Charles Ramirez Berg has suggested, Doc is aligned with the carnivalesque in his often blatantly uncouth defiance of WASP social norms and class distinctions (he will thumb his nose at the Law and Order League as the coach pulls out).[18] Doc's strategy of comic defiance is echoed in the soundtrack, as the hymn "Shall We Gather at the River?" (the accompaniment to Dallas's forced march) goes into an idiosyncratic orchestration (piccolo, bassoon, drum).[19] Their mock walk to the guillotine ends at the steps of the saloon, which Doc enters to obtain a drink. Dallas sits on the steps of the saloon to wait for the stagecoach.

As in the opening scene of the film, what is absent is as important at this moment as what is present in supporting *Stagecoach*'s ultimate alignment of the prostitute with moral goodness, "family values," and civilized refinement. To have Dallas enter the saloon would unequivocally link her to the economic exchange of her sexuality because prostitutes frequently were hired out as "companions" in saloons. Such a social space would not necessarily have "classed" its male customers, but it would certainly have "classed" its female participants as sexually degraded. Although Dallas's alignment with traditional feminine virtues may be a radical break with both generic (and censorship) norms of Hollywood of 1939, it follows a narrative logic established in early frontier literature. It reveals, in fact, that *Stagecoach* is imbricated in many of the same contradictions of class evident in the narrative traditions of the Western genre and the genre's literary origins.

Barry Keith Grant has drawn astute parallels between qualities evident in Ford's Westerns and in James Fenimore Cooper's *Leatherstocking Tales*, noting, for example, that the outlaw hero of *Stagecoach*, the Ringo Kid (John Wayne) and other Ford/Wayne heroes are "in the mythic mold of Natty [Bumppo]."[20] Grant links Cooper's political conservatism and his oppositional stance toward Jacksonian democracy to his novels' "progressive retreat into a mythic past" where "his hero Natty moved further away, both spatially and temporally."[21] I wish to push the point of Cooper's sociopolitical conservatism further in terms of its impact on class issues in his novels and call attention to the contradictions present in early literary Westerns that are reproduced in *Stagecoach*'s construction of class and, especially, in its construction of its central romantic couple, the Ringo Kid and Dallas.

Cooper considered a society where class privileges were erased and equality between the classes expected a dangerous "bastard democracy."[22] As Henry Nash Smith notes in *Virgin Land*, Cooper was not alone in holding such views: "The concept of a classless society appealed only to a radical minority, and was constantly in danger of being obliterated by the much older and deeper belief in social stratification. . . . The ideal of social subordination, of a hierarchy of classes, of a status system, had the weight of centuries behind it."[23] Cooper and the writers of Westerns who followed him worked within the format of the sentimental novel, and the requirements of this form left them feeling, says Smith, "under some compulsion to extend the application of the sounding platitudes of democracy and equality from politics to social and economic life. They faced a continual struggle to reconcile their almost instinctive regard for refinement with their democratic theories and their desire to find some values in the unrefined West."[24] Although Cooper's depictions of the wilderness valorize nature and the nobility of the wilderness hunter, he "stoutly resisted the tendency to break down distinctions between social classes."[25] Cooper followed his own, pre-Turnerian notion of social stages in which the goal was to replace the primitive stage of the frontier with higher orders of civilization, marked by the formation of a gentry class. The civilizing of the primitive, agricultural frontier would inevitably bring with it other stages of development.

Henry Nash Smith suggests that many Ur-texts of the Western, including Cooper's *Leatherstocking Tales*, created characters who represented the genre's ongoing struggle with the problematics of class embodied in the clash of primitivism with civilized culture. Although Cooper appreciated the spiritual values, the moral sublimity that accrued in men associated with the wilderness, his ideal society could not "be realized under the conditions of rough equality that prevail in the earliest stages of settlement."[26] Smith suggests that Cooper started with "a genteel hero, a heroine, and assorted villains, and the faithful guide."[27] At first, says Smith, Natty's primitive prowess "could be exploited with little regard for graduations in rank. But the problem of the hunter's [social] status could not be permanently ignored. The response of readers to this symbol of forest freedom and virtue created a predicament for the novelist by revealing to him that his most vital character occupied a technically inferior position both in the social system and in the form of the sentimental novel as he was using it."[28] For Leatherstocking to become the romantic hero, he was obliged to fall in love with a heroine, and Cooper "had to construct a female character sufficiently refined and genteel but sufficiently low in social status to receive the addresses of the hunter and scout without a shocking and indecent violation of the proprieties."[29] Cooper could never construct an appropriate heroine for Bumppo, just as he could never solve the question of Leatherstocking's place in society because of class issues. As a result, Cooper's Natty Bumppo, the prototypical Western hero, could develop only into "an anarchic and self-contained atom – hardly even a monad – alone in a hostile, or at best a neutral, universe."[30]

Ford embraces what Cooper rejected, a "bastard democracy" in which the lowest are regarded as equal to society's highest. *Stagecoach* romanticizes the lower, working classes of the frontier even as it appears to uphold a kind of Turnerian and Jeffersonian view of the American West as a utopian space that goes through different stages of development. As a result, *Stagecoach* may approach the classless frontier much differently than Cooper, but in no less contradictory a fashion. Dependent also on an evolutionary hypothesis of frontier development, the film creates a contradictory picture of class, one that is not easily resolved in narrative terms, but one entirely consistent with the contradictions with regard to class that are evident in Cooper, the literary origins of the Western, and Turner's historical theories regarding frontier democracy.

Just as the key problematic for Cooper was his hero and coping with the ideological implications of social stages of frontier development, so too these issues are key to Ford's delineation of frontier society in relation to the ideal of democracy and the troubling issue of class at the frontier. To be a Western, *Stagecoach* needs a hero who represents wilderness nobility and primitive prowess, but unlike Cooper's Leatherstocking, the Ringo Kid is not a "monad" apart from frontier society. The film also establishes him as a landowner (his ranch in Mexico), and his desire for revenge is based on family loyalty. All along the journey, his familial and social links to the community are foregrounded. He knows Buck (and his family); Curley was a friend of his father, as is Chris; Doc once set the arm of his brother. Nevertheless, he is an escaped convict, one whom the "better" elements of society (like Gatewood) regard as "notorious." "Isn't Ringo a fine boy," declares Buck after the stage picks up Ringo, and, indeed, Marshal Curley and the film confirm Buck's assessment.

Anticipating later Ford Westerns in which the hero is judged according to how he treats Native Americans, the hero in *Stagecoach* is judged as to how he treats women.[31] Ringo is blind to the fact that Dallas is a prostitute and is being ostracized as a social outcast (he thinks they are avoiding him). Then, in the first dinner sequence, Ringo and Dallas are treated like two criminals who have lost their right to vote in the determination of the journey. Curley announces that he holds the Kid's "proxy" and does not think of asking Dallas what she wants to do until he is prompted by Ringo.

Curley: "Now, Mrs. Mallory, I ain't goin' to put a lady in danger without she votes for it." ... "What's your vote, mister?"

Ringo: "Where's your manners, Curley? Ain't you going to ask the other lady first?"

Dallas is not a lady, so she doesn't count, even in the "bastard democracy" of the West. Thus, when Ringo wants to protect Dallas and to give her full access to democratic frontier society, the other characters can only look quizzically on his gesture as illogical. Ringo's intervention and Dallas's startled response to it, however, are given enormous emotional weight by the film's visuals. In one of the single most breathtaking moments in *Stagecoach* (or in any Ford film), a medium shot shows Dallas, dropped very, very low in the frame, against a white wall. She suddenly looks up and out of the frame. This is a stylistic break that registers the emotional power of Ringo's intervention. As a result, contrary to everyone else, including the normally class-tolerant frontiersmen (Buck and Curley), he treats her like "the other lady," a moniker denied to her by everyone else until Mr. Peacock's affirmation of her goodness after the birth scene, when he calls for a specifically Christian model of tolerance: "Let's not forget the ladies, bless them – let us have a little Christian charity one for the other." While the other passengers may, at this moment, refuse to confirm this "new" identity for Dallas and even regard it as a gross misrecognition, Dallas (and the film) does nothing to suggest that Ringo is wrong. According to the moral judgment of the film (not the characters), Ringo's moral superiority rests in his desire to restore to Dallas the public (moral) identity she deserves to possess for reasons apart from the deployment of her sexuality. Through Ringo's inclusive gesture, the film celebrates the notion of the democratizing, class-leveling function of the West as a form of the "bastard democracy" that functions to right the wrong of social ostracization and class division perpetuated by an arrogant WASP middle class. Here, in an unexpected way, are the seeds of an analysis of American social and economic inequalities that extends far beyond the norms of the genre, even if they ultimately cannot escape the contradictions implicated ideologically in that genre's conceptualization.

However surprising it may appear, Ford's *Stagecoach*, like Cooper's *Leatherstocking Tales*, also needs a refined heroine, but one "sufficiently low in social status" to pair with a sexually innocent hero who is also a convicted murderer.[32] Contrary to some readings of the film, Dallas is not a frontier whore with a "heart of gold" who undergoes transformation (and thus reformation). Dallas's lack of whorishness contrasts remarkably with, for example, Marlene Dietrich's showy saloon singer/prostitute in *Destry Rides Again* (1939) or Ona Munson's colorful Belle Watling in *Gone with the Wind* (1939).[33] This lack functions to confirm Dallas's adherence to middle-class, eastern notions of proper femininity, as do her shame and lack of social defiance. Dallas is all along a nice girl (just as Ringo thinks she is) whose fundamental, proper feminine characteristics (maternal nurturing, altruistic selflessness) surface in a crisis situation. Lucy Mallory resists acknowledging Dallas's goodness: "I'm afraid she sat up all night while I slept." But in spite of its marked resistance to doing so, "good society" ultimately cannot continue to misrecognize Dallas as a member of the underclass aligned with moral depravity (and worse).

Yet, as radical as it is to have Dallas, the prostitute, as the hero's love interest, *Stagecoach*'s most radical divergence from the genre's longstanding feminine stereotypes is to suggest that a prostitute could, and even should, be a mother. In fact, it suggests that she is the best material for motherhood. To accomplish this remarkable association of Dallas with normative maternity, Lucy Mallory is visually isolated from her own offspring and appears with "Little Coyote" in only one scene (when Doc comes in to check on how she is doing after the birth). Otherwise, Lucy Mallory is completely displaced by the visual inscription of Dallas and the newborn as the "madonna and child." Dallas holds the infant to show her to Buck, Curley, and the male passengers gathered in the hallway. And it is in this scene that she and Ringo exchange long looks that confirm their romantic attraction, which leads to a marriage proposal – not sex. In conventional terms of reading class, Dallas might be dismissed as functioning as a "wet-nurse" to the aristocratic woman, but it is clear that Dallas symbolically displaces Lucy as the "madonna" rather than merely supplementing her. When the stagecoach reaches the salt flats, it is attacked by the Apaches. Dallas, not Lucy, holds the baby in her arms, looks at it, and, despairing of the newborn's future, collapses in tears over the tiny bundle. By way of contrast, there is no indication that Lucy is even thinking of her child. At this moment, she is wedged into a corner against the side of the coach, looking away from her child. She prays and is oblivious even to the fact that Hatfield is poised to shoot her with his last bullet to keep her from falling into the hands of the Apaches.[34] The construction of Dallas and Ringo conforms to the observation made in relation to early Western literature by Smith: "The values that are occasionally found in the West are anomalous instances of conformity to a standard that is actually foreign to the region. This principle is exemplified in the Western heroines, who seem to be worthy of admiration only in proportion as they have escaped from the crudity and vulgarity of their surroundings, either by virtue of birth elsewhere, or through the possession of an implausible innate refinement."[35] To avoid the kind of class dilemma that Natty Bumppo creates for Cooper, Ford's solution is to have Dallas and Ringo emerge as natural aristocrats, morally superior beings who have not been made coarse and cynical by the degrading social experiences imposed upon them (through streetwalking or jail).

Stagecoach overtly rejects the eastern elites on the coach. Yet, paradoxically, in constructing a hero and heroine who both possess an "implausible innate refinement," the film succumbs to the inherent class distinctions embedded in the theory of social stages that posits refinement and middle-class, "eastern" norms as the standard of value. Ringo and Dallas do possess a "Western freshness" that contrasts with "eastern over sophistication." They also escape the kind of cultural primitivism (especially revealed in language) that typifies *Stagecoach* characters like Buck, Chris, and Curley, or Chihuahua in *My Darling Clementine*, or Link Appleyard in *The Man Who Shot Liberty Valance* (1962). Frontier illiteracy, coarseness, grotesque physicality, and multicultural, interethnic sexual mixing are all left to the secondary, supporting characters (Buck, Curley, Chris, Doc, Billy Pickett) who provide *Stagecoach* with its primary comic material. As a consequence, although they are subject to social degradation as members of the class of criminals, Dallas and Ringo do not represent difference aligned with barbaric or primitive values associated with the most primitive stage of frontier life. On the contrary, they both embody the best of civilization's values – altruism, sensitivity, regard for family and marriage, a sense of tolerance and fair play, and good manners. Their behavior and motivations adhere to criteria of refinement that, following Smith's observations regarding Cooper, actually betray an "unconscious devotion to class distinctions."[36] While Ringo's desire for revenge for his family might be linked to lawlessness or "savagery," Dallas, superior even to refined heroines of Westerns such as Molly in Owen Wister's novel *The Virginian* (1902), is able to turn him away from this goal (although circumstance sets his course on it once again). As a consequence, she is a powerful force for civilization, and Ringo is a gentle man capable of being persuaded to turn away from violence. This strategy of constructing his hero and heroine reveals the attempt of Ford's film to skirt the logic of Cooper's conservatism as well as of Turner's theory of civilization in which refinement "is believed to increase steadily as one moves from primitive simplicity and coarseness toward the complexity and polish of urban life."[37]

Many scholars have emphasized how, by the end of the journey, the stagecoach's occupants, with the exception of Gatewood, have coalesced into a community. Certainly, the scene in which the men gather around Dallas as she holds Mrs. Mallory's baby is the most persuasive image of a cohesive community momentarily unconscious of its differences. But have the class-divided occupants of the stagecoach become a unified community, as so many have argued? Does *Stagecoach* affirm class solidarity and a utopian resolution to class differences? I suggest that what *Stagecoach* offers is not a true and complete reconciliation of classes but an apparent victory of one and defeat of the other. Western democratic egalitarianism versus eastern elitism – which can triumph? What social stage will be in ascendancy?

It first should be noted that during the journey, upper- and middle-class "easterners" are of little help in guaranteeing the survival of the group. When they are attacked, Curley calls for Ringo's assistance, and they and Buck literally keep the stage afloat (in the river-crossing sequence) and moving across the salt flats as the Apaches attack. It is Doc and Dallas who minister to Lucy Mallory when she is ready to deliver her baby, and Doc who ostensibly saves Peacock's life and attempts to help the dying Hatfield. Then, at the end of the stagecoach's journey, the travelers' arrival at Lordsburg also undercuts the value of temporary class reconciliation. Certainly, Lucy and Peacock do say goodbye to Dallas, and the warmth of their sentiments indicates a reversal of their previous attitudes. They do not turn against the lower class once they are out of danger. However, Mr. Peacock employs the same "salesman's" line about visiting

The men gather around Dallas with Mrs. Mallory's baby in a Fordian image of community. (Museum of Modern Art/Film Stills Archive)

him in Kansas City, Kansas, that he used with Jerry the bartender in Tonto, and Lucy's words are just that, words, as she and her baby are hustled off to the hospital by middle-class women more restrained in their attitude toward Dallas but still reminiscent of the League ladies of Tonto. The middle- and upper-class easterners (Peacock, Lucy Mallory, Hatfield, Gatewood) are all dispersed: Peacock and Lucy to the hospital, Hatfield to the morgue, Gatewood to jail. The elites are made irrelevant to the final sequence of the film and its resolution of the problems that impede the union of the hero and heroine, who must confront their pasts. This is where Ringo must face the Plummer brothers and Dallas is forced to reveal her life as a prostitute to him. The irrelevancy of the socially "superior" classes to the safe passage of the stagecoach and to the resolution of the main protagonists' conflicts may be read as Ford's way of asserting the functional inferiority of the social elite, their lack of vitality and adaptation to Western democracy, and, of course, their ultimate irrelevancy to the primary concerns of the Western as a myth.

The final Lordsburg sequence emerges as a remarkable statement on working-class solidarity. It brings the "dregs" of Western society to the foreground as heroic and "glorified." As the last of the elites are dispersed, the representatives of the working/lower classes – Buck, Ringo, Doc, and Dallas – gather around the front of the stagecoach. At the same time, a parallel gathering occurs in a local saloon, where Luke Plummer, his girlfriend, and his hired hands are joined by Luke's brothers. It is against these enemies that Doc, Curley, and Buck will all attempt to help Ringo: Curley arms him, Buck attempts to confuse his enemies, and Doc attempts to disarm them. In the end, the working/lower classes must fend for themselves – support one another and, finally, change the rules altogether as the lawman (Curley) lets his prisoner (Ringo) escape.

This famous ending of *Stagecoach*, in which Dallas and Ringo are "saved from the blessings of civilization," is an ambivalent one but fully in keeping with the ongoing difficulties of conceptualizing the frontier as a classless, utopian democracy. The ideal couple, waiting to be returned to the oppression of society (prison and prostitution), is released by their surrogate fathers (Doc and Curley) to go to the haven of Ringo's ranch in Mexico. The ending suggests that social forces which seek to reestablish the order of civilization are too strong. They will make it an impossibility for Dallas to assume her true "natural" vocation as wife and mother and for Ringo to reenter society as the "good cowhand" he yearns to be once again. *Stagecoach*'s final rejection of "the blessings of civilization" is only a partial one, however. In keeping with a long tradition in sentimental Western literature, Ringo and Dallas possess refined virtues that uphold rather than overturn middle-class eastern values.[38] As Robin Wood has said, "their proposed future embraces precisely the fundamentals on which civilization is built."[39] But they cannot reenter a civilization that promises to become even more stratified and even less tolerant of class differences. The dangers of the social phase that brings civilization fully to the frontier can be overcome only by leaving them behind.

Stagecoach acknowledges the dangers of social stratification brought by increasing social development and refinement. The undemocratic and intolerant tendencies in the advanced phase of frontier development are criticized by the film, but the longstanding and often contradictory "theory" of frontier development that underscores this picture of U.S. society is not. In the final sequence, Ford glorifies the dregs at the expense of the elite, but in the end, the film adheres to the notion of U.S. development as a history of advancing stages of social development. With the arrival of advanced stages in development, social structures are hardened so that the mainstream can reassert its right to pass judgment on others marked as different by class, ethnicity, race, or moral "inferiority."

Stagecoach may imply that individuals can momentarily overcome these hierarchical differences and achieve social cohesion, but the ending of the film suggests the dystopic dimensions of the arrival of civilization at the frontier and the ultimate impossibility of preserving the best of Western values (social tolerance and class indifference). Indeed, by sending Ringo and Dallas to Mexico, the film acknowledges that even a temporary defeat of class hierarchies is contrary to the logic of western development and the force of "history." Escape across the border is the only solution. *Stagecoach*, like James Fenimore Cooper's *Leatherstocking Tales* and Frederick Jackson Turner's theory of frontier history, remains caught in contradictory cultural and historical claims regarding the ideological implications of the frontier experience. That experience, whether fictionalized, lived, or theorized, cannot escape the complications of class, gender, or American democracy itself.

NOTES

1. Frederick Jackson Turner, dedication address for a high school in Portage, Wisconsin, January 1, 1896, as reported in the Portage *Weekly Democrat*, January 3, 1896 (clipping, Turner Papers, Henry E. Huntington Library), quoted in Henry Nash Smith, *Virgin Land: The American West as Symbol and Myth* (Cambridge, Mass.: Harvard University Press, 1950 [1978]), p. 254.

2. Robin Wood, "'*Shall* We Gather at the River?': The Late Films of John Ford," reprinted in Gaylyn Studlar and Matthew Bernstein, eds., *John Ford Made Westerns: Filming the Western in the Sound Era* (Bloomington: Indiana University Press, 2001), p. 14. My argument may seem to share something with that of Richard Slotkin, who has argued that many of Ford's Westerns, including the cavalry trilogy, actually address contemporary national concerns. See Slotkin, *Gunfighter Nation: The Myth of the Frontier in Twentieth-Century America* (New York: Harper Perennial, 1992), pp. 328–43, 347–65.

3. See Frederick Jackson Turner, *Rereading Frederick Jackson Turner: The Significance of the Frontier in American History and Other Essays* (New York: Holt, 1994); "The Significance..." was originally published in *Annual Report of the American Historical Association for the Year 1893* (Washington, D.C.: Government Printing Office, 1894), pp. 199–227. On Turner, see also Smith, *Virgin Land*, p. 225. For Jefferson's views, see Andrew A. Lipscomb, ed., *The Writings of Thomas Jefferson*, 20 vols. (Washington, D.C.: 1904–5), vol. 4, p. 509.

4. Frederick Jackson Turner, *The Frontier in American History* (New York: Holt, 1920), pp. 255, 267, quoted in Smith, *Virgin Land*, p. 254.

5. Richard Slotkin says that *Stagecoach* is derived from B-Westerns that dominated the first decade of the talkies. *Gunfighter Nation*, p. 304. The role of *Stagecoach* in reviving the A-Western and reestablishing the genre's popularity is, perhaps, somewhat exaggerated, as Matthew Bernstein suggests in *Walter Wanger: Hollywood Independent* (Berkeley: University of California Press, 1994), p. 149. See also Thomas Schatz's essay in this volume.

6. Joan Dagle, "Linear Patterns and Ethnic Encounters in the Ford Western," in Studlar and Bernstein, eds., *John Ford Made Westerns*, p. 106. On the visual articulation of relationships through eyeline matches and editing, see also Nick Browne, "The Spectator-in-the-Text: The Rhetoric of *Stagecoach*," *Film Quarterly* 29, no. 2 (Winter 1975–6), pp. 26–38. Reprinted in Phillip Rosen, ed., *Narration, Apparatus, Ideology* (New York: Columbia University Press, 1991), pp. 102–19.

7. Smith, *Virgin Land*, p. 223.

8. *Ibid.*, p. 255.

9. See Turner, *The Significance of the Frontier in American History*, pp. 199–227. See also Ray Allen Billington, *Frederick Jackson Turner: Historian, Teacher, Scholar* (New York: Oxford University Press, 1973), pp. 82–131; and for a discussion relating Turner's theory of progress to performative and popular frontier iconography, see Richard White, "Frederick Jackson Turner and Buffalo Bill," in James R. Grossman, ed., *The Frontier in American Culture* (Berkeley: University of California Press, 1994), pp. 6–65.

10. On music in *Stagecoach* and its sources, see Kathryn Kalinak, "'The Sound of Many Voices': Music in John Ford's Westerns," in Studlar and Bernstein, eds., *John Ford Made Westerns*, pp. 184–5.

11. For a woman to travel alone might appear to be a serious violation of Victorian norms, but there is evidence to suggest that such behavior was not unusual in the frontier West. Whether reflecting social reality or registering wishfulfilling fantasy, numerous observers of the time remarked at length on the courtesy exhibited to solo women travelers by otherwise rough frontiersmen. See Glenda Riley, *Women and Indians on the Frontier, 1825–1915* (Albuquerque: University of New Mexico Press, 1984), pp. 47–9.

12. In this regard, the attempts by the Children's Aid Society of New York to relocate thousands of orphans to the Plains states is an example of social reformers' undemocratic use of the West as a social safety valve.

13. The lack of military status and professional success implied by a posting to a frontier assignment is given considerable attention in Ford's *Fort*

Apache (1948) in the careers of both Col. Owen Thursday and Capt. Sam Collingwood.

14. This construction of Lucy Mallory and Hatfield has some remarkable parallels with the representation of Mary Todd and Stephen Douglas as a "couple" in Ford's *Young Mr. Lincoln* (1939) before Mary's interest in Abraham Lincoln overrides her class condescension toward him.

15. Ford's depiction of the Law and Order League offers a pointed caricature of middle-age, middle-class femininity. Yet, this apparently all-female force is historically accurate, at least in the sense of demonstrating white middle-class women's organized attacks on legalized prostitution during this period (the 1880s). As John D'Emilio and Estelle Freedman point out in *Intimate Matters: A History of Sexuality in America* (New York: Harper & Row, 1988), the social purity movement became a powerful force in the 1870s-1890s in fighting for a single sexual standard and in attempting to keep women, especially working-class, immigrant women, from falling into prostitution because of the corrupting influence of men. See pp. 150–1.

16. In explaining why frontier boarding houses did not seem to adhere to Victorian protocol regarding male visitors to rooms, Cathy Luchetti and Carol Olwell note: "Perhaps, once it was clear that a woman did not belong to a father, husband, or other male relative, she was automatically considered promiscuous, and society lost interest in her activities." *Women of the West* (St. George, Utah: Antelope Island Press, 1982), p. 33.

17. On prostitution in the West, see Luchetti and Olwell, *Women of the West*, pp. 33–5.

18. See Charles Ramirez Berg, "The Margin as Center: The Multicultural Dynamics of John Ford's Westerns," in Studlar and Bernstein, eds., *John Ford Made Westerns*, pp. 79–80.

19. See Kalinak in Studlar and Bernstein, eds., *John Ford Made Westerns*, pp. 184–5.

20. Barry Keith Grant, "Two Rode Together: John Ford and James Fenimore Cooper," in Studlar and Bernstein, eds., *John Ford Made Westerns*, p. 207.

21. *Ibid.*, p. 208.

22. Smith, *Virgin Land*, p. 215.

23. *Ibid.*

24. *Ibid.*, p. 223.

25. *Ibid.*, p. 212.

26. *Ibid.*, p. 223.

27. *Ibid.*, p. 88.

28. *Ibid.*, p. 64. Leslie Fiedler emphasizes the impossible place of the woman in *The Leatherstocking Tales*, which he traces to Natty's commitment to nature above all. Fiedler asks, "In an age of Romance, what can one do with the hero who, *in essence and by definition cannot get the girl?*" (emphasis in the original). *Love and Death in the American Novel*, rev. ed. (New York: Stein and Day, 1975), p. 209.

29. Smith, *Virgin Land*, p. 65.

30. *Ibid.*, p. 89.

31. See Dagle, "Linear Patterns and Ethnic Encounters," p. 110.

32. Bernstein details how "the Breen Office rejected Ford and Nichols's treatment in toto because of its sympathetic portrayal of Dallas," among other objectionable points (including Doc Boone's constant drunkenness). The first draft of the script, says Bernstein, "followed Geoffrey Shurlock's suggestion that 'no specific references' to Dallas's prostitution be uttered." *Walter Wanger: Hollywood Independent*, p. 148.

33. Belle Watling actually embraces her social ostracization. This is evident especially when she visits Melanie Wilkes (Olivia de Havilland) to keep the latter from calling on her (presumably at the bordello). Belle protests when Melanie says that she would not be ashamed to publicly thank Belle as a friend for saving her husband's life: "Wouldn't be fittin'"...protests Belle. Motherhood and whoredom co-exist in Belle's life, but they are not socially compatible. She feels compelled to ship her son off to private school to keep him from knowing about her (much as Dallas tries to prevent Ringo from entering Lordsburg to keep him ignorant of her life).

34. No Ford scholar appears to have remarked on the appearance of the dead woman at the ferry stop. She appears as if she were a creation straight out of Hatfield's imagination as a beautiful young ingenue with long, fair hair. She is absolutely contrary in appearance to those hard-won, late-middle-age women who so often inhabit Ford's West, especially the stage stops and frontier outposts, such as Jane Darwell as Miss Florie in *3 Godfathers* (1948), "Ma" (Mary Gordon) in *Fort Apache*, and Billy Pickett's wife (Marga Daighton) in an earlier scene in *Stagecoach*.

35. Smith, *Virgin Land*, p. 229.

36. *Ibid.*, p. 230.

37. *Ibid.*, p. 229.

38. Robin Wood says of the way station dinner scene that it "sets the artificial Southern gallantry of the fallen gentleman Hatfield against the natural courtesy of the outlaw Ringo; and sets the 'cultivated' sensibility of cavalry wife Lucy Mallory against the natural sensitivity of the fallen Dallas." "Shall We Gather at the River?", pp. 31–2.

39. *Ibid.*, p. 32.

6 *Stagecoach* and the Quest for Selfhood

Stagecoach, in its day, was more often characterized as a melodrama than as a Western. And it is true that what we might call the salvation of a woman, as well as the formation of a romantic couple, is central to *Stagecoach*'s narrative. Yet on the whole the roles of women in *Stagecoach*, and in John Ford's films in general, seem much more conventional than in the Hollywood movies of the 1930s and 1940s that Stanley Cavell has dubbed "comedies of remarriage" and "melodramas of the unknown woman."[1] In the course of *Stagecoach*, not one but two women achieve a new perspective. However, neither Dallas nor Lucy has much in common with the heroic leading women of such films as *The Philadelphia Story* (1940) or *Now, Voyager* (1942), women who are passionately committed to their quests for selfhood.

Stagecoach seems to have more to do with such matters as social class and prejudice. On those matters, the film judges American society – "civilization" – to be wanting. In the end, when Curley (allied with Doc) subverts the "rule of law" he is sworn to uphold, Dallas and Ringo are free to "settle down" on his ranch – but only south of the border, in Mexico, a place outside "civilization," to which they will never be free to return.

What does Dallas want? She wants to be a mother, for one thing. And she wants Ringo. At first, she tries to get him to forget revenge and go off right away to his ranch in Mexico, where she will join him – but only after she fulfills her duty to serve Lucy and her baby. Dallas is even a step ahead of Ringo. Anticipating that he will agree, she has his rifle ready for him. And for the moment he is willing to defer, or forgo, his revenge.

If at that point Ringo had not been stopped – or, rather, stopped himself, when he saw the Apache smoke signals – from riding off to his ranch, as Dallas had suggested, to be joined by her once the stagecoach carried Lucy and her baby safely to Lordsburg, he would have failed to play his part in fighting off the marauding Apaches. Everyone's blood – including Dallas's – would then have been on his hands. So *Stagecoach* cannot be saying that Ringo should have run off to his ranch. Then is the film saying that it is wrong to run away – to avoid what is not to be avoided? And is this a principle that holds for women as well as for men?

Once in Lordsburg, of course, Ringo could still forgo revenge and propose to Dallas that she wait until he gets out of prison. Or he could forgo revenge and escape to his ranch with Dallas. True, he has given his word to Curley, the U.S. marshal, but in order to kill the Plummers, he has to break his promise, in any case ("I lied to you, Curley. I got three [bullets] left"). We accept – and, it seems, Curley accepts – that facing this moment of reckoning with the Plummers *is* something Ringo "has to do," given the reality that, although the law has men as honorable as Curley to enforce it, the rule of Law has not yet been firmly established in such a place as Lordsburg. Once Ringo has successfully completed this task, turning himself in to Curley is the second thing he "has to do."

Dallas, too, "has to do" two things. One is to let Ringo know who she is in society's eyes – a prostitute – so that he has a fair chance to reject her once he knows the truth. As they approach the red-light district, she tells him not to follow her any farther. But she knows he will. And, movingly, when he does learn the "truth" – I like to believe he always knew it – he does not disappoint her. Saying "Wait here," he then goes off to kill the Plummers before returning, so he thinks, to bid her "au revoir" until he finishes serving his jail time ("We ain't never gonna say goodbye," he has already said to her). When Curley and Doc Boone conspire to dispatch Ringo – accompanied by Dallas – not back to jail but to the freedom – and exile – of his ranch in Mexico, *Stagecoach* may seem to enjoy a happy ending. But it is an ending that forsakes the utopianism of genres like the remarriage comedy and the melodrama of the unknown woman, which affirm the possibility – at least, the hope – of reconciling the human aspirations of their characters with the injustices of American society as it stands. "In fact," as Tag Gallagher notes in his book on John Ford (a book that, with all its perversities, remains the most illuminating critical study of the director's work), "no other Ford western gives a more cynical verdict on the notion of the West as synthesis of nature and civilization."[2] *Stagecoach's* Lordsburg and Tonto – sleazy towns filled with "mean, intolerant, aggressive people" – are far less enlightened places than, for example, the Shinbone of *The Man Who Shot Liberty Valance* (1962). The fact that Ringo and Dallas escape "the blessings of civilization" is no more a happy ending than are the conclusions of Ford's non-Western films of the period, such as *Young Mr. Lincoln* (1939), *The Grapes of Wrath* (1940), or *How Green Was My Valley* (1941). By running off with Dallas to his ranch in Mexico, Ringo escapes from the problems of American society rather than confronting them. He offers *us*, who cannot escape, no solution or reason for optimism.

The second thing Dallas "has to do" is cater to Lucy and her newborn baby, putting their well-being ahead of her own, until the stagecoach reaches Lordsburg and others can relieve her of her duty. To contemporary sensibilities – mine, for one – it rankles that *Stagecoach* seems to be endorsing Dallas's notion that it is her "duty" to serve Lucy, as if it is natural, even noble, for one of society's outcasts to value a "respectable" woman's happiness more than her own. When Dallas momentarily succeeds in persuading Ringo to ride off to his ranch right now, even though that means sacrificing his wish for vengeance, but then tells him that she will have to meet him later because continuing to cater to Lucy and the baby is something she "has to do," I think of her not as being noble but as chickening out, failing to rise to the occasion, like the aviator André, the "modern hero" in Renoir's *The Rules of the Game* (1939), who tells Christine that he would like to run off with her now but has to wait until he ties up some loose ends, because there are *rules* about such things.

In any case, to suggest that Dallas thinks of serving Lucy and her baby as her "duty" does not register an even more rankling element of her motivation. As Gallagher notes, it is an element highlighted in

Dudley Nichols's script, for example in his description of the moment Dallas presents Lucy's newborn infant to the male passengers.

> The last trace of hardness has vanished from Dallas as she holds the infant in her arms, and there is a glow of wonder in her face. She stands for a moment in the doorway, a smile in her eyes...Her experience of the last few hours has deeply affected her, taken all the defiance out of her face, and softened it into beauty.[3]

To be sure, Ford's realization of this moment considerably downplays the screenplay's claim that it represents a grand epiphany. As Gallagher notes, "Dallas has all along been eager to be pleasant; she does not abruptly shift attitudes; she is merely relieved momentarily from self-shame, which soon returns."[4] Nonetheless, Nichols's rather nauseating idea that witnessing the miracle of birth transforms hard-edged, defiant Dallas by bringing out in her the softness, the nurturing maternal quality that is the true essence – the beauty – of womanhood is so crucial to *Stagecoach*'s screenplay that vestiges of it inevitably remain in the completed film.

It is important to keep in mind, though, that as Ford films it, there is a profound ambiguity to the moment Gallagher singles out. Smiling as she cradles Lucy's baby in her arms, Dallas happily and proudly presents the infant to the assembled men. But among those men is one who means the world to Dallas. The emotional heart of this passage is the exchange of looks between Ringo and Dallas that Ford registers in a pair of big closeups.

Ringo's trace of a smile registers his approval of Dallas. She is his kind of woman. But what kind of woman is she? What does he see in her face at this moment? What do we see? On Dallas's face, as we view it in this extraordinary closeup, there is a "glow of wonder," no doubt. But does this glow reveal the quality Nichols envisioned, the beauty of a woman who knows, and becomingly submits to, her subordinate place? Or is her glowing smile, as she frankly meets Ringo's unwavering gaze, smoldering with desire, like his?

In his useful monograph on *Stagecoach*, Edward Buscombe dwells at some length on the ensuing scene, in which Ringo observes Dallas going outside for some air and follows her. The scene "is no more than a bridge between the previous one, in which the passengers digest the news of the baby's birth, and the following one, in which Ringo will finally declare his feeling for Dallas."[5] In this scene, Buscombe notes, there is a "calm beauty...which is in excess of the demands of the narrative, but not superfluous to our satisfaction as an audience." It is a key to Ford's cinema, Buscombe argues, that every scene, every shot, is, like this one, "more than just functional to the narrative; there is always some added value" – some special beauty or pleasure, whether it results from "a particular felicity of framing, or the subtlety with which the actors are blocked, or an elegant camera movement."[6]

Gallagher makes a similar point when he argues that in *Stagecoach*, "interest in the characters stems from their interaction, from subtle details of gesture, intonation, and staging, and from tension between the type and the individual inhabiting it."[7] But Gallagher's formulation has the advantage over Buscombe's in that it recognizes that Ford's cinematic style is not fruitfully thought of as "adding value" to narratives that are in principle separable from that style. Rather, Ford's stylistic choices are internal to his narratives, play essential roles in making them – and in revealing them to be – the narratives they are. (The problem with Buscombe's formulation, it is worth noting, is one endemic to the field of film studies, which in the 1970s adopted an anti-narrative bias it has not yet fully outgrown.)

In the scene in question, for example, the calm beauty of the passage, the satisfying mood created largely through framing and lighting, cannot really be said to be "in excess of the demands of the narrative." The satisfaction the scene provides suggests, rather, that its specific mood, its calm beauty, is somehow *demanded* by the film's narrative. Or, at least, that this scene, as Ford presents it, is a satisfying response – perhaps not the only possible one – to the narrative's demands.

As Buscombe describes it, the scene begins with "Ringo, screen left, leaning against the wall, looking down a dark corridor, away from the camera. Dallas comes out of a doorway on the right and, without seeing Ringo, turns and walks off toward the door in long shot. Ringo moves to follow her; the camera remains still, watching him walk away."[8] Actually, Dallas is already in the corridor – already being watched by Ringo, in the foreground of the frame, and by us – as she walks away from the camera and toward the door in the background. And what is most noteworthy about this deep-focus shot, visually, is not the darkness of the corridor but the way that darkness emphasizes the brightness of the luminous doorway, which is doubled by its bright reflection on the ground. The doorway frames Dallas's silhouetted figure – the light coming through the door is what casts her figure in silhouette – even as the doorway's reflection frames her shadow in a perfect frame-within-the-frame.[9]

The doubling of Dallas's image within this frame resonates with the film's repeated assertions that there is a split between her social role, who she is in the eyes of society, and who she is in Ringo's eyes – and ours. Beyond this, the deep-focus cinematography emphasizes both the three-dimensionality of this space and the flatness of its pro-jected image, both the reality and the unreality of the world on film. As Dallas walks, her figure diminishes in size, the exaggerated fore-shortening creating the impression that when she reaches the end of this tunnel, she will cross over to another world, the world from which this beautiful light is emanating. The woman who appears in this frame is at once a real human being and an uncanny apparition –

 an emanation of that other world to which she finds herself drawn. What makes the effect magical, rather than nightmarish, is Dallas's beauty as she calmly walks toward the light, and the beauty of the light itself, which makes the frame seem to glow from within.

Ford elides Dallas's entrance into this charged space. Then, too, in the previous scene (in which Dallas presents Lucy's baby to the male passengers and secretly exchanges looks with Ringo), Ford downplays Dallas's exit from the room, rendering it almost invisible, and alto-gether refrains from showing Ringo's exit, which is separate from Dallas's (although presumably cued by it, whether consciously or not). In that scene, the mostly comical exchanges among the other men, which culminate in Doc's relieved "Whew," serve to distract us from attending to Dallas's and Ringo's almost simultaneous exits. This enhances our sense that when we next view Dallas and Ringo, in the corridor, they appear out of nowhere, as if magically transported to another dimension. And the corridor's charged space itself appears as if conjured by magic.

Again, when this shot begins, Dallas is already in the corridor, already walking toward the light at the end of the tunnel. We do not, as Buscombe claims, see Dallas come out of a doorway and, not seeing Ringo, turn and walk toward the door.[10] We have no idea whether she knows he is there, whether she is wordlessly inviting him to follow. Our sense is that she is so absorbed in her private thoughts as to be under a spell. Surely, her "private thoughts" are about the baby she helped bring into the world, about the miracle of birth, about her own all-but-abandoned dream of being a mother. Surely, too, she is thinking sweet thoughts about Ringo. Even if she does not know he is there, surely she imagines his presence, wishes for it. And surely Ringo, himself under a spell, senses or, at least, imagines this.

Before Ringo performs the fateful gesture of following Dallas down the corridor, he looks back, almost directly at the camera. This gesture has a realistic motivation – presumably, Ringo is checking to make sure that Curley isn't watching. It also has an uncanny aspect. It reminds us that the *camera* is watching. *We* are watching. Like us, Ringo is outside the space of the corridor, looking in. When he looks back toward the camera and then follows Dallas into the depths of this space, it is as if, like Buster Keaton in *Sherlock, Jr.* (1924), he is breaching the barrier-that-is-no-real-barrier of the movie screen. It is as if he is entering, awake, the world of his dream.

The scene in question, in any case, is not really a bridge between the scene in which the male passengers digest the fact of the baby's birth and the following conversation in which Ringo finally declares his feelings to Dallas. It is a bridge, specifically, between the smoldering looks that pass between Ringo and Dallas, which are the emotional heart of the preceding scene, as we have said, and the ensuing conversation, which takes place outside, when he catches up to her and, separated from her by a wooden fence, at once awakens and breaks her heart by proposing marriage. But to say that the scene is a bridge is not to deny its importance. In a metaphysical mood, *Stagecoach* is reminding us that all film scenes are bridges. The medium of film,

itself, is a bridge (between past and present, between fantasy and reality, between film-maker and viewer).

The moment Ringo begins follow-ing Dallas, Chris (Chris-Pin Martin), the Mexican station-keeper, emerges from a side door, and Ford cuts, on this action, to a two-shot of Ringo and Chris. It is a beautifully lit shot, in which Chris is in profile on the left of the screen, Ringo on the right with his

back to the camera, his face, catching the light, half-turned toward Chris. Within this framing, Chris – heretofore a stereotyp-ically comical Mexican, gratifyingly treated here by Ford, with respect – informs Ringo that all three Plummers are now in Lordsburg. Ringo then bends down to the

to light his cigarette, the smoke shin-ing white as it drifts through the lamp-light. He resumes walking down the cor-ridor, watched by Chris and by the calm, steady camera until he disappears from view through the door.

As is clear from the language of my de-scription, Ford tries to film the exchange between Ringo and Chris, which serves an expository function, in such a way as to sustain the metaphysical mood, the air of unreality, of the previous shot. Ford does not want to break the spell because he wants it to infuse the ensuing conversation between Ringo and Dallas. But Ford, I find, is not entirely successful in this. Inevitably, Chris's intrusion to some degree dissipates the magical mood of the passage as a whole and does so to the detriment of the film. It is one of many points in *Stagecoach* at which Dudley Nichols's screenplay seems to me to be thwarting Ford's deeper instincts as a director. In all honesty, though, I must add that there are also points in the film at which Ford, himself, seems to disappoint me.

Gallagher is right in pointing out how frequent an occurrence it is for a Ford character to intimate a depth beyond what seems his or her familiar type. The "tight juxtaposing of so many archetypes in archetypal adventures" evident in *Stagecoach*, Gallagher writes,

> seems an extreme application of Ford's vignette techniques of characterization (whereby a hypertypical cameo immediately defines a character); yet vignetting is blended with extended character development, and the result becomes a sort of archetypal fireworks show of increasing brilliance, as Ford freely plays each situation to an extreme degree of stylization and composes vignette "magic moments."[11]

Throughout most of the film, for example, Buck mostly acts like a simpleton. But when the stagecoach reaches its destination, he looks Ringo squarely in the eye and says, simply, "Lordsburg." The gravity of his voice and demeanor reveal him to be a man who is capable, despite his apparent oafishness, of recognizing the fatefulness of this moment. Ford gives every character, except for the reprehensible Gatewood, at least one bit of business that reveals the character to have unsuspected depth.

In doing so, we might note, Ford repeatedly employs a motif that amounts to a stylistic signature. Literally dozens of times, Ford incorporates into a scene – most frequently, he ends the scene with it – a lingering reaction shot – we might more accurately call it a "reactionless shot" – in which a character stares, more or less without expression, and more or less in the direction of the camera. For example, shortly after Ringo joins the motley group on their fateful stagecoach ride to Lordsburg, he mentions that his brother was murdered. This revelation is followed by a closeup detailing Dallas's reaction, then by a reaction shot of Peacock and Doc. The sequence concludes with a frontal "reactionless  shot" of Ringo. Such a shot does not specify *what* the character is thinking or feeling. It asserts only that he or she *is* thinking and feeling, that this is a human being who possesses a depth, an inner life, not reducible to the familiar features of a type. But because *as* individuals the characters in *Stagecoach* remain all but completely undeveloped, I sometimes find myself feeling that Ford is employing this device merely for effect, that he is trying to make us feel for characters that his film has failed to invest with any real depth (whatever "real depth," in a movie character, may actually come to).

Then, too, if Dallas were played not by Claire Trevor but by Marlene Dietrich – Walter Wanger's original choice for the role – or, say, Barbara Stanwyck, or, for that matter, the Maureen O'Hara of Ford's own *How Green Was My Valley*, or if Ford had directed Trevor differently, *Stagecoach* would not give the impression, as it does, that Dallas has so little sense of herself that she feels crushed by an unjust society's judgment of her. A Dietrich, a Stanwyck, or an O'Hara would never whine with self-pity, as Ford has Trevor do almost every time she opens her mouth. If one views *Stagecoach* with the sound muted, Trevor is magnificent – a woman of strength and unfathomable inner resources. But when Ford has her speak the words the screenplay gives her to speak, her voice is almost always pitched at the edge of hysteria and grates on the ears – at least, my ears – like chalk on a blackboard. Louise Platt, as Lucy, is likewise splendid – except when she speaks. She delivers all her lines, not hysterically, but in an impersonal, uninflected voice that would never pass the lips of a Katharine Hepburn, say (who, in *Mary of Scotland* [1936], successfully imprinted a sense of her strength and intelligence on a Ford film of the period).

In *Stagecoach*, in other words, Ford has both leading women speak their lines in voices terminally lacking in spunk. How striking a contrast is John Wayne's Ringo Kid! Viewers who know Wayne only from his later films might well be surprised by how young-looking – and beautiful – he was as a thirty-one-year-old. But his voice already possessed that magic that can turn the most basic of lines ("A man could live there . . . And a woman"; "I asked you to marry me, didn't I?"; "We ain't never gonna say goodbye"; "I gotta know where you live, don't I?"; "Wait here") into poetry – not the poetry of poetry, but the poetry of film speech, the poetry in the fact that just this human being is speaking just these words in just this way at just this moment.

To further specify both what I find wonderful and what I find disappointing in *Stagecoach*, and to further pursue themes that have already made their appearance in the present essay, I will conclude by examining in detail three passages that revolve around the relationship, or lack of a relationship, between Dallas and Lucy. The first is the initial encounter – or non-encounter – between the two women, when first Dallas and then Lucy board the stagecoach bound for Lordsburg. The second is the passage in which, as Gallagher puts it, "Dallas the whore [offends] propriety by sitting next to Lucy the lady, who, by the morals of the day, must register shock."[12] This is the sequence from *Stagecoach* that has received by far the most critical attention to date, having been the object of a highly influential analysis by Nick Browne that was, in turn, the object of an almost equally extended critique in Gallagher's book on Ford.[13] The third is the final encounter – or, again, non-encounter – between the two women when they disembark in Lordsburg and go their separate ways.

THE INITIAL ENCOUNTER

As Buck calls out the names of the stops the stagecoach is scheduled to make, Lucy, accompanied by two other "respectable" women, is in the middle of the frame walking toward the camera. There is a cut

to Dallas, with her chaperones from the Law and Order League, also walking toward the camera, but not centered in the frame. Dallas exits the frame, as two men stare after her. Cut to a shot, more or less from their point of view, of Dallas raising her leg so as to board the coach. At the sound of

a wolf-whistle coming from offscreen, she looks toward the camera, and there is a cut back to the two men, viewed from the same angle,

but closer. They wink suggestively. There is a cut back to Dallas, who does a little curtsy in mocking appreciation of their mocking appreciation of her. Then comes a medium shot of Dallas in the coach, framed in profile, breathing deeply, but otherwise showing no reaction. In this shot, the camera angle, hence the screen direction, is strangely reversed.

This is followed by a shot of the stagecoach that returns to the original angle – and frames Dallas through the frame-within-the-frame of the open door, looking almost at the camera – as Peacock and then Doc Boone clamber on board. Then there is a cut to a shot of one of the "respectable" women, Mrs. Whitney, and Lucy. The fact that Lucy

is in the middle of this frame, looking at something offscreen, has the effect of retroactively revealing the preceding shot to be – or turning it into – something like a shot from her point of view.

When Mrs. Gatewood enters the frame, saying "Mrs. Whitney, you're not going to let your friend travel with…," Lucy seems to be looking past this woman to the stagecoach (to Doc? to Dallas?). As the woman says these words, Lucy – only reluctantly taking her eyes off what she is looking at – looks momentarily at Mrs. Whitney, then back, turning the following shot – a reprise of the medium shot of Dallas in profile – into one that, although the angle is reversed, *feels* as if it is from Lucy's point of view. On the hurt-ful words "…that creature," Dallas turns, looking almost toward the camera, as she endures them. Presumably, Dallas is hiding her eyes from the respectable women who so strongly disapprove of her. And yet, as Ford presents this view to us, it *feels* as if Dallas, as she endures Mrs. Whitney's "She's right, Lucy," is *meeting*, not avoiding, Lucy's gaze.

Not as candid about her social prejudices as the other woman, Mrs. Whitney adds, "Besides, you're not well enough to travel." When Lucy replies, in a matter-of-fact tone, "It's only a few hours, Nancy; I'm quite all right," she addresses Nancy's concern for her medical condition (we soon learn that Lucy is pregnant, the "blessed event" expected at any moment). And she avoids addressing the alleged impropriety of traveling in a coach with such a "creature" as Dallas. As Lucy says these words, she looks briefly at her friend, as politeness requires. But it is clear that Lucy only *reluctantly* pulls her eyes away, even for a moment, from the object of her fascination. Even before Lucy finishes speaking her lines, her gaze has already returned to Dallas. As this description makes clear, what is most surprising – and remarkable – about this passage is its emphatic, repeated intimations that there is a mysterious bond, an unspoken mutual attraction, between Dallas and Lucy.

THE ENCOUNTER AT THE WAY STATION

The second sequence begins about a third of the way into the film. The stagecoach has stopped at a way station. Geronimo is reported

to be in the vicinity. The passengers are to vote to decide whether to return to Tonto or press on toward Lordsburg. They vote to go on. As the wife of the innkeeper, Billy Pickett (Francis Ford), enters with a pot full of food, there is a cut to an "objective" view of the whole room, with Lucy, in the right foreground, sitting at the head of the table,

then to a shot more or less from Lucy's point of view, as Dallas passes behind Ringo toward a chair by the wall. As Ringo says, "Sit down here, ma'am," their gazes meet.

In an "objective" shot, Gatewood, Doc, Pickett, Hatfield, and Lucy all turn their eyes to Ringo and Dallas. Then there is a

cut to a shot – from Lucy's point of view? – of Ringo helping Dallas with her chair, the camera dollying in as Ringo takes a seat beside her. Her eyes are downcast, averted from the camera (from Lucy?). When finally Dallas looks up, our impression is that she is glancing at someone – Lucy – out of the corner of her eye.

As we hear the offscreen sound of a plate being picked up, presumably by Ringo, there is a cut to an almost frontal medium closeup of Lucy. The fact that as this shot begins she is staring at someone,

presumably Dallas, suggests that this shot is from Dallas's point of view. This suggestion is seconded when Lucy's gaze momentarily wavers a bit, as if in reaction to Dallas's no longer merely glancing at her, but decisively meeting her gaze. Then there is a medium closeup of Dallas, angled obliquely to register Lucy's point of view. At the head of this shot, Dallas is almost fiercely meeting Lucy's gaze. This confirms that the preceding shot of Lucy was, indeed, from Dallas's point of view. Since Dallas is meeting Lucy's gaze by staring at her out of the corner of her eye, of course Ford makes the shot of Lucy almost frontal, while he shoots Dallas from an oblique angle.

Within this frame, Dallas looks down, thinks for a moment, then lowers her gaze even more. Lost in thought, she seems on the verge of saying or doing something, or at least formulating some idea or judgment, when there is a cut to the "objective" shot. Gatewood takes a plate of food being passed (by Ringo, offscreen) and holds it out to Lucy. At the head of this shot, Lucy is still looking at Dallas. But then she, too, lowers her gaze, lost in thought.

All the while staring at Lucy, Hatfield takes the plate from Gatewood and holds it out to her, but she makes no move to take it from him. Then Hatfield puts the plate down and directs his gaze at Dallas and Ringo, evidently assuming that it is Dallas's proximity, forced on Lucy by Ringo's improper invitation for her to join him, that is keeping Lucy from eating. There is a cut to Dallas and Ringo, in almost the same

framing as earlier, but now from Hatfield's point of view, not Lucy's; then a cut back to the "objective" shot. Hatfield says to Lucy, "May I find you another place, Mrs. Mallory? It's cooler by the window." Finally, Lucy emerges from her absorption with her private thoughts enough to look up, and there is a cut to Dallas (who is still looking down) and Ringo (who is looking at Hatfield and Lucy), then again back to the "objective" shot. Lucy turns her eyes toward Hatfield, then in the general direction of Dallas (but now looking "through," not at, her). As Hatfield pulls out her chair, Lucy says "Thank you" in her usual impersonal, uninflected voice, and exits the frame, followed by Hatfield. Gatewood, too, begins to get up, and there is a cut to the establishing shot, from the head of the table, that opened the sequence.

Lucy, Hatfield, and Gatewood take new seats at the other end of the table as Ringo watches and Dallas stares ahead of her. There is a cut to a frontal medium two-shot of Dallas and Ringo. Ringo turns to Dallas, looks down, looks back at the others, and says, to his plate, "Looks like I got the plague, don't it." Dallas looks briefly at Ringo, then down and away, saying, or whining, as quiet music begins, "No. No, it's not you." "Well, I guess you can't break out of prison and into society on the same morning," Ringo says, and gets up, angrily. She takes his arm to stop him. "Please." She looks into his eyes. "Please," she repeats, this time without a trace of a whine. Then she removes her hand, looks away, and passes him a bowl of chili. She is about to serve him, but, taking the ladle from her, he serves her. Then, as the music continues, there is a cut to a general shot of the whole room – almost a reprise of the shot that opened the entire sequence – as the camera dollies in.

As Nick Browne reads the sequence, we spectators share Lucy's gaze, but not Dallas's.[14] Experiencing the sequence as though it were narrated by Lucy, Browne claims, we find ourselves implicated when Lucy repudiates Dallas. Yet our emotional identification with Dallas is so strong that we are prompted to repudiate Lucy's claim to occupy a position of moral authority. Repudiating Lucy's gaze, we thus repudiate the position we, ourselves, have occupied. According to Browne, Ford "masks" his activity as narrator, becomes "invisible," and employs Lucy as "a visible persona ... to constitute and make legible and continuous the depicted space, by referring shots on the screen alternately to the authority of her eye or the place of her body, [so that] the story seems to tell itself [and seems to deny] the existence of a narrator different from the character."[15]

Gallagher contests Browne's reading by arguing, shrewdly, that it mistakenly approaches Ford as though he were Hitchcock. Hitchcock allows his camera to assume one subjective point of view after another. Ford, however, exacts "empathetic distance," as Gallagher puts it, in every shot. He argues that we experience every Ford shot, even those that are from a character's literal point of view, *as* a Ford shot, an expression of Ford's narrating presence. Thus we are never, as Browne claims, so implicated in Lucy's repudiation of Dallas that we are provoked to repudiate our own position, as well as hers. We see *that* Lucy and the other intolerant characters view Dallas in a way that social custom decrees, a way that is "far less empathetic toward their victims" than is the way of seeing vouchsafed to us by Ford's narration.

Ford makes this particularly clear, Gallagher argues, by showing Dallas from Lucy's perspective even before he shows Lucy staring at Dallas from that perspective. Importantly, Gallagher adds, although Ford shows Dallas from Lucy's perspective, he never shows Lucy from Dallas's perspective. If Ford were to show Lucy from Dallas's perspective, "[t]he conflict and the terror such a perspective would convey would detract from the greater, philosophic question." That question is, Gallagher claims, *"How can they act that way?"*[16]

But what way *does* Lucy act? Despite their disagreements, Gallagher is in accord with Browne on the crucial point that Ford does not balance the subjective shots from Lucy with matching subjective shots from Dallas, thereby emphasizing "Dallas's passive victimhood and Lucy's active aggression, and also Dallas's inferior position."[17] As is clear from our close reading of the passage, however, on this crucial point Browne and Gallagher are both in error. Ford *does* show Lucy from Dallas's perspective, just as he shows Dallas from Lucy's perspective.

And Browne and Gallagher are likewise both in error when they characterize Dallas as the "passive victim" and Lucy the "active aggressor" in their exchange of glances. Hatfield simply assumes that Lucy disapproves of "impropriety" as strongly as he does and chivalrously takes it upon himself to rescue her from her proximity to

Dallas. Too much the southern gentleman to state his real reason, he invites Lucy to move with him to the far end of the table where "it's cooler." Thoughtful after her unsettling exchange of glances with Dallas, and in any case perplexed that she cannot quite place the familiar-looking southerner who is going out of his way to be so considerate to her, Lucy politely says "Thank you" and follows Hatfield's lead. But at no point can Lucy really be said to be "repudiating" Dallas, or, for that matter, to be claiming for herself a position of moral authority. As in his presentation of the first encounter between Dallas and Lucy, Ford's presentation here again intimates that these two women, although they do not know what to make of each other, nonetheless find themselves mysteriously drawn to each other.

THE FINAL ENCOUNTER

When we arrive at the final encounter between Dallas and Lucy, we viewers hope – and therefore expect – that there will at last be a clear acknowledgment, each for the other, on the order of Dallas's last conversation with Mr. Peacock, in which he calls her "Miss Dallas" and invites her to visit his family some day.

"Respectable" women from the town – no doubt members of Lordsburg's Law and Order League – are welcoming Lucy to Lordsburg. One of these women, perhaps a nurse, says to Lucy, "Where's the baby, dear?" Without saying a word, Lucy looks screen right. There is a cut to Dallas, who is at this moment stepping down from the stagecoach, holding the baby. As Dallas walks toward the women, the camera pans left with her, until she meets up with the nurse (if she is a nurse), who takes the baby away from her and then exits the scene, accompanied by the other "respectable" women, who likewise say nothing to Dallas. As the women are walking off, we hear Lucy – she is barely visible at the lower left of the frame – say "Dallas...." There is a cut to a low-angle shot of

Dallas, then to a high-angle shot of Lucy. "... If there's ever anything I can do for...." Lucy cuts herself off, stares, then lowers her gaze, swallowing hard. There is a cut back to Dallas, who says, with a rueful smile, "I know," then takes off her coat and hands it to someone out of the frame. There is a cut to a longer shot as Lucy pulls the coat over herself as she is carried away on her stretcher, her gaze locked with Dallas's. Then Dallas steps back and turns away, the camera reframing with her as she picks up her bags, stares at them, then looks up. From her point of view, we see soldiers arrive.

Dallas has earned Lucy's respect, as well as her gratitude. We know that Lucy knows this. We know that Dallas knows that Lucy knows this. When Dallas steps down from the stagecoach, cradling the baby in her arms, it provides Lucy with a perfect opportunity to say in public what she privately knows to be true. But even when the baby is wordlessly taken away from Dallas, Lucy remains silent. Only when the other women have departed the scene does she speak. And then she finds herself saying something utterly impersonal. But then – this is one of the most mysterious moments of the film – Lucy stops herself. She is suddenly at a loss. Surely at this moment she recognizes – and recognizes that Dallas, too, recognizes – the inadequacy of what she was about to say, of anything she could now say, given her failure, just now, to put in a good word for Dallas when it might have counted for something.

Dallas's "I know" is spoken with no special hostility, but no real warmth, either. We hear in her voice only a trace of her usual self-pitying whine. But it is enough to register not only that Dallas is disappointed with Lucy but also that Lucy's failure comes as no surprise to her.

Ford refrains from suggesting, in other words, that a redemptive communion takes place between these two women. They are ships that pass in the night. But why? Why cannot Ford bring himself to allow Dallas and Lucy the kind of mutual recognition that, say, Stella and Helen achieve in *Stella Dallas* (1937), when despite the unbridgeable barriers that separate them, they nonetheless share an unspoken understanding? Lucy is condemned to civilization, while Dallas is condemned to live outside it or, as it will turn out, to escape from it. But neither woman embraces, nor even accepts, her own, or the other woman's, placement. Why not?

Dallas's whole existence, Gallagher writes in a fine passage,

> is a kind of dream; every moment, not just this one, has its glow or gloom, its warmth or chill; an accepting baby on one hand and a repelling propriety on the other dramatically define the boundaries of Dallas's affective consciousness, and thus exacerbate the vibrant oscillations twixt hope and despair with which Dallas experiences Ringo's presence.... And it is this melodramatized representation of inner experience that Ford aims for.[18]

But the fact that Ford aims for such a "melodramatized" representation of Dallas's – and, for that matter, Lucy's – inner experience means that he wishes to represent them as irreparably split, as incapable of becoming whole. This aspiration helps keep him from finding in these women the capacity for change, the hopefulness, the spunk, that enables the heroines of remarriage comedies and melodramas of the unknown woman to embrace so wholeheartedly their heroic quest for selfhood.

NOTES

1. That classical Hollywood movies inherit the philosophical perspective of American transcendentalism – a tradition of thought that affirms the possibility and necessity of relying on one's own experience, and on the acknowledgment of others, to achieve selfhood – is an idea articulated by Cavell in his indispensable books *Pursuits of Happiness: The Hollywood Comedy of Remarriage* (Cambridge, Mass.: Harvard University Press, 1981) and *Contesting Tears: Hollywood Melodramas of the Unknown Woman* (Chicago: University of Chicago Press, 1996). Cavell demonstrates how the genres he studies work through the Emersonian problematic of self-reliance and conformity and thereby sustain serious conversations with their – our – culture on such matters as the human need for society and the equal need to escape it, the search for community, and the fate of the American dream.
2. Tag Gallagher, *John Ford: The Man and His Films* (Berkeley: University of California Press, 1986), p. 161.
3. Quoted in Paul Jensen, "Dudley Nichols," in Richard Corliss, ed., *The Hollywood Screenwriters* (New York: Avon, 1972), p. 118.
4. Gallagher, *John Ford*, p. 150.
5. Edward Buscombe, *Stagecoach* (London: British Film Institute, 1992), p. 55.
6. *Ibid.*, p. 56.
7. Gallagher, *John Ford*, p. 149.
8. Buscombe, *Stagecoach*, p. 56.

9. In *Shadow of a Doubt* (1943), when Uncle Charles, having just learned that the police were off his trail, stops on the stairs and turns to face the camera, Hitchcock cuts to a shot, from Charles's point of view, that I find strikingly reminiscent of this shot from *Stagecoach*. In Hitchcock's shot, young Charlie, centered in an almost symmetrical frame, is beautifully backlit by the doorway that frames her. Her figure is doubled by her shadow, which is perfectly framed by the doorway's reflection on the floor. In *Hitchcock – The Murderous Gaze*, I argue that this shot is an instance of a motif – I call it Hitchcock's "tunnel image" – that recurs in virtually every one of the director's films. See my *Hitchcock – The Murderous Gaze* (Cambridge, Mass.: Harvard University Press, 1982), pp. 224, 236, 290, 361.
10. Buscombe, *Stagecoach*, p. 56.
11. Gallagher, *John Ford*, p. 149.
12. *Ibid.*, p. 153.
13. Nick Browne, "The Spectator-in-the-Text: The Rhetoric of *Stagecoach*," *Film Quarterly* 34, no. 2 (Winter 1975–6), pp. 26–38. Gallagher, pp. 153–60.
14. Browne, "The Spectator-in-the-Text," pp. 35–7.
15. *Ibid*.
16. Gallagher, *John Ford*, p. 160.
17. *Ibid.*, pp. 153–4.
18. Browne, "The Spectator-in-the-Text," pp. 150–1.

Reviews of *Stagecoach*

STAGECOACH

Welford Beaton

Reprinted from *The Hollywood Spectator* (February 18, 1939).

One of the greatest of all Westerns. And one of the most interesting Hollywood possibly could have for study. It is superb entertainment, but take it apart and we discover all the story it has could be told comfortably between the two ends of one reel of film. That interests me because one of the beliefs the *Spectator* has expressed at intervals during the past decade is that the story is not the thing of most importance to screen entertainment, that what really matters is the manner of telling what story there is – that it is the medium that entertains. Film producers as a whole know too little about their medium to give them confidence to test a theory. Walter Wanger apparently is an exception. *Stagecoach* is evidence of his willingness to put to a test the theory that the medium, not the story, is the thing. He takes us with a stagecoach on a trip across a stretch of Western territory at a time when prowling Indians made it perilous. After one brush with the Redskins, the coach gets through; at the destination one of the passengers kills the three desperadoes who had killed his father and brother. There you have all the story there is. And for one hour and thirty-three minutes it is gripping entertainment. It is a *Grand Hotel* on wheels.

Only great screen craftsmanship could elongate so slim a story without stretching it too thin in spots. In Dudley Nichols, writer, and John Ford, director, Wanger had a team with many notable screen achievements to its credit, but no other I can recall matches *Stagecoach* as an example of cinematic skill. Quite extraordinary is the manner in which Dudley has strung together a series of little incidents, snatches of dialogue, gems of humor, to enlist our interest in a strangely assorted group of people – a young woman of commercial virtue, the refined young wife of an army officer, a drunken doctor, a timid whiskey peddler, an escaped prisoner on his way back to jail, a pompous banker who is absconding, a stagecoach reinsman who is not brave but bravely carries on, a United States marshal, resolute, fearless, sentimental. They are the people whom the stagecoach carries into and out of danger. Another, a professional gambler with a gallant side, falls victim to an Indian bullet. Each of these people has his or her individual problem, and all of them are worked into the script with a literary version of the skill a juggler displays when he keeps an equal number of balls in the air simultaneously, each ball being a separate unit, but it is as a group they hold our interest.

When John Ford was given the Nichols script he must have seen it as a series of pictures, he could not have read it as a story in words. Its literal translation in screen terms would have achieved poor results. It essentially was a script we had to *see*, one containing only one chase and a triple killing. And Ford makes us see it, and makes the seeing continuously thrilling. It is a production of tremendous physical sweep of pictorial grandeur, of superb beauty which the preview audience greeted with rounds of applause. Photography has the velvety warmth of masterly graded light and shade, not the gaudiness of Technicolor which cheapens so many screen productions. To the cameras of Bert Glennon and Ray Binger we are indebted for some of the most imposing pictures that ever adorned a screen. Through all the feast for our eyes to feed on, Director Ford weaves strongly the thread of human values. He gives us no hero, no heroine – just the people I have mentioned, each to himself being the most important, but to you and me being only one of the group. The forward progression of the story is one of the most brilliant exhibitions of sustained filmic motion the screen has given us in recent years of the talkie era. We have the feeling all the time that we are pressing onward with the characters, going with them on their perilous journey, hoping with them that they will reach their destination in safety. And for that, we have John Ford to thank.

As for the individual mention of cast members, no more evenly balanced set of characterizations ever has been presented, the prominence of the individual plays being dependent entirely on the length of his or her role. Hundreds appear in the picture, and all of them are merely human beings whom we are permitted to see as they live their lives. Claire Trevor, as the prostitute, earns our instant sympathy and retains it throughout, her performance being the most penetrating she has to her credit. John Wayne seemed born for the part he plays, but the same might be said of the others in the most prominent roles, Andy Devine, John Carradine, Thomas Mitchell, George Bancroft, Louise Platt, Donald Meek, Berton Churchill. In all its technical aspects the production maintains the high level of the writing, direction, and acting. Cutting the film presented some nice problems, particularly in a sequence in which a few score mounted Indians attack the stagecoach, and which, incidentally, is an intensely thrilling sequence. Otho Lovering, editorial supervisor, and Dorothy Spencer and Walter Reynolds, editors, deserve praise for their skillful assembling of the film. The excellent results achieved with the sound recorded by Frank Mayer have much to do with the success of the production.

STAGECOACH

Frank S. Nugent

Reprinted from the *New York Times* (March 3, 1939). Reprinted with permission of the *New York Times*.

In one superbly expansive gesture, which we (and the Music Hall) can call *Stagecoach*, John Ford has swept aside ten years of artifice and talkie compromise and has made a motion picture that sings a song of camera. It moves, and how beautifully it moves, across the plains of Arizona, skirting the sky-reaching mesas of Monument Valley, beneath the piled-up cloud banks which every photographer dreams about, and through all the old-fashioned, but never really outdated, periods of prairie travel in the scalp-raising seventies, when Geronimo's Apaches were on the warpath. Here, in a sentence, is a movie of the grand old school, a genuine rib-thumper and a beautiful sight to see.

Mr. Ford is not one of your subtle directors, suspending sequences on the wink of an eye or the precisely calculated gleam of a candle in a mirror. He prefers the broadest canvas, the brightest colors, the widest brush and the boldest possible strokes. He hews to the straight narrative line with the well-reasoned confidence of a man who has seen that narrative succeed before. He takes no shadings from his characters: either they play it straight or they don't play at all. He likes his language simple and he doesn't want too much of it. When his Redskins bite the dust, he expects to hear the thud and see the dirt spurt up. Above all, he likes to have things happen out in the open, where his camera can keep them in view.

He has had his way in *Stagecoach* with Walter Wanger's benison, the writing assistance of Dudley Nichols and the complete cooperation of a cast which had the sense to appreciate the protection of being stereotyped. You should know, almost without being told, the station in life (and in frontier melodrama) of the eight passengers on the Overland stage from Tonto to Lordsburg.

To save time, though, here they are: "Doc" Boone, a tipsy man of medicine; Major Hatfield, professional gambler, once a Southern gentleman and a gentleman still; Dallas, a lady of such transparently dubious virtue that she was leaving Tonto by popular request; Mrs. Mallory, who, considering her condition, had every reason to be hastening to her army husband's side; Mr. Gatewood, an absconding banker and windbag; Mr. Peacock, a small and timid whiskey salesman destined by Bacchus to be Doc Boone's traveling companion; Sheriff Wilcox and his prisoner, the Ringo Kid. The driver, according to the rules, has to be Slim Summerville or Andy Devine; Mr. Devine got the call.

So onward rolls the stage, nobly sped by its six stout-hearted bays, and out there, somewhere behind the buttes and crags, Geronimo is lurking with his savage band, the United States Cavalry is biding its time to charge to the rescue and the Ringo Kid is impatiently awaiting his cue to stalk down the frontier-town street and blast it out with the three Plummer boys. But foreknowledge doesn't cheat Mr. Ford of his thrills. His attitude, if it spoke its mind, would be: "All right, you know what's coming, but have you ever seen it done like this?" And once you've swallowed your heart again, you'll have to say, "No, sir! Not like this!"

His players have taken easily to their chores, all the way down the list from Claire Trevor's Dallas to Tom Tyler's Hank Plummer. But the cutest coach-rider in the wagon, to our mind, was little Donald Meek as Mr. Peacock, the whiskey-drummer. That, of course, is not meant as a slight to Thomas Mitchell as the toping Dr. Boone, to Louise Platt as the wan Mrs. Mallory, George Bancroft as the sheriff or John Wayne as the Ringo Kid. They've all done nobly by a noble horse opera, but none so nobly as its director. This is one stagecoach that's powered by a Ford.

THE VIEW IS NICE

John Mosher

Reprinted from *The New Yorker* (March 4, 1939).

The movies I've seen lately suggest that kind of party you get caught in out in the country, where you have to be thankful there is at least some scenery. It's the landscape that saves your life. For the sake of the view, you forgive all. In *Stagecoach*, the view is certainly something, and it hardly matters at all what goes on. The credit for the valuable things in this film unquestionably belongs to the cameramen, the Messrs. Glennon and Binger, both of whom, I discover, were involved in the making of *The Hurricane*, which had its pictorial moments, you may remember, and to a Mr. Ned Scott, evidently a stranger without any recorded history, who is held responsible for the "still photography." Being an old-fashioned "Western" with a story of Arizona and New Mexico, *Stagecoach* at least provides an opportunity for the camera experts to focus on handsome mountains, deserts, valleys, streams, and beautiful horizons. Toward the end, for a big climax, John Ford has directed an Indian battle – arrows flying straight into the coach and missing heroes and heroines by mere inches – which must have forced the cameramen, except Mr. Scott, I assume, to whisk about with their implements. The narrative follows all the classic rules of "Westerns," including the inevitable expectant mother, always present on these difficult journeys, whose great experience complicates the general scuffle and harasses the valiant. The actors and actresses are mostly familiar persons, like Claire Trevor, and some genuine Apaches, so we are told, have bolted out of the reservation to contribute their little bit toward the progress of art.

Filmography

Note: Only films directed and/or produced by Ford are listed here. Information on the early films in which Ford appears as an actor, the films directed by others in which he was involved, and the few episodes of television shows he directed can be found in the filmographies contained in the books on Ford by Gallagher, Davis, and Bogdanovich (see Select Bibliography), to which the present one is indebted.

THE TORNADO (1917)
Production: Universal
Director: John Ford (as Jack Ford)
Cast: John Ford (Jack Dayton, the No-Gun Man), Jean Hathaway (his Irish mother), John Duffy (Slick, his partner), Peter Gerald (Pendleton), Elsie Thornton (Bess), Duke Worne (Lesparre)

THE TRAIL OF HATE (1917)
Production: Universal
Director: John Ford (as Jack Ford)
Screenwriter: John Ford (as Jack Ford)
Cast: John Ford (Lt. Jack Brewer), Duke Worne (Capt. Dana Holden), Louise Granville (Madge)

THE SCRAPPER (1917)
Production: Universal
Director: John Ford (as Jack Ford)
Screenwriter: John Ford (as Jack Ford)
Cinematographer: Ben Reynolds

Cast: John Ford (Buck Logan), Louise Granville (Helen Dawson), Duke Worne (Jerry Martin), Jane Hathaway (Martha Hayes)

THE SOUL HERDER (1917)
Production: Universal
Director: John Ford (as Jack Ford)
Screenwriter: George Hively
Cinematographer: Ben Reynolds
Cast: Harry Carey (Cheyenne Harry), Jean Hersholt (the parson), Elizabeth Jones (Mary Ann), Fritzi Ridgeway (June Brown), Vester Pegg (Topeka Jack), Hoot Gibson (Chuck Rafferty), Bill Gettinger (Bill Young)

CHEYENNE'S PAL (1917)
Production: Universal
Director: John Ford (as Jack Ford)
Screenplay: Charles J. Wilson, Jr., from a story by Ford
Cinematographer: Friend F. Baker
Cast: Harry Carey (Cheyenne Harry), Jim Corey (Noisy Jim), Gertrude Aster (dance-hall girl), Hoot Gibson

STRAIGHT SHOOTING (1917)
Production: Universal
Director: John Ford (as Jack Ford)
Screenplay: George Hively
Cinematographer: George Scott
Cast: Harry Carey (Cheyenne Harry), Molly Malone (Joan Sims), Duke Lee (Thunder Flint), Vester Pegg (Placer Fremont), Hoot Gibson (Sam Turner), George Berrell (Sweetwater Sims), Ted Brooks (Ted Sims), Milt Brown (Black-Eye Pete)

THE SECRET MAN (1917)
Production: Universal
Director: John Ford (as Jack Ford)
Screenwriter: George Hively
Cinematographer: Ben Reynolds
Cast: Harry Carey (Cheyenne Harry), Morris Foster (Harry Beaufort), Elizabeth Jones (his child), Steve Clemente (Pedro), Vester Pegg (Bill), Elizabeth Sterling (Molly), Hoot Gibson (Chuck Fadden)

A MARKED MAN (1917)
Production: Universal
Director: John Ford (as Jack Ford)
Screenplay: George Hively, from a story by Ford
Cinematographer: John W. Brown
Cast: Harry Carey (Cheyenne Harry), Molly Malone (Molly Young),
    Harry Rattenbury (Young), Vester Pegg (Kent), Mrs. Townsend
    (Harry's mother), Bill Gettinger (sheriff), Hoot Gibson

BUCKING BROADWAY (1917)
Production: Universal
Director: John Ford (as Jack Ford)
Screenplay: George Hively
Cinematographer: John W. Brown
Cast: Harry Carey (Cheyenne Harry), Molly Malone (Helen Clayton),
    L. M. Wells (Ben Clayton), Vester Pegg (Capt. Thornton)

THE PHANTOM RIDERS (1918)
Production: Universal
Director: John Ford (as Jack Ford)
Screenplay: George Hively, from a story by Henry McRae
Cinematographer: John W. Brown
Cast: Harry Carey (Cheyenne Harry), Molly Malone (Molly), Buck
    Connor (Pebble), Bill Gettinger (Dave Bland), Vester Pegg (leader of
    the Phantom Riders), Jim Corey (foreman)

WILD WOMEN (1918)
Production: Universal
Director: John Ford (as Jack Ford)
Screenwriter: George Hively
Cinematographer: John W. Brown
Cast: Harry Carey (Cheyenne Harry), Molly Malone (the princess),
    Martha Maddox (the queen)

THIEVES' GOLD (1918)
Production: Universal
Director: John Ford (as Jack Ford)
Screenwriter: George Hively, from the story "Back to the Right Train"
    by Frederick R. Bechdolt
Cinematographer: John W. Brown

Cast: Harry Carey (Cheyenne Harry), Molly Malone (Alice Norris), L. M. Wells (savage), Vester Pegg (outlaw)

THE SCARLET DROP (1918)
Production: Universal
Director: John Ford (as Jack Ford)
Screenwriter: George Hively, from a story by Ford
Cinematographer: Ben Reynolds
Cast: Harry Carey (Kaintuck Cass), Molly Malone (Molly Calvert), Vester Pegg (Capt. Marley Calvert), M. K. Wilson (Graham Lyons)

HELL BENT (1918)
Production: Universal
Director: John Ford (as Jack Ford)
Screenwriter: John Ford, Harry Carey
Cinematographer: Ben Reynolds
Cast: Harry Carey (Cheyenne Harry), Neva Gerber (Bess Thurston), Duke Lee (Cimarron Bill), Vester Pegg (Jack Thurston), Joseph Harris (Beau)

A WOMAN'S FOOL (1918)
Production: Universal
Director: John Ford (as Jack Ford)
Screenwriter: George Hively, from the novel *Lin McLean* by Owen Wister
Cinematographer: Ben Reynolds
Cast: Harry Carey (Lin McLean), Betty Schade (Katy), Roy Clark (Tommy Lusk), Molly Malone (Jessamine)

THREE MOUNTED MEN (1918)
Production: Universal
Director: John Ford (as Jack Ford)
Screenwriter: Eugene B. Lewis
Cinematographer: John W. Brown
Cast: Harry Carey (Cheyenne Harry), Joe Harris (Buck Masters), Neva Gerber (Lola Masters), Harry Carter (warden's son)

THE CRAVING (1919)
Production: Universal
Directors: Francis Ford and John Ford (as Jack Ford)
Screenwriter: Francis Ford

Cast: Francis Ford (Carroll Wayles), Mae Gaston (Beaulah Grey), Peter Gerald (Ala Kasarib), Duke Worne (Dick Wayles), Jean Hathaway (Mrs. Wayles)

ROPED (1919)
Production: Universal
Director: John Ford (as Jack Ford)
Screenwriter: Eugene B. Lewis
Cinematographer: John W. Brown
Cast: Harry Carey (Cheyenne Harry), Neva Gerber (Aileen Judson Brown), Molly McConnell (Mrs. Judson Brown), J. Farrell MacDonald (butler), Arthur Shirley (Ferdie Van Duzen)

THE FIGHTING BROTHERS (1919)
Production: Universal
Director: John Ford (as Jack Ford)
Screenwriter: George Hively, from a story by George C. Hull
Cinematographer: John W. Brown
Cast: Pete Morrison (Sheriff Pete Larkin), Hoot Gibson (Lonnie Larkin), Yvette Mitchell (Conchita), Jack Woods (Ben Crawley), Duke Lee (Slim)

A FIGHT FOR LOVE (1919)
Production: Universal
Director: John Ford (as Jack Ford)
Screenwriter: Eugene B. Lewis
Cinematographer: John W. Brown
Cast: Harry Carey (Cheyenne Harry), Joe Harris (Black Michael), Neva Gerber (Kate McDougall), Mark Fenton (Angus McDougall), J. Farrell MacDonald (priest), Princess Neola Mae (Little Fawn), Chief Big Tree (Swift Deer)

BY INDIAN POST (1919)
Production: Universal
Director: John Ford (as Jack Ford)
Screenwriter: H. Tipton Steck, from the story "The Trail of the Billy-Doo" by William Wallace Cook
Cast: Pete Morrison (Jode McWilliams), Duke Lee (Pa Owens), Magda Lane (Peg Owens), Ed Jones (Stumpy), Jack Woods (Dutch), Harley Chambers (Fritz), Hoot Gibson (Chub), Jack Walters (Andy), Otto Myers (Swede), Jim Moore (Two-Horns)

THE RUSTLERS (1919)
Production: Universal
Director: John Ford (as Jack Ford)
Screenwriter: George Hively
Cinematographer: John W. Brown
Cast: Pete Morrison (Ben Clayburn), Helen Gibson (Nell Wyndham),
   Jack Woods (Sheriff Buck Farley), Hoot Gibson (deputy)

BARE FISTS (1919)
Production: Universal
Director: John Ford (as Jack Ford)
Screenwriter: Eugene B. Lewis, from a story by Bernard McConville
Cinematographer: John W. Brown
Cast: Harry Carey (Cheyenne Harry), Molly McConnell (his mother),
   Joseph Girard (his father), Howard Ensteadt (Bud), Betty Schade
   (Conchita), Vester Pegg (Lopez), Joe Harris (Boone Travis), Anna Mae
   Walthall (Ruby)

GUN LAW (1919)
Production: Universal
Director: John Ford (as Jack Ford)
Screenwriter: H. Tipton Steck
Cinematographer: John W. Brown
Cast: Peter Morrison (Dick Allen), Hoot Gibson (Bart Stevens, alias
   Smoke Gublen), Helen Gibson (Letty), Jack Woods (Cayuse Yates),
   Otto Myers, Ed Jones, H. Chambers (Yates's gang)

THE GUN PACKER (1919)
Production: Universal
Director: John Ford (as Jack Ford)
Screenwriter: Karl R. Coolidge, from a story by John Ford and Harry
   Carey
Cinematographer: John W. Brown
Cast: Ed Jones (Sandy McLoughlin), Pete Morrison ("Pearl Handle"
   Wiley), Magda Lane (Rose McLoughlin), Jack Woods (Pecos Smith),
   Hoot Gibson (outlaw leader), Jack Walters (Brown), Duke Lee (Buck
   Landers), Howard Enstaedt (Bobby McLoughlin)

RIDERS OF VENGEANCE (1919)
Production: Universal
Producer: P. A. Powers

Director: John Ford (as Jack Ford)
Screenwriters: John Ford and Harry Carey
Cinematographer: John W. Brown
Cast: Harry Carey (Cheyenne Harry), Seena Owen (the girl), Joe Harris
    (Sheriff Gale Thurman), J. Farrell MacDonald (Buell), Jennie Lee
    (Harry's mother), Glita Lee (Virginia)

THE LAST OUTLAW (1919)
Production: Universal
Director: John Ford (as Jack Ford)
Screenwriter: H. Tipton Steck, from a story by Evelyne Murray
    Campbell
Cinematographer: John W. Brown
Cast: Ed "King Fisher" Jones (Bud Coburn), Richard Cumming (Sheriff
    Brownlo), Lucille Hutton (Idaleen Coburn), Jack Walters
    (Chad Allen)

THE OUTCASTS OF POKER FLAT (1919)
Production: Universal
Producer: P. A. Powers
Director: John Ford (as Jack Ford)
Screenwriter: H. Tipton Steck, from the stories "The Outcasts of Poker
    Flat" and "The Luck of Roaring Camp" by Bret Harte
Cinematographer: John W. Brown
Cast: Harry Carey (Square Shootin' Lanyon; John Oakhurst), Cullen
    Landis (Billy Lanyon; Tommy Oakhurst), Gloria Hope (Ruth Watson;
    Sophy)

THE AGE OF THE SADDLE (1919)
Production: Universal
Producer: P. A. Powers
Director: John Ford (as Jack Ford)
Screenwriter: George Hively, from a story by B. J. Jackson
Cinematographer: John W. Brown
Cast: Harry Carey (Cheyenne Harry Henderson), Joe Harris
    (Sheriff "Two Gun" Hildebrand), Duke R. Lee (Sheriff
    Faulkner), Peggy Pearce (Madeline Faulkner), Jack Walters
    (Inky O'Day), Vester Pegg (gambler), Zoe Ray and Howard
    Ensteadt (the children), Ed "King Fisher" Jones (Home Sweet
    Holmes), William Cartwright (Humpy Anderson), Andy
    Devine

THE RIDER OF THE LANE (1919)
Production: Universal
Producer: P. A. Powers
Director: John Ford (as Jack Ford)
Screenwriter: H. Tipton Steck, from the story "Jim of the Rangers" by
   G. P. Lancaster
Cinematographer: John W. Brown
Cast: Harry Carey (Jim Kyneton), Gloria Hope (Betty), Vester Pegg (Nick
   Kyneton), Theodore Brooks (the kid), Joe Harris (Buck Souter), Jack
   Woods (Jack West), Duke R. Lee (Capt. Graham Saltire), Claire
   Anderson (Roseen), Jennie Lee (mother)

A GUN FIGHTIN' GENTLEMAN (1919)
Production: Universal
Producer: P. A. Powers
Director: John Ford (as Jack Ford)
Screenwriter: Hal Hoadley, from a story by John Ford and Harry Carey
Cinematographer: John W. Brown
Cast: Harry Carey (Cheyenne Harry), Barney Sherry (John Merritt),
   Kathleen O'Conner (Helen Merritt), Lydia Yeamans Titus (her aunt),
   Harry von Meter (Earl of Jollywell), Duke R. Lee (Buck Regan), Joe
   Harris (Seymour), Johnny Cooke (the old sheriff), Ted Brooks (the
   youngster)

MARKED MEN (1919)
Production: Universal
Producer: P. A. Powers
Director: John Ford (as Jack Ford)
Screenwriter: H. Tipton Steck, from the story "The Three Godfathers"
   by Peter B. Kyne
Cinematographer: John W. Brown
Editors: Frank Lawrence, Frank Atkinson
Cast: Harry Carey (Cheyenne Harry), J. Farrell MacDonald (Tom
   "Placer" McGraw), Joe Harris (Tom Gibbons), Winifred Westover
   (Ruby Merrill), Ted Brooks (Tony Garcia), Charles Lemoyne (Sheriff
   Pete Cushing), David Kirby (Warden "Bruiser" Kelly)

THE PRINCE OF AVENUE A (1920)
Production: Universal
Director: John Ford (as Jack Ford)

Screenwriter: Charles J. Wilson Jr., from a story by Charles and Frank
   Dazey
Cinematographer: John W. Brown
Cast: James J. "Gentleman Jim" Corbett (Barry O'Conner), Mary
   Warren (Mary Tompkins), Harry Northrup (Edgard Jones),
   Cora Drew (Mary O'Conner), Richard Cummings (Patrick
   O'Conner), Frederick Vroom (William Tompkins), Mark Fenton
   (Father O'Toole)

THE GIRL IN NO. 29 (1920)
Production: Universal
Director: John Ford (as Jack Ford)
Screenwriter: Philip J. Hurn, from the story "The Girl in the Mirror" by
   Elizabeth Jordan
Cinematographer: John W. Brown
Cast: Frank Mayo (Laurie Devon), Harry Hilliard (Rodney Bangs), Claire
   Anderson (Doris Williams), Elinor Fair (Barbara Devon), Bull
   Montana (Abdullah, the strangler), Ray Ripley (Ransome Shaw),
   Robert Bolder (Jacob Epstein)

HITCHIN' POSTS (1920)
Production: Universal
Director: John Ford (as Jack Ford)
Screenwriter: George C. Hull, from a story by Harold M. Schumate
Cinematographer: Benjamin Kline
Cast: Frank Mayo (Jefferson Todd), Beatrice Burnham (Ophelia
   Bereton), Joe Harris (Raoul Castiga), J. Farrell MacDonald (Joe
   Alabam), Mark Fenton (Col. Carl Bereton), Dagmar Godowsky
   (octoroon), Duke R. Lee (Col. Lancy), C. E. Anderson (steamboat
   captain), M. Biddulph (Maj. Gray)

JUST PALS (1920)
Production: William Fox
Director: John Ford (as Jack Ford)
Screenwriter: Paul Schofield, from a story by John McDermott
Cinematographer: George Schneiderman
Cast: Buck Jones (Bim), Helen Ferguson (Mary Bruce), George E. Stone
   (Bill), Duke R. Lee (sheriff), William Buckley (Harvey Cahill), Edwin
   Booth Tilton (Dr. Stone), Eunice Murdock Moore (Mrs. Stone)

THE BIG PUNCH (1921)
Production: William Fox
Director: John Ford (as Jack Ford)
Screenwriters: John Ford and Jules Furthman, from the story "Fighting Back" by Furthman
Cinematographer: Frank Good
Cast: Buck Jones (Buck), Barbara Bedford (Hope Standish), George Siegmann (Flash McGraw), Jack Curtis (Jed), Jennie Lee (Buck's mother), Jack McDonald and Al Fremont (Jed's friends)

THE FREEZE OUT (1921)
Production: Universal
Director: John Ford (as Jack Ford)
Screenwriter: George C. Hull
Cinematographer: Harry C. Fowler
Cast: Harry Carey (Ohio, the stranger), Helen Ferguson (Zoe Whipple), Charles Lemoyne (Denver Red), J. Farrell MacDonald (Bobtail McGuire), Lydia Yeamans Titus (Mrs. McGuire)

THE WALLOP (1921)
Production: Universal
Director: John Ford (as Jack Ford)
Screenwriter: George C. Hull, from the story "The Girl He Left Behind Him" by Eugene Manlove Rhodes
Cinematographer: Harry C. Fowler
Cast: Harry Carey (John Wesley Pringle), Joe Harris (Barela), Charles Lemoyne (Matt Lisner), J. Farrell MacDonald (Neuces River), Mignonne Golden (Stella Vorhis), Bill Gettinger (Christopher Foy), Noble Johnson (Espinol), C. E. Anderson (Applegate), Mark Fenton (Maj. Vorhis)

DESPERATE TRAILS (1921)
Production: Universal
Director: John Ford (as Jack Ford)
Screenwriter: Elliott J. Clawson, from the story "Christmas Eve at Pilot Butte" by Courtney Riley Cooper
Cinematographers: Harry C. Fowler, Robert DeGrasse
Cast: Harry Carey (Bert Carson), Irene Rich (Mrs. Walker), George E. Stone (Danny Boy), Helen Field (Carrie), Barbara La Marr (Lady Lou), George Siegmann (Sheriff Price), Charles Insley (Dr. Higgins), Ed Coxen (Walter A. Walker)

ACTION (1921)
Production: Universal
Director: John Ford (as Jack Ford)
Screenwriter: Harvey Gates, from the story "The Mascotte of the Three
    Star" by J. Allen Dunn
Cinematographer: John W. Brown
Cast: Hoot Gibson (Sandy Brooke), Francis Ford (Soda Water Manning),
    J. Farrell MacDonald (Mormon Peters), Buck Conners (Pat Casey),
    Byron Munson (Henry Meekin), Ed "King Fisher" Jones (Art Smith)

SURE FIRE (1921)
Production: Universal
Director: John Ford (as Jack Ford)
Screenwriter: George C. Hull, from the story "Bransford of Rainbow
    Ridge" by Eugene Manlove Rhodes
Cinematographer: Virgil G. Miller
Cast: Hoot Gibson (Jeff Bransford), Molly Malone (Marian Hoffman),
    Reeves "Breezy" Eason Jr. (Sonny), Harry Carter (Rufus Coulter),
    Murdock MacQuarrie (Major Parker), Fritzi Brunette (Elinor Parker),
    George Fisher (Burt Rawlings), Charles Newton (Leo Ballinger), Jack
    Woods (Brazos Bart), Jack Walters (Overland Kid), Joe Harris
    (Romero), Steve Clemente (Gomez)

JACKIE (1921)
Production: William Fox
Director: John Ford (as Jack Ford)
Screenwriter: Dorothy Yost, from a story by Countess Helena Barcynska
    (Marguerite Florence Helene Jervis Evans)
Cinematographer: George Schneiderman
Cast: Shirley Mason (Jackie), William Scott (Mervyn Carter), Harry
    Carter (Bill Bowman), George E. Stone (Benny), John Cooke (Winter),
    Elsie Bambrick (Millie)

LITTLE MISS SMILES (1922)
Production: William Fox
Director: John Ford (as Jack Ford)
Screenwriter: Dorothy Yost, from the story "Little Aliens" by Myra Kelly
Cinematographer: David Abel
Cast: Shirley Mason (Esther Aaronson), Gaston Glass (Dr. Jack
    Washton), George Williams (Papa Aaronson), Martha Franklin
    (Mama Aaronson), Arthur Rankin (Dave Aaronson)

SILVER WINGS (1922)
Production: William Fox
Directors: John Ford (Prologue, as Jack Ford), Edwin Carewe
Screenwriter: Paul H. Sloane
Cinematographers: Joseph Ruttenberg, Robert Kurle
Cast: Mary Carr (Anna Webb), Lynn Hammond (John Webb), Knox
    Kincaid (John), Joseph Monahan (Harry), Maybeth Carr (Ruth),
    Claude Brook (Uncle Andrews), Robert Hazleton (priest), Florence
    Short (widow)

THE VILLAGE BLACKSMITH (1922)
Production: William Fox
Director: John Ford (as Jack Ford)
Screenwriter: Paul H. Sloane, from a poem by Henry Wadsworth
    Longfellow
Cinematographer: George Schneiderman
Cast: William Walling (John Hammond), Virginia True Boardman (his
    wife), Virginia Valli (Alice Hammond), David Butler (Bill Hammond),
    Tully Marshall (Squire Ezra Brigham), Francis Ford (Asa Martin),
    Bessie Love (Rosemary Martin), Mark Fenton (Dr. Brewster)

THE FACE ON THE BARROOM FLOOR (1923)
Production: William Fox
Director: John Ford (as Jack Ford)
Screenwriters: Eugene B. Lewis and G. Marion Burton, from the poem
    by Hugh Antoine D'Arcy
Cinematographer: George Schneiderman
Cast: Henry B. Walthall (Robert Stevens), Ruth Clifford (Marion Von
    Vleck), Alma Bennett (Lottie), Norval McGregor (governor), Michael
    Dark (Henry Drew), Gus Saville (fisherman)

THREE JUMPS AHEAD (1923)
Production: William Fox
Director: John Ford (as Jack Ford)
Screenwriter: John Ford (as Jack Ford)
Cinematographer: Daniel B. Clark
Cast: Tom Mix (Steve Clancy), Alma Bennett (Annie Darrell), Virginia
    True Boardman (Mrs. Darrell), Edward Piel (Taggit), Joe E. Girard
    (Annie's father), Francis Ford (Virgil Clancy), Margaret Joslin (Juliet),
    Henry Todd (Cicero), Buster Gardner (Brutus)

CAMEO KIRBY (1923)
Production: William Fox
Director: John Ford
Screenwriter: Robert N. Lee, from the play by Harry Leon Wilson and
    Booth Tarkington
Cinematographer: George Schneiderman
Cast: John Gilbert (Cameo Kirby), Gertrude Olmstead (Adele Randall),
    Alan Hale (Col. Moreau), William E. Lawrence (Col. Randall), Jean
    Arthur (Ann Playdell), Richard Tucker (Cousin Aaron)

NORTH OF HUDSON BAY (1923)
Production: William Fox
Director: John Ford
Screenwriter: Jules Furthman
Cinematographer: Daniel B. Clark
Cast: Tom Mix (Michael Dane), Kathleen Kay (Estelle MacDonald),
    Jennie Lee (Dane's mother), Frank Cameau (Cameron MacDonald),
    Eugene Pallette (Peter Dane), Will Walling (Angus MacKenzie), Frank
    Leigh (Jeffrey Clough), Fred Kohler (Armand LeMoir)

HOODMAN BLIND (1923)
Production: William Fox
Director: John Ford
Screenwriter: Charles Kenyon, from the play by Henry Arthur Jones and
    Wilson Barrett
Cinematographer: George Schneiderman
Cast: David Butler (Jack Yeulette), Gladys Hulette (Yeulette; Jessie
    Walton), Regina Connelly (Jessie Walton, the first), Frank Campeau
    (Mark Lezzard), Marc MacDermott (John Linden), Trilby Clark
    (Mrs. Linden), Eddie Gribbon (Battling Brown), Jack Walters
    (Bull Yeaman)

THE IRON HORSE (1924)
Production: William Fox
Director: John Ford
Screenwriters: Charles Kenyon, from a story by Kenyon and John
    Russell
Cinematographers: George Schneiderman, Burnett Guffey
Music: Erno Rapee
Cast: George O'Brien (Davy Brandon), Madge Bellamy (Miriam Marsh),
    Charles Edward Bull (Abraham Lincoln), William Walling (Thomas

Marsh), Fred Kohler (Deroux), Cyril Chadwick (Peter Jesson), Gladys Hulette (Ruby), James Marcus (Judge Haller), Francis Powers (Sgt. Slattery), J. Farrell MacDonald (Cpl. Casey), James Welch (Pvt. Schultz), Colin Chase (Tony), Walter Rogers (Gen. Dodge), Jack O'Brien (Dinny), George Waggner (Buffalo Bill Cody), John Padjan (Wild Bill Hickok), Charles O'Malley (Maj. North), Delbert Mann (Charles Crocker), Chief Big Tree (Cheyenne chief), Chief White Spear (Sioux chief), Stanhope Wheatcroft (John Hay)

HEARTS OF OAK (1924)
Production: William Fox
Director: John Ford
Screenwriter: Charles Kenyon, from the play by James A. Herne
Cinematographer: George Schneiderman
Cast: Hobert Bosworth (Terry Dunnivan), Pauline Starke (Chrystal), Theodore von Eltz (Ned Fairweather), James Gordon (John Owen), Francis Powers (Grandpa Dunnivan), Jennie Lee (Grandma Dunnivan), Francis Ford

LIGHTNIN' (1925)
Production: William Fox
Director: John Ford
Screenwriter: Frances Marion, from the play by Winchell Smith and Frank Bacon
Cinematographer: Joseph A. August
Cast: Jay Hunt (Lightnin' Bill Jones), Madge Bellamy (Millie), Edythe Chapman (Mother Jones), Wallace McDonald (John Marvin), J. Farrell MacDonald (Judge Lemuel Townsend), Ethel Clayton (Margaret Davis), Richard Travers (Raymond Thomas), James Marcus (Sheriff Blodgett)

KENTUCKY PRIDE (1925)
Production: William Fox
Director: John Ford
Screenwriter: Dorothy Yost
Cinematographers: George Schneiderman, Edmund Reek
Cast: Henry B. Walthall (Roger Beaumont), J. Farrell MacDonald (Mike Donovan), Gertrude Astor (Mrs. Beaumont), Malcolm Waite (Greve Carter), Belle Stoddard (Mrs. Donovan), Winston Miller (Danny Donovan)

THE FIGHTING HEART (1925)
Production: William Fox
Director: John Ford
Screenwriter: Lillie Hayward, from "Once to Every Man" by Larry Evans
Cinematographer: Joseph H. August
Cast: George O'Brien (Danny Bolton), Billie Dove (Doris Anderson),
    J. Farrell MacDonald (Jerry), Diana Miller (Helen Van Allen), Victor
    McLaglen (Soapy Williams), Bert Woodruff (Grandfather Bolton),
    James Marcus (Judge Maynard), Lynn Cowan (Chub Morehouse),
    Harvey Clark (Dennison), Francis Ford (town fool), Francis Powers
    (John Anderson)

THANK YOU (1925)
Production: William Fox
Director: John Ford
Screenwriter: Frances Marion, from the play by Winchell Smith and
    Tom Cushing
Cinematographer: George Schneiderman
Cast: George O'Brien (Kenneth Jamieson), Jacqueline Logan (Diana
    Lee), Alec Francis (David Lee), J. Farrell MacDonald (Andy), Cyril
    Chadwick (Mr. Jones), Edith Bostwick (Mrs. Jones), Vivian Ogden
    (Miss Glodgett), James Neill (Dr. Cobb), George Fawcett
    (Jamieson Sr.)

THE SHAMROCK HANDICAP (1926)
Production: William Fox
Director: John Ford
Screenwriter: John Stone, from a story by Peter B. Kyne
Cinematographer: George Schneiderman
Cast: Leslie Fenton (Neil Ross), J. Farrell MacDonald (Con O'Shea),
    Janet Gaynor (Sheila O'Hara), Claire McDowell (Molly O'Shea),
    Willard Louis (Orville Finch), Andy Clark (Chesty Morgan), George
    Harris (Benny Ginsburg)

3 BAD MEN (1926)
Production: William Fox
Director: John Ford
Screenwriters: John Ford and John Stone, from the novel *Over the Border*
    by Herman Whitaker
Cinematographer: George Schneiderman
Cast: George O'Brien (Dan O'Malley), Olive Borden (Lee Carlton),

J. Farrell MacDonald (Mike Costigan), Tom Santschi (Bull Stanley), Frank Campeau (Spade Allen), Louis Tellegen (Sheriff Layne Hunter), George Harris (Joe Minsk), Jay Hunt (old prospector), Priscilla Bonner (Millie Stanley), Otis Harlan (Zack Lesley), Walter Perry (Pat Monahan)

THE BLUE EAGLE (1926)
Production: William Fox
Director: John Ford
Screenwriter: L. G. Rigby, from the story "The Lord's Referee" by Gerald Beaumont
Cinematographer: George Schneiderman
Cast: George O'Brien (George Darcy), Janet Gaynor (Rose Cooper), William Russell (Big Tim Ryan), Robert Edeson (Father Joe), David Butler (Nick Galvani), Phillip Ford (Limpy Darcy), Ralph Sipperly (Slats Mulligan), Margaret Livingston (Mary Rohan), Jerry Madden (Baby Tom), Harry Tenbrook (Bascom), Lew Short (Capt. McCarthy)

UPSTREAM (1927)
Production: William Fox
Director: John Ford
Screenwriter: Randall H. Faye, from the story "The Snake's Wife" by Wallace Smith
Cinematographer: Charles G. Clarke
Cast: Nancy Nash (Gertie King), Earle Foxe (Eric Brasingham), Grant Withers (Jack LeVelle), Raymond Hitchcock (star boarder), Lydia Yeamans Titus (Miss Breckenridge), Emile Chautard (Campbell Mandare), Ted McNamara and Sammy Cohen (dance team), Francis Ford (juggler)

MOTHER MACHREE (1928)
Production: William Fox
Director: John Ford
Screenwriter: Gertrude Orr, from lyrics and song by Rida Johnson Young
Cinematographer: Chester Lyons
Editors: Katherine Hilliker, H. H. Caldwell
Cast: Belle Bennett (Ellen McHugh), Neil Hamilton (Brian McHugh), Philippe Lacy (Brian, as child), Pat Someset (Bobby De Puyser), Victor McLaglen (Terence O'Dowd), Ted McNamara (Harper of

Wexford), William Platt (Pips), John MacSweeney (priest), Jacques
Rollens (Signor Bellini), Rodney Hildebrand (Brian McHugh Sr.)

FOUR SONS (1928)
Production: William Fox
Director: John Ford
Screenwriter: Philip Klein, from the story "Grandma Bernle Learns Her
    Letters" by I. A. R. Wylie
Cinematographers: George Schneiderman, Charles G. Clarke
Editor: Margaret V. Clancey
Music: Carli Elinor
Cast: Margaret Mann (Frau Bernle), James Hall (Joseph Bernle),
    Charles Morton (Johann Bernle), George Meeker (Andres Bernle),
    Francis X. Bushman Jr. (Franz Bernle), June Collyer (Annabelle
    Bernle), Albert Gran (postman), Earle Foxe (Major Von Stomm),
    Frank Reicher (headmaster), Jack Pennick (Joseph's American friend),
    Archduke Leopold of Austria (German captain)

HANGMAN'S HOUSE (1928)
Production: William Fox
Director: John Ford
Screenwriters: Marion Orth and Willard Mack, from the novel by Brian
    Oswald Donn-Byrne
Cinematographer: George Schneiderman
Editor: Margaret V. Clancey
Cast: Victor McLaglen (Citizen Hogan), Hobart Bosworth (James
    O'Brien, Lord Chief Justice), June Collyer (Connaught O'Brien), Larry
    Kent (Dermott McDermott), Earle Foxe (John D'Arcy), Eric Mayne
    (legionnaire colonel), Joseph Burke (Neddy Joe), Belle Stoddard (Anne
    McDermott), John Wayne

NAPOLEON'S BARBER (1928)
Production: William Fox
Director: John Ford
Screenwriter: Arthur Caesar, from his own play
Cinematographer: George Schneiderman
Cast: Otto Matiesen (Napoleon), Frank Reicher (the barber), Natalie
    Golitzin (Josephine), Helen Ware (barber's wife), Philippe De Lacy
    (barber's son), Russell Powell (blacksmith)

RILEY THE COP (1928)
Production: William Fox
Director: John Ford
Screenwriters: James Gruen, Fred Stanley
Cinematographer: Charles G. Clarke
Editor: Alex Troffey
Cast: J. Farrell MacDonald (Aloysius Riley), Louise Fazenda (Lena Krausmeyer), Nancy Drexel (Mary), David Rollins (Davy Collins), Harry Schultz (Hans Krausmeyer), Billy Bevan (Paris cab driver), Mildred Boyd (Caroline)

STRONG BOY (1929)
Production: William Fox
Director: John Ford
Screenwriters: James Kevin McGuinness, Andrew Bennison, and John McLain, from the story by Frederick Hazlett Brennan
Cinematographer: Joseph H. August
Cast: Victor McLaglen (William "Strong Boy" Bloss), Leatrice Joy (Mary McGregor), Clyde Cook (Pete), Slim Summerville (Slim), Kent Sanderson (Wilbur Watkins), Tom Wilson (baggage master), Jack Pennick (baggage man), Eulalie Jensen (the queen), David Torrence (railroad president), J. Farrell MacDonald (Angus McGregor), Dolores Johnson (usherette), Douglas Scott (Wobby), Robert Ryan (porter)

THE BLACK WATCH (1929)
Production: William Fox
Director: John Ford
Screenwriters: James Kevin McGuinness, John Stone, and Frank Barber, from the novel *King of the Khyber Rifles* by Talbot Mundy
Cinematographer: Joseph H. August
Editor: Alex Troffey
Art Director: William Darling
Cast: Victor McLaglen (Capt. Donald King), Myrna Loy (Yasmani), Roy D'Arcy (Rewa Ghunga), Pat Somerset (Highlanders' officer), David Rollins (Lt. Malcolm King), Mitchell Lewis (Mohammed Khan), Walter Long (Harem Bey), Frank Baker and David Percy (Highlanders' officers), Lumsden Hare (colonel), Cyril Chadwick (Major Twynes), David Torrence (Marechal), Francis Ford (Major MacGregor)

SALUTE (1929)
Production: William Fox
Director: John Ford
Screenwriter: James Kevin McGuinness, from the story by Tristram
  Tupper and John Stone
Cinematographer: Joseph H. August
Editor: Alex Troffey
Cast: William Janney (Midshipman Paul Randall), Helen Chandler
  (Nancy Wayne), Stepin Fetchit (Smoke Screen), Frank Albertson
  (Midshipman Albert Edward Price), George O'Brien (Cadet John
  Randall), Joyce Compton (Marion Wilson), Cliff Dempsey (Major
  Gen. Somers), Lumsden Hare (Rear Adm. Randall), David Butler
  (navy coach), Rex Bell (cadet), John Breeden, Ward Bond, John
  Wayne (midshipmen)

MEN WITHOUT WOMEN (1930)
Production: William Fox
Director: John Ford
Screenplay: Dudley Nichols, from the story "Submarine" by John Ford
  and James Kevin McGuinness
Cinematographer: Joseph H. August
Editor: Paul Weatherwax
Art Director: William S. Darling
Music: Peter Brunelli, Glen Knight
Cast: Kenneth MacKenna (Burke), Frank Albertson (Price), Paul Page
  (Handsome), Pat Somerset (Lt. Digby, R.N.), Walter McGrail (Cobb),
  Stuart Erwin (Jenkins), Warren Hymer (Kaufman), J. Farrell
  MacDonald (Costello), Roy Stewart (Capt. Carson), Warner
  Richmond (Lt. Commander Bridewell), Harry Tenbrook (Winkler),
  Ben Hendricks Jr. (Murphy), George LeGuere (Pollosk), Charles
  Gerrard (Weymouth), John Wayne, Robert Parrish, Frank Baker

BORN RECKLESS (1930)
Production: William Fox
Director: John Ford
Screenwriter: Dudley Nichols, from the novel *Louis Beretti* by Donald
  Henderson Clarke
Cinematographer: George Schneiderman
Editor: Frank E. Hull
Art Director: Jack Schulze

Cast: Edmond Lowe (Louis Beretti), Catherine Dale Owen (Joan Sheldon), Lee Tracy (Bill O'Brien), Margaret Churchill (Rosa Beretti), Warren Hymer (Big Shot), Pat Somerset (Duke), William Harrigan (Good News Brophy), Frank Albertson (Frank Sheldon), Ferike Boros (Ma Beretti), J. Farrell MacDonald (district attorney), Paul Porcasi (Pa Beretti), Eddie Gribbon (Bugs), Mike Donlin (Fingy Moscovitz), Ben Bard (Joe Bergman), Paul Page (Ritzy Reilly), Joe Brown (Needle Beer Grogan), Jack Pennick and Ward Bond (soldiers), Roy Stewart (district attorney Cardigan)

UP THE RIVER (1930)
Production: William Fox
Director: John Ford
Screenwriter: Maurine Watkins with John Ford and William Collier
Cinematographer: Joseph H. August
Editor: Frank E. Hull
Set Designer: Duncan Cramer
Music: Joseph McCarthy, James F. Hanley
Cast: Spencer Tracy (St. Louis), Warren Hymer (Dannemora Dan), Humphrey Bogart (Steve), Claire Luce (Judy), Joan Lawes (Jean), Sharon Lynn (Edith LaVerne), George McFarlane (Jessup), Gaylord Pendleton (Morris), Morgan Wallace (Frosby), William Collier Sr. (Pop), Robert E. O'Connor (warden), Louise MacIntosh (Mrs. Massey), Edythe Chapman (Mrs. Jordan), Johnny Walker (Happy), Noel Francis (Sophie), Pat Somerset (Beauchamp), Robert Parrish

SEAS BENEATH (1931)
Production: William Fox
Director: John Ford
Screenwriter: Dudley Nichols, from the story by James Parker Jr.
Cinematographer: Joseph H. August
Editor: Frank E. Hull
Cast: George O'Brien (Commander Bob Kinglsey), Marion Lessing (Anna Marie Von Steuben), Warren Hymer (Lug Kaufman), William Collier Sr. (Mugs O'Flaherty), John Loder (Franz Schilling), Walter C. "Judge" Kelly (Chief Mike "Guns" Costello), Walter McGrail (Joe Cobb), Henry Victor (Ernst Von Steuben), Larry Kent (Lt. MacGregor), Gaylord Pendleton (Ens. Richard Cabot), Mona Maris (Lolita), Nat Pendleton (Butch Wagner), Harry Tenbrook (Winkler), Francis Ford (trawler captain), Frank Baker

THE BRAT (1931)
Production: Fox Film
Director: John Ford
Screenwriters: Sonya Levien, S. N. Behrman, and Maud Fulton, from
the play by Fulton
Cinematographer: Joseph H. August
Editor: Alex Troffey
Cast: Sally O'Neil (the brat), Alan Dinehart (MacMillan Forester), Frank
Albertson (Stephen Forester), Virginia Cherrill (Angela), June Collyer
(Jane), J. Farrell MacDonald (Timson), William Collier Sr. (judge),
Ward Bond (policeman)

ARROWSMITH (1931)
Production: Samuel Goldwyn/United Artists
Producer: Samuel Goldwyn
Director: John Ford
Screenwriter: Sidney Howard, from the novel by Sinclair Lewis
Cinematographer: Ray June
Editor: Hugh Bennett
Art Director: Richard Day
Music: Alfred Newman
Cast: Ronald Colman (Dr. Martin Arrowsmith), Helen Hayes (Leora),
A. E. Anson (Prof. Gottlieb), Richard Bennett (Sondelius), Claude
King (Dr. Tubbs), Beulah Bondi (Mrs. Tozer), Myrna Loy (Joyce
Lanyon), Russell Hopton (Terry Wicket), DeWitt Jennings (Mr. Tozer),
John Qualen (Henry Novak), Adele Watson (Mrs. Novak), Lumsden
Hare (Sir Robert Fairland), Ward Bond (policeman), Frank Baker (ship
captain)

AIR MAIL (1932)
Production: Universal
Producer: Carl Laemmle Jr.
Director: John Ford
Screenwriters: Dale Van Every and Lt. Commander Frank W. Wead,
from the story by Wead
Cinematographer: Karl Freund
Cast: Pat O'Brien (Duke Talbot), Ralph Bellamy (Mike Miller),
Gloria Stuart (Ruth Barnes), Lillian Bond (Irene Wilkins), Russell
Hopton ("Dizzy" Wilkins), Slim Summerville (Slim McCune),
Frank Albertson (Tommy Bogan), Leslie Fenton (Tony Dressel),
David Landau (Pop), Tom Corrigan (Sleepy Collins), William Daly

(Tex Lane), Francis Ford (passenger), Jim Thorpe (Indian), Jack
Pennick

FLESH (1932)
Production: Metro-Goldwyn-Mayer
Director: John Ford
Screenwriters: Leonard Praskins, Edgar Allen Woolf, and (uncredited)
   William Faulkner, from the story by Edmund Goulding, with
   dialogue by Moss Hart
Cinematographer: Arthur Edeson
Editor: William S. Gray
Cast: Wallace Beery (Polokai), Karen Morley (Lora Nash), Ricardo Cortez
   (Nicky), Jean Hersholt (Mr. Herman), John Miljan (Joe Willard),
   Vince Barnett (waiter), Herman Bing (Pepi), Greta Meyer (Mrs.
   Herman), Ed Brophy (Dolan), Ward Bond (wrestler), Nat Pendleton

PILGRIMAGE (1933)
Production: Fox Film
Director: John Ford
Screenwriters: Philip Klein and Barry Connors, from the story "Gold
   Star Mother" by I. A. R. Wylie, with dialogue by Dudley Nichols
Cinematographer: George Schneiderman
Editor: Louis R. Loeffler
Art Director: William Darling
Music: R. H. Bassett
Cast: Henrietta Crosman (Hannah Jessop), Heather Angel (Suzanne),
   Norman Foster (Jim Jessop), Marian Nixon (Mary Saunders), Maurice
   Murphy (Gary Worth), Lucille LaVerne (Mrs. Tally Hatfield), Charles
   Grapewin (Dad Saunders), Hedda Hopper (Mrs. Worth), Robert
   Warwick (Major Albertson), Betty Blythe (Janet Prescot), Francis Ford
   (Mayor Elmer Briggs), Louise Carter (Mrs. Rogers), Jay Ward (Jim
   Saunders), Francis Rich (nurse), Adele Watson (Mrs. Simms), Jack
   Pennick (sergeant)

DOCTOR BULL (1933)
Production: Fox Film
Director: John Ford
Screenwriter: Paul Green, from the novel *The Last Adam* by James
   Gould Cozzens
Cinematographer: George Schneiderman
Music: Samuel Kaylin

Cast: Will Rogers (Dr. Bull), Marian Nixon (May Tripping), Berton
    Churchill (Herbert Banning), Louise Dresser (Mrs. Banning), Howard
    Lally (Joe Tripping), Rochelle Hudson (Virginia Banning), Vera Allen
    (Janet Cardmaker), Tempe Pigotte (Grandma), Elizabeth Patterson
    (Aunt Patricia), Ralph Morgan (Dr. Verney), Andy Devine (Larry
    Ward), Nora Cecil (Aunt Emily), Francis Ford (mayor)

THE LOST PATROL (1934)
Production: RKO
Executive Producer: Merian C. Cooper
Director: John Ford
Screenwriters: Dudley Nichols and Garrett Fort, from the story "Patrol"
    by Philip MacDonald
Cinematographer: Harold Wenstrom
Editor: Paul Weatherwax
Art Directors: Van Nest Polglase, Sidney Ullman
Music: Max Steiner
Cast: Victor McLaglen (sergeant), Boris Karloff (Sanders), Wallace Ford
    (Morelli), Reginald Denny (George Brown), J. M. Kerrigan
    (Quincannon), Billy Bevan (Herbert Hale), Alan Hale (cook),
    Brandon Hurst (Bell), Douglas Walton (Pearson), Sammy Stein
    (Abelson), Howard Wilson (flyer), Neville Clark (Lt. Hawkins),
    Paul Hanson (Jock Mackay), Francis Ford, Frank Baker

THE WORLD MOVES ON (1934)
Production: Fox Film
Producer: Winfield Sheehan
Director: John Ford
Screenwriter: Reginald C. Berkeley
Cinematographer: George Schneiderman
Art Director: William Darling
Music: Max Steiner, Louis De Francesco, R. H. Bassett, David Buttolph,
    Hugo Friedhofer, and George Gershwin
Cast: Madeleine Carroll (Mrs. Warburton; Mary Warburton), Franchot
    Tone (Richard Girard), Lumsden Hare (Gabriel Warburton; Sir John
    Warburton), Raul Roulien (Carlos Girard; Henri Gerard), Reginald
    Denny (Erik von Gerhardt), Siegfried Rumann (Baron von Gerhardt),
    Louise Dresser (Baronness von Gerhardt), Stepin Fetchit (Dixie),
    Dudley Diggs (Mr. Manning), Frank Melton (John Girard), Brenda
    Fowler (Mrs. Girard), Russell Simpson (notary public), Walter McGrail

(French novelist), Frank Moran (Culbert), Jack Pennick and Francis Ford (legionnaires)

JUDGE PRIEST (1934)
Production: Fox Film
Producer: Sol Wurtzel
Director: John Ford
Screenwriters: Dudley Nichols and Lamar Trotti, from stories by Irvin S. Cobb
Cinematographer: George Schneiderman
Music: Samuel Kaylin
Cast: Will Rogers (Judge William Priest), Henry B. Walthall (Rev. Ashby Brand), Tom Brown (Jerome Priest), Anita Louise (Ellie May Gillespie), Rochelle Hudson (Virginia Maydew), Berton Churchill (Sen. Horace K. Maydew), David Landau (Bob Gillis), Brenda Fowler (Mrs. Caroline Priest), Hattie McDaniel (Aunt Dilsey), Stepin Fetchit (Jeff Poindexter), Frank Melton (Flem Tally), Roger Imhof (Billy Gaynor), Charley Grapewin (Sgt. Jimmy Bagby), Francis Ford (juror no. 12), Robert Parrish

THE WHOLE TOWN'S TALKING (1935)
Production: Columbia
Producer: Lester Cowan
Director: John Ford
Screenwriter: Jo Swerling, from the novel by W. R. Burnett, with dialogue by Robert Riskin
Cinematographer: Joseph H. August
Editor: Viola Lawrence
Cast: Edward G. Robinson (Arthur Ferguson Jones; Killer Mannion), Jean Arthur (Miss "Bill" Clark), Wallace Ford (Mr. Healy), Arthur Byron (Mr. Spencer), Arthur Hohl (Det. Sgt. Michael Boyle), Donald Meek (Mr. Hoyt), Paul Harvey (J. G. Carpenter), Edward Brophy (Slugs Martin), J. Farrell MacDonald (warden), Etienne Girardot (Mr. Seaver), James Donlon (Howe), Joseph Sawyer, Francis Ford, Robert Parrish

THE INFORMER (1935)
Production: RKO
Associate Producer: Cliff Reid
Director: John Ford
Screenwriter: Dudley Nichols, from the novel by Liam O'Flaherty

Cinematographer: Joseph H. August
Editor: George Hively
Art Directors: Van Nest Polglase, Charles Kirk
Music: Max Steiner
Cast: Victor McLaglen (Gypo Nolan), Heather Angel (Mary McPhillip),
  Preston Foster (Dan Gallagher), Margo Graham (Katie Madden),
  Wallace Ford (Frankie McPhillip), Una O'Connor (Mrs. McPhillip),
  J. M. Kerrigan (Terry), Joseph Sawyer (Bartley Mulholland), Neil
  Fitzgerald (Tommy Conner), Donald Meek (Pat Mulligan), D'Arcy
  Corrigan (the blind man), Leo McCabe (Donahue), Gaylord
  Pendleton (Daley), Francis Ford (Judge Flynn), May Boley (Mrs.
  Betty), Grizelda Harvey (girl), Dennis O'Dea (street singer), Jack
  Mulhall (lookout), Robert Parrish (soldier), Frank Moran, Frank Baker,
  Clyde Cook

STEAMBOAT ROUND THE BEND (1935)
Production: Fox Film/20th Century–Fox
Producer: Sol M. Wurtzel
Director: John Ford
Screenwriters: Dudley Nichols and Lamar Trotti, from the story by Ben
  Lucian Burman
Cinematographer: George Schneiderman
Editor: Alfred De Gaetano
Art Director: William Darling
Musical Director: Samuel Kaylin
Cast: Will Rogers (Dr. John Pearly), Anne Shirley (Fleety Belle), Eugene
  Pallette (Sheriff Rufe Jefers), John McGuire (Duke), Berton Churchill
  ("The New Moses"), Stepin Fetchit (George Lincoln Washington),
  Francis Ford (Efe), Irvin S. Cobb (Capt. Eli), Roger Imhof (Pappy),
  Raymond Hatton (Matt Abel), Charles B. Middleton (Fleety's father),
  Jack Pennick (ringleader)

THE PRISONER OF SHARK ISLAND (1936)
Production: 20th Century–Fox
Producer: Darryl F. Zanuck
Director: John Ford
Screenwriter: Nunnally Johnson
Cinematographer: Bert Glennon
Editor: Jack Murray
Art Director: William Darling
Musical Director: Louis Silvers

Cast: Warner Baxter (Dr. Samuel A. Mudd), Gloria Stuart
(Mrs. Peggy Mudd), Claude Gillingwater (Col. Jeremiah
Milford Dyer), Arthur Byron (Mr. Erickson), O. P. Heggie
(Dr. McIntyre), Harry Carey (commander of Ft. Jefferson),
Francis Ford (Cpl. O'Toole), John Carradine (Sgt. Rankin),
Frank McGlynne Sr. (Abraham Lincoln), Douglas Wood
(Gen. Ewing), Joyce Kay (Martha Mudd), Fred Kohler Jr.
(Sgt. Cooper), Francis McDonald (John Wilkes Booth), J. M.
Kerrigan (Judge Maiben), Jack Pennick (soldier), Robert Parrish,
Frank Baker

MARY OF SCOTLAND (1936)
Production: RKO
Producer: Pandro S. Berman
Director: John Ford
Screenwriter: Dudley Nichols, from the play by Maxwell Anderson
Cinematographer: Joseph H. August
Editor: Jane Loring
Art Directors: Van Nest Polglase, Carroll Clark
Music: Max Steiner
Cast: Katharine Hepburn (Mary Stuart), Fredric March (Bothwell),
Florence Eldridge (Elizabeth), Douglas Walton (Darnley), John
Carradine (David Rizzio), Monte Blue (Messager), Jean Fenwick (Mary
Seton), Robert Barrat (Morton), Gavin Muir (Leicester), Ian Keith
(James Stuart Moray), Moroni Olsen (John Knox), Donald Crisp
(Huntley), William Stack (Ruthven), Molly Lamont (Mary
Livingston), Walter Byron (Sir Francis Walsingham), Ralph Forbes
(Randolph), Alan Mowbray (Throckmorton), Lionel Belmore (English
fisherman), Doris Lloyd (his wife), D'Arcy Corrigan (Kirkcaldy), Mary
Gordon (nurse), Frank Baker (Douglas), Lionel Pape (Burghley), Cyril
McLaglen (Faudoncide), Earle Foxe (Duke of Kent), Brandon Hurst
(Arian)

THE PLOUGH AND THE STARS (1936)
Production: RKO
Associate Producers: Cliff Reid, Robert Sisk
Director: John Ford
Screenwriter: Dudley Nichols, from the play by Sean O'Casey
Cinematographer: Joseph H. August
Editor: George Hively
Art Director: Van Nest Polglase

Music: Nathaniel Shilkret

Cast: Barbara Stanwyck (Mora Clitheroe), Preston Foster (Jack Clitheroe), Barry Fitzgerald (Fluther Good), Dennis O'Day (young Covey), Eileen Crowe (Bessie Burgess), Arthur Shields (Padraic Pearse), Erin O'Brien Moore (Rosie Redmond), Brandon Hurst (Sgt. Tinley), F. J. McCormick (Capt. Brennon), Una O'Conner (Maggie Corgan), Moroni Olsen (Gen. Connolly), J. M. Kerrigan (Peter Flynn), Neil Fitzgerald (Lt. Kangon), Bonita Granville (Mollser Gogan), Cyril McLaglen (Cpl. Stoddart), Mary Gordon (woman), Lionel Pape (English officer), Gaylord Pendleton, Doris Lloyd, D'Arcy Corrigan, Frank Baker

WEE WILLIE WINKIE (1937)

Production: 20th Century–Fox

Producer: Darryl F. Zanuck

Director: John Ford

Screenwriters: Ernest Pascal and Julian Josephson, from the story by Rudyard Kipling

Cinematographer: Arthur Miller

Editor: Walter Thompson

Art Director: William Darling

Music: Louis Silvers

Cast: Shirley Temple (Priscilla Williams), Victor McLaglen (Sgt. MacDuff), C. Aubrey Smith (Col. Williams), June Lang (Joyce Williams), Michael Whalen (Lt. "Coppy" Brandes), Cesar Romero (Khoda Khan), Constance Collier (Mrs. Allardyce), Douglas Scott (Mott), Gavin Muir (Capt. Bibberbeigh), Willie Fung (Mohammed Dihn), Brandon Hurst (Bagby), Lionel Pape (Major Allardyce), Clyde Cook (Pipe Major Sneath), Cyril McLaglen (Cpl. Tummel), Pat Somerset (officer)

THE HURRICANE (1937)

Production: Samuel Goldwyn/United Artists

Producer: Samuel Goldwyn

Director: John Ford

Screenwriters: Dudley Nichols and (uncredited) Ben Hecht, from the novel by Charles Nordhoff and James Norman Hall

Cinematographer: Bert Glennon

Editor: Lloyd Nosler

Art Directors: Richard Day, Alexander Golitzen

Music: Alfred Newman

Cast: Dorothy Lamour (Marama), Jon Hall (Terangi), Mary Astor
(Mrs. DeLaage), C. Aubrey Smith (Father Paul), Thomas Mitchell
(Dr. Kersaint), Raymond Massey (Gov. Eugene DeLaage), John
Carradine (guard), Jerome Cowan (Capt. Nagle), Al Kikume
(Chief Meheir), Kuulei DeClercq (Tita)

FOUR MEN AND A PRAYER (1938)
Production: 20th Century–Fox
Producer: Darryl F. Zanuck
Director: John Ford
Screenwriters: Richard Sherman, Sonya Levien, Walter Ferris, and
(uncredited) William Faulkner, from the novel by David Garth
Cinematographer: Ernest Palmer
Editor: Louis R. Loeffler
Art Directors: Bernard Herzbrun, Rudolph Sternad
Music: Louis Silvers, Ernst Toch
Cast: Loretta Young (Lynn Cherrington), Richard Greene (Geoffrey
Leigh), George Sanders (Wyatt Leigh), David Niven (Christopher
Leigh), William Henry (Rodney Leigh), C. Aubrey Smith (Col.
Loring Leigh), J. Edward Bromberg (Gen. Torres), Alan Hale (Farnoy),
John Carradine (Gen. Adolfo Arturo Sebastian), Reginald Denny
(Douglas Loveland), Berton Churchill (Martin Cherrington), Claude
King (Gen. Bryce), John Sutton (Capt. Drake), Barry Fitzgerald
(Mulcahy), Cecil Cunningham (Pyer), Frank Baker (defense attorney),
Lionel Pape (coroner), Brandon Hurst (jury foreman)

SUBMARINE PATROL (1938)
Production: 20th Century–Fox
Producer: Darryl F. Zanuck
Director: John Ford
Screenwriters: Rian James, Darrell Ware, Jack Yellen, and (uncredited)
William Faulkner, from the novel *The Splinter Fleet* by John
Milholland
Cinematographer: Arthur Miller
Editor: Robert Simpson
Art Directors: William Darling and Hans Peters
Music Director: Arthur Lange
Cast: Richard Greene (Perry Townsend III), Nancy Kelly (Susan Leeds),
Preston Foster (Lt. John C. Drake), George Bancroft (Capt. Leeds),
Slim Summerville (Ellsworth "Spuggs" Flicketts – "Cookie"), Joan
Valerie (Anne), John Carradine (Matt McAllison), Warren Hymer

(Rocky Haggerty), Henry Armetta (Luigi), Douglas Fowley (Brett),
J. Farrell MacDonald (Quincannon), Dick Hogan (Johnny), Maxie
Rosenbloom (Sgt. Joe Duffy), Ward Bond (Olaf Swanson), Robert
Lowery (Sparks), Charles Tannen (Kelly), George E. Stone (Irving
Goldfarb), Moroni Olsen (Capt. Wilson), Jack Pennick (Guns
McPeck), Elisha Cook Jr. ("Professor" Pratt)

STAGECOACH (1939)
Production: Wanger/United Artists
Executive Producer: Walter Wanger
Director: John Ford
Screenwriter: Dudley Nichols, based on the story "Stage to Lordsburg"
    by Ernest Haycox
Cinematographer: Bert Glennon
Editors: Otho Lovering, Dorothy Spence, and Walter Reynolds
Art Director: Alexander Toluboff
Music: American folk songs adapted by Richard Hageman, W. Franke
    Harling, John Leipold, Leo Shuken, and Louis Gruenberg
Cast: John Wayne (Ringo Kid), Claire Trevor (Dallas), Thomas Mitchell
    (Dr. Josiah Boone), John Carradine (Hatfield), Andy Devine (Buck
    Rickabaugh), Donald Meek (Samuel Peacock), Louise Platt (Lucy
    Mallory), George Bancroft (Curley Wilcox), Berton Churchill (Henry
    Gatewood), Tim Holt (Lt. Blanchard), Tom Tyler (Luke Plummer),
    Chris-Pin Martin (Chris), Elvira Rios (Yakima, his wife), Francis Ford
    (Billy Pickett), Marga Ann Daighton (Mrs. Pickett), Walter McGrail
    (Capt. Sickels), Harry Tenbrook (telegraph operator), Jack Pennick
    (Jerry, the bartender), Brenda Fowler (Mrs. Gatewood), Joseph
    Rickson (Hank Plummer), Vester Pegg (Ike Plummer), Chief Big
    Tree (Indian scout), Yakima Canutt (cavalry scout), Franklyn
    Farnum (Deputy), Duke Lee (Lordsburg sheriff), Frank Baker (scalded
    corpse)

YOUNG MR. LINCOLN (1939)
Production: Cosmopolitan/20th Century–Fox
Executive Producer: Darryl F. Zanuck
Producer: Kenneth McGowan
Director: John Ford
Screenwriter: Lamar Trotti
Cinematographer: Bert Glennon
Editor: Walter Thompson
Art Directors: Richard Day and Mark Lee Kirk

Music: Alfred Newman

Cast: Henry Fonda (Abraham Lincoln), Alice Brady (Abigail Clay),
 Marjorie Weaver (Mary Todd), Eddie Collins (Efe Turner),
 Pauline Moore (Ann Rutledge), Arleen Whelan (Sarah Clay),
 Richard Cromwell (Matt Clay), Ward Bond (John Palmer Cass),
 Donald Meek (John Felder), Spencer Charters (Judge
 Herbert A. Bell), Eddie Quillan (Adam Clay), Milburn Stone
 (Stephen Douglas), Cliff Clark (Sheriff Billings), Robert Lowery
 (juror), Charles Tannen (Ninian Edwards), Francis Ford (Sam Boone),
 Fred Kohler Jr. (Scrub White), Dorris Bowdon (uncredited, Carrie Sue
 Clay), Kay Linaker (Mrs. Edwards), Russell Simpson (Woolridge),
 Robert Homans (Mr. Clay), Jack Pennick (Big Buck), Harry Tyler
 (hairdresser), Charles Halton (Hawthorne), Elizabeth Jones

DRUMS ALONG THE MOHAWK (1939)

Production: 20th Century–Fox

Executive Producer: Darryl F. Zanuck

Producer: Raymond Griffith

Director: John Ford

Screenwriters: Lamar Trotti, Sonya Levien, and (uncredited) William
 Faulkner, from the novel by Walter D. Edmonds

Cinematographers: Bert Glennon and Ray Rennahan

Editor: Robert Simpson

Art Directors: Richard Day and Mark Lee Kirk

Music: Alfred Newman

Cast: Claudette Colbert (Lana Borst Martin), Henry Fonda (Gilbert
 Martin), Edna May Oliver (Mrs. McKlennan), Eddie Collins (Christian
 Reall), John Carradine (Caldwell), Dorris Bowdon (Mary Reall), Jessie
 Ralph (Mrs. Weaver), Arthur Shields (Fr. Rosenkranz), Robert Lowery
 (John Weaver), Roger Imhof (Gen. Nicholas Herkimer), Francis
 Ford (Joe Boleo), Ward Bond (Adam Hartmann), Kay Linaker
 (Mrs. Demooth), Russell Simpson (Dr. Petry), Chief Big Tree (Blue
 Back), Spencer Charters (Fisk), Jack Pennick (Amos), Charles Tannen
 (Robert Johnson), Lionel Pape (general), Arthur Aylesworth (George),
 Frank Baker (commander of colonial troops), Elizabeth Jones
 (Mrs. Reall), Mae Marsh

THE GRAPES OF WRATH (1940)

Production: 20th Century–Fox

Producer: Darryl F. Zanuck

Director: John Ford
Screenwriter: Nunnally Johnson, from the novel by John Steinbeck
Cinematographer: Gregg Toland
Editor: Robert Simpson
Art Directors: Richard Day and Mark Lee Kirk
Music: Alfred Newman
Cast: Henry Fonda (Tom Joad), Jane Darwell (Ma Joad), John Carradine
  (Casey), Charley Grapewin (Grampa Joad), Dorris Bowdon
  (Rosasharn), Russell Simpson (Pa Joad), O. Z. Whitehead (Al), John
  Qualen (Muley), Eddie Quillan (Connie), Zeffie Tilbury (Grandma
  Joad), Frank Sully (Noah), Frank Darien (Uncle John), Darryl Hickman
  (Winfield), Shirley Mills (Ruth Joad), Grant Mitchell (guardian), Ward
  Bond (policeman), Frank Faylen (Tim), Joe Sawyer (accountant),
  Harry Tyler (Bert), Charles B. Middleton (conductor), Roger Imhof
  (Thomas), Arthur Aylesworth (father), David Hughes (Frank), Charles
  Tannen (Joe), Cliff Clark (townsman), Robert Homans (Spencer),
  Irving Bacon (conductor), Mae Marsh, Francis Ford, Jack Pennick

THE LONG VOYAGE HOME (1940)
Production: Argosy Pictures/Wanger/United Artists
Producer: Walter Wanger
Director: John Ford
Screenwriter: Dudley Nichols, from the one-act plays "The Moon of the
  Caribbees," "In the Zone," "Bound East for Cardiff" and "The Long
  Voyage Home" by Eugene O'Neill
Cinematographer: Gregg Toland
Editor: Sherman Todd
Art Director: James Basevi
Music: Richard Hageman
Cast: Thomas Mitchell (Aloysius Driscoll), John Wayne (Ole Olsen), Ian
  Hunter (Thomas Fenwick – "Smitty"), Barry Fitzgerald (Cocky),
  Wilfred Lawson (captain), Mildred Natwick (Freda), John Qualen
  (Axel Swanson), Ward Bond (Yank), Joe Sawyer (Davis), Arthur
  Shields (Donkeyman), J. M. Kerrigan (Crimp), David Hughes (Scotty),
  Billy Bevan (Joe), Cyril McLaglen (mate), Robert E. Perry (Paddy),
  Jack Pennick (Johnny Bergman), Harry Tenbrook (Max), Lionel Pape

TOBACCO ROAD (1941)
Production: 20th Century–Fox
Producer: Darryl F. Zanuck

Director: John Ford
Screenwriter: Nunnally Johnson, from the play by Jack Kirkland and
    novel by Erskine Caldwell
Cinematographer: Arthur Miller
Editor: Barbara McLean
Art Directors: Richard Day and James Basevi
Music: David Buttolph
Cast: Charley Grapewin (Jeeter Lester), Marjorie Rambeau (Sister
    Bessie), Gene Tierney (Ellie May Lester), William Tracy (Dude Lester),
    Elizabeth Patterson (Ada Lester), Dana Andrews (Dr. Tim), Slim
    Summerville (Henry Peabody), Ward Bond (Lov Bensey), Grant
    Mitchell (George Payne), Zeffie Tilbury (Grandma Lester), Russell
    Simpson (sheriff), Spencer Charters (employee), Harry Tyler (auto
    salesman), Irving Bacon (teller), Charles Halton (mayor), Jack
    Pennick (deputy sheriff), Francis Ford (vagabond)

SEX HYGIENE (1941)
Production: Audio Productions/U.S. Army
Producer: Darryl F. Zanuck
Director: John Ford
Cinematographer: George Barnes
Editor: Gene Fowler Jr.
Cast: Charles Trowbridge, Robert Lowery, George Reeves

HOW GREEN WAS MY VALLEY (1941)
Production: 20th Century–Fox
Producer: Darryl F. Zanuck
Director: John Ford
Screenwriter: Philip Dunne, from the novel by Richard Llewellyn
Editor: James B. Clark
Art Directors: Richard Day and Nathan Juran
Music: Alfred Newman
Cast: Walter Pidgeon (Mr. Gruffydd), Maureen O'Hara (Angharad
    Morgan), Donald Crisp (Gwilym Morgan), Sara Allgood
    (Mrs. Beth Morgan), Anna Lee (Bronwyn Morgan),
    Roddy McDowell (Huw Morgan), John Loder (Ianto Morgan),
    Patrick Knowles (Ivor Morgan), Richard Fraser (Davy Morgan),
    James Monks (Owen Morgan), Barry Fitzgerald (Cyfartha),
    Morton Lowry (Mr. Jonas), Arthur Shields (Mr. Parry), Ann Todd
    (Ceiwen), Frederick Worlock (Dr. Richard), Evan E. Evans
    (Gwinlyn), Rhys Williams (Dai Bando), Lionel Pape (Old

Evans), Mae Marsh (miner's wife), Frank Baker, Irving Pichel
(narrator)

THE BATTLE OF MIDWAY (1942)
Production: U.S. Navy/20th Century–Fox
Director: Lt. Comdr. John Ford, USNR
Narration written by John Ford, Dudley Nichols, and James Kevin
  McGuinness
Cinematographers: John Ford, Jack McKenzie, Lt. Kenneth M. Pier, and
  Gregg Toland
Editors: John Ford and Robert Parrish
Music: Alfred Newman

TORPEDO SQUADRON (1942)
Production: U.S. Navy
Director: Lt. Comdr. John Ford, USNR

DECEMBER 7TH (1943)
Production: U.S. Navy
Directors: Lt. Comdr. John Ford, USNR, and Lt. Gregg Toland, USNR
Cinematographer: Gregg Toland
Editor: Robert Parrish
Music: Alfred Newman

WE SAIL AT MIDNIGHT (1943)
Production: Crown Film Unit/U.S. Navy
Director: Lt. Comdr. John Ford, USNR
Narration written by Clifford Odets
Music: Richard Addinsell

THEY WERE EXPENDABLE (1945)
Production: Metro-Goldwyn-Mayer
Producer: John Ford
Director: John Ford
Screenwriter: Frank W. Wead, from the book by William L. White
Cinematographer: Joseph H. August
Editors: Frank E. Hull and Douglas Biggs
Art Directors: Cedric Gibbons and Malcolm F. Brown
Music: Herbert Stothert
Cast: Robert Montgomery (Lt. John Brickley), John Wayne (Lt. Rusty
  Ryan), Donna Reed (Lt. Sandy Davis), Jack Holt (Gen. Martin), Ward

Bond (Boots Mulcahey), Louis Jean Heydt (Ohio), Marshall
Thompson (Snake Gardner), Russell Simpson (Dad), Leon Ames
(Major Morton), Paul Langton (Andy Andrews), Arthur Walsh
(Jones), Donald Curtis (Shorty Long), Cameron Mitchell (George
Cross), Jeff York (Tony Aiken), Murray Alper (Slug Mahan), Harry
Tenbrook (Larsen), Jack Pennick (Doc Charlie), Charles Trowbridge
(Adm. Blackwell), Betty Blythe (officer's wife), Wallace Ford, Tom
Tyler, Frank Baker

MY DARLING CLEMENTINE (1946)
Production: 20th Century–Fox
Producer: Samuel G. Engel
Director: John Ford
Screenwriters: Samuel G. Engel and Winston Miller, from the story by
  Sam Hellman, based on the book *Wyatt Earp, Frontier Marshall* by
  Stuart N. Lake
Cinematographer: Joseph P. McDonald
Editor: Dorothy Spencer
Art Directors: James Basevi and Lyle R. Wheeler
Music: Cyril J. Mockridge
Cast: Henry Fonda (Wyatt Earp), Linda Darnell (Chihuahua), Victor
  Mature (Doc John Holliday), Walter Brennan (Old Man Clanton),
  Tim Holt (Virgil Earp), Ward Bond (Morgan Earp), Cathy Downs
  (Clementine Carter), Alan Mowbray (Granville Thorndyke), John
  Ireland (Billy Clanton), Grant Withers (Ike Clanton), Roy Roberts
  (mayor), Jane Darwell (Kate Nelson), Russell Simpson (John
  Simpson), Francis Ford (Dad – old soldier), J. Farrell MacDonald
  (Mac), Don Garner (James Earp), Jack Pennick (stagecoach driver),
  Fred Libby (Phin Clanton), Earle Fox (gambler), Mae Marsh

THE FUGITIVE (1947)
Production: Argosy Pictures/RKO
Producers: John Ford and Merian C. Cooper
Director: John Ford
Screenwriter: Dudley Nichols, from the novel *The Labyrinthine
  Ways/The Power and the Glory* by Graham Greene
Cinematographer: Gabriel Figueroa
Editor: Jack Murray
Art Director: Alfred Ybarra
Music: Richard Hageman
Cast: Henry Fonda (a fugitive), Dolores Del Rio (an Indian woman),

Pedro Armendariz (police lieutenant), Ward Bond (El Gringo), Leo
Carrillo (chief of police), J. Carroll Naish (police spy), Robert
Armstrong (police sergeant), Chris-Pin Martin (organ player), John
Qualen (doctor), Fortunio Bonanova (governor's cousin), Miguel
Inclan (hostage)

FORT APACHE (1948)
Production: Argosy Pictures/RKO
Producers: John Ford and Merian C. Cooper
Director: John Ford
Screenwriter: Frank S. Nugent, from the story "Massacre" by James
    Warner Bellah
Cinematographer: Archie Stout
Editor: Jack Murray
Art Director: James Basevi
Music: Richard Hageman
Cast: John Wayne (Capt. Kirby York), Henry Fonda (Lt. Col. Owen
    Thursday), Shirley Temple (Philadelphia Thursday), John Agar
    (Lt. Michael O'Rourke), Ward Bond (Sgt. Major O'Rourke), George
    O'Brien (Capt. Sam Collingwood), Victor McLaglen (Sgt. Mulcahy),
    Pedro Armendariz (Sgt. Beaufort), Anna Lee (Mrs. Collingwood),
    Irene Rich (Mrs. O'Rourke), Guy Kibbee (Dr. Wilkins), Grant Withers
    (Silas Meachum), Miguel Inclan (Cochise), Jack Pennick (Sgt.
    Shattuck), Mae Marsh (Mrs. Gates), Dick Foran (Sgt. Quincannon),
    Frank Ferguson (newspaperman), Francis Ford (bartender), Hank
    Worden (Southern recruit), Harry Tenbrook (courier), Frank Baker
    and Ben Johnson (stunt riders)

3 GODFATHERS (1948)
Production: Argosy Pictures/Metro-Goldwyn-Mayer
Producers: John Ford and Merian C. Cooper
Director: John Ford
Screenwriters: Laurence Stallings and Frank S. Nugent, from the story
    by Peter B. Kyne
Cinematographer: Winton C. Hoch
Editor: Jack Murray
Art Director: James Basevi
Music: Richard Hageman
Cast: John Wayne (Robert Marmaduke Sangster Hightower), Pedro
    Armendariz (Pedro Roca Fuerte), Harry Carey Jr. (William
    Kearney – "the Abilene Kid"), Ward Bond (Perley "Buck" Sweet),

Mildred Natwick (mother), Charles Halton (Mr. Latham), Jane Darwell (Miss Florie), Mae Marsh (Mrs. Perly Sweet), Guy Kibbee (judge), Dorothy Ford (Ruby Latham), Ben Johnson, Michael Dugan, Don Summers (patrolmen), Hank Worden (deputy sheriff), Jack Pennick (Luke – train conductor), Francis Ford (drunk), Fred Libby (deputy sheriff), Ruth Clifford (woman in bar)

SHE WORE A YELLOW RIBBON (1949)
Production: Argosy Pictures/RKO
Producers: John Ford and Merian C. Cooper
Director: John Ford
Screenwriters: Frank S. Nugent and Laurence Stallings, from the story "War Party" by James Warner Bellah
Cinematographer: Winton C. Hoch
Editor: Jack Murray
Art Director: James Basevi
Music: Richard Hageman
Cast: John Wayne (Capt. Nathan Brittles), Joanne Dru (Olivia), John Agar (Lt. Flint Cohill), Ben Johnson (Sgt. Tyree), Harry Carey Jr. (Lt. Pennell), Victor McLaglen (Sgt. Quincannon), Mildred Natwick (Mrs. Abbey Allshard), George O'Brien (Major Mack Allshard), Arthur Shields (Dr. O'Laughlin), Francis Ford (barman), Harry Woods (Karl Rynders), Chief Big Tree (Pony That Walks), Noble Johnson (Red Shirt), Cliff Lyons (Trooper Cliff), Tom Tyler (Quayne), Jack Pennick (Sgt. Major), Bill Gettinger (officer), Don Summers (Jenkins), Fred Libby (Cpl. Krumrein), Frank Baker

WHEN WILLIE COMES MARCHING HOME (1950)
Production: 20th Century–Fox
Producer: Fred Kohlmar
Director: John Ford
Screenwriters: Mary Loos and Richard Sale, from the story "When Leo Comes Marching Home" by Sy Gomberg
Cinematographer: Leo Tover
Editor: James B. Clark
Art Director: Lyle R. Wheeler
Music: Alfred Newman
Cast: Dan Dailey (Bill Kluggs), Corinne Calvet (Yvonne), Colleen Townsend (Marge Fettles), Lloyd Corrigan (Major Adams), William Demarest (Herman Kluggs), James Lydon (Charles Fettles), Evelyn Varden (Gertrude Kluggs), Charles Halton (Mr. Fettles), Mae Marsh

(Mrs. Fettles), Jack Pennick (sergeant), Don Summers (MP Sherve), Harry Tenbrook (Joe), Hank Worden (choir leader), Charles Trowbridge (Gen. Merrill), Kenneth Tobey (Lt. K. Geiger), Whit Bissell (Lt. Handley), Frank Baker, J. Farrell MacDonald, Vera Miles

WAGON MASTER (1950)
Production: Argosy Pictures/RKO
Producers: John Ford and Merian C. Cooper
Director: John Ford
Screenwriters: Frank S. Nugent and Patrick Ford
Cinematographer: Bert Glennon
Editor: Jack Murray
Art Director: James Basevi
Music: Richard Hageman, with songs by Stan Jones sung by the Sons of the Pioneers
Cast: Ben Johnson (Travis Blue), Harry Carey Jr. (Sandy Owens), Joanne Dru (Denver), Ward Bond (Elder Wiggs), Charles Kemper (Uncle Shiloh Clegg), Alan Mowbray (Dr. A. Locksley Hall), Jane Darwell (Sister Ledeyard), Ruth Clifford (Fleuretty Phyffe), Russell Simpson (Adam Perkins), James Arness (Floyd Clegg), Fred Libby (Reese Clegg), Hank Worden (Luke Clegg), Mickey Simpson (Jesse Clegg), Francis Ford (Mr. Peachtree), Cliff Lyons (sheriff of Crystal City), Don Summers (Sam Jenkins), Jim Thorpe (Navajo)

RIO GRANDE (1950)
Production: Argosy Pictures/Republic
Producers: John Ford and Merian C. Cooper
Director: John Ford
Screenwriter: James Kevin McGuinness, from the story "Mission with No Record" by James Warner Bellah
Cinematographer: Bert Glennon
Editor: Jack Murray
Art Director: Frank Hotaling
Music: Victor Young, with songs sung by the Sons of the Pioneers
Cast: John Wayne (Lt. Col. Kirby Yorke), Maureen O'Hara (Mrs. Yorke), Harry Carey Jr. (Trooper Daniel Boone), Chill Wills (Dr. Wilkins), J. Carroll Naish (Gen. Philip Sheridan), Victor McLaglen (Sgt. Quincannon), Grant Withers (deputy marshal), Peter Ortiz (Capt. St. Jacques), Steve Pendleton (Capt. Prescott), Karolyn Grimes (Margaret Mary), Alberto Morin (lieutenant), Stan Jones (sergeant), Fred Kennedy (Heinze), Jack Pennick, Pat Wayne (regimental singers)

THIS IS KOREA! (1951)
Production: U.S. Navy/Republic
Director: Rear Adm. John Ford, USNR
Narration written by James Warner Bellah and Frank S. Nugent
Cinematographers: Charles Bohuy, Bob Rhea, and Mark Armistead

THE QUIET MAN (1952)
Production: Argosy Pictures/Republic
Producers: John Ford and Merian C. Cooper
Director: John Ford
Screenwriter: Frank S. Nugent, from the story by Maurice Walsh
Cinematographer: Winton C. Hoch
Editor: Jack Murray
Art Director: Frank Hotaling
Music: Victor Young
Cast: John Wayne (Sean Thornton), Maureen O'Hara (Mary Kate
    Danaher), Barry Fitzgerald (Michaeleen Og Flynn), Ward Bond
    (Fr. Peter Lonergan), Victor McLaglen (Red Will Danaher), Mildred
    Natwick (Mrs. Sarah Tillane), Francis Ford (Dan Tobin), Eileen Crowe
    (Elizabeth Playfair), May Craig (woman at railroad station), Arthur
    Shields (Rev. Cyril Playfair), Charles FitzSimmons (Forbes), Sean
    McClory (Owen Glynn), Jack McGowran (Feeney), Ken Curtis
    (Dermot Fahy), Mae Marsh (Fr. Paul's mother), Harry Tenbrook
    (policeman), Hank Worden (trainer in flashback), Frank Baker

WHAT PRICE GLORY (1952)
Production: 20th Century–Fox
Producer: Sol C. Siegel
Director: John Ford
Screenwriters: Phoebe and Henry Ephron, from the play by Maxwell
    Anderson
Cinematographer: Joseph MacDonald
Editor: Dorothy Spencer
Art Directors: Lyle R. Wheeler and George W. Davis
Music: Alfred Newman
Cast: James Cagney (Capt. Flagg), Corinne Calvet (Charmaine), Dan
    Dailey (Sgt. Quirt), William Demarest (Cpl. Kiper), Craig Hill
    (Lt. Aldrich), Robert Wagner (Lewisohn), Marisa Pavan (Nichole
    Bouchard), Casey Adams (Lt. Moore), James Gleason (Gen. Cokely),
    Wally Vernon (Lipinsky), Henry Letondal (Cognac Pete), Fred Libby

(Lt. Schmidt), Ray Hyke (Mulcahy), Paul Fix (Gowdy), James Lilburn (young soldier), Henry Morgan (Morgan), Dan Borzage (Gilbert), Jack Pennick (Ferguson), Tom Tyler (Capt. Davis), Charles FitzSimmons (Capt. Wickham)

THE SUN SHINES BRIGHT (1953)
Production: Argosy Pictures/Republic
Producers: John Ford and Merian C. Cooper
Director: John Ford
Screenwriter: Laurence Stallings, from the stories "The Sun Shines
    Bright," "The Mob from Massac," and "The Lord Provides" by Irvin
    S. Cobb
Cinematographer: Archie Stout
Editor: Jack Murray
Art Director: Frank Hotaling
Music: Victor Young
Cast: Charles Winninger (Judge William Pittman Priest), Arleen
    Whelan (Lucy Lee Lake), John Russell (Ashby Corwin), Stepin Fetchit
    (Jeff Poindexter), Russell Simpson (Dr. Lewt Lake), Ludwig Stössel
    (Herman Felsburg), Francis Ford (Brother Finney), Paul Hurst (Sgt.
    Jimmy Bagby), Mitchell Lewis (Andy Radcliffe), Grant Withers (Buck),
    Milburn Stone (Horace K. Maydew), Dorothy Jordan (Lucy's mother),
    Slim Pickens (Sterling), Jane Darwell (Amora Ratchitt), Mae Marsh
    (Amora's companion), Jack Pennick (Beaker), Patrick Wayne
    (cadet)

MOGAMBO (1953)
Production: Metro-Goldwyn-Mayer
Producer: Sam Zimbalist
Director: John Ford
Screenwriter: John Lee Mahin, from the play "Red Dust" by Wilson
    Collison
Cinematographers: Robert Surtees and Fredrick A. Young
Editor: Frank Clarke
Art Director: Alfred Junge
Cast: Clark Gable (Victor Marswell), Ava Gardner (Eloise Y. Kelly), Grace
    Kelly (Linda Nordley), Donald Sinden (Donald Nordley), Philip
    Stainton (John Brown Pryce), Erick Pohlmann (Leon Boltchak),
    Laurence Naismith (Skipper John), Dennis O'Dea (Fr. Joseph), Asa
    Etula (native male)

THE LONG GRAY LINE (1955)
Production: Rota Productions/Columbia
Producer: Robert Arthur
Director: John Ford
Screenwriter: Edward Hope, from *Bringing Up the Brass*, the
   autobiography of Marty Maher with Nardi Reeder Champion
Cinematographer: Charles Lawton Jr.
Editor: William Lyon
Art Director: Robert Peterson
Music Adaptation: George Duning
Cast: Tyrone Power (Martin Maher), Maureen O'Hara (Mary
   O'Donnell), Robert Francis (James Sunstrom Jr.), Donald Crisp (old
   Martin), Ward Bond (Capt. Herman J. Koehler), Betsy Palmer (Kitty
   Carter), Phil Carey (Charles Dotson), William Leslie (Red Sundstrom),
   Harry Carey Jr. (Dwight Eisenhower), Patrick Wayne (Cherub
   Overton), Sean McClory (Dinny Maher), Peter Graves (Sgt. Rudolph
   Heinz), Milburn Stone (Capt. John Pershing), Erin O'Brien-Moore
   (Mrs. Koehler), Martin Milner (Jim O'Carberry), Jack Pennick
   (Tommy)

THE RED, WHITE AND BLUE LINE (1955)
Production: U.S. Treasury Dept./Columbia
Director: John Ford (?)
Screenwriter: Edward Hope
Cinematographer: Charles Lawton Jr.
Narrated by Ward Bond

MISTER ROBERTS (1955)
Production: Orange Productions/Warner Bros.
Producer: Leland Hayward
Director: John Ford
Screenwriters: Frank S. Nugent and Joshua Logan, from the play by
   Logan and Thomas Heggen and the novel by Heggen
Cinematographer: Winton C. Hoch
Editor: Jack Murray
Art Director: Art Loel
Music: Franz Waxman
Cast: Henry Fonda (Lt. Roberts), James Cagney (captain), Jack Lemmon
   (Ens. Frank Thurlow Pulver), William Powell (Doc), Ward Bond (CPO
   Dowdy), Betsy Palmer (Lt. Ann Girard), Phil Carey (Mannion), Nick
   Adams (Reber), Harry Carey Jr. (Stefanowski), Ken Curtis (Dolan),

Frank Aletter (Gerhart), Fritz Ford (Lidstrom), Buck Kartalian (Mason), William Henry (Lt. Billings), William Hudson (Olson), Studdy Kruger (Schlemmer), Harry Tenbrook (Cookie), Pat Wayne (Bookser), Dan Borzage (Jonesey), Martin Milner (shore patrol officer), Jack Pennick (marine sergeant)

THE SEARCHERS (1956)
Production: C. V. Whitney Pictures/Warner Bros.
Producers: Merian C. Cooper and C. V. Whitney
Director: John Ford
Screenwriter: Frank S. Nugent, from the novel by Alan LeMay
Cinematographer: Winton C. Hoch
Editor: Jack Murray
Art Directors: Frank Hotaling and James Basevi
Music: Max Steiner
Cast: John Wayne (Ethan Edwards), Jeffrey Hunter (Martin Pawley), Vera Miles (Laurie Jorgensen), Ward Bond (Capt. Rev. Samuel Clayton), Natalie Wood (Debbie Edwards), John Qualen (Lars Jorgensen), Olive Carey (Mrs. Jorgensen), Henry Brandon (Chief Scar), Ken Curtis (Charlie McCorry), Harry Carey Jr. (Brad Jorgensen), Antonio Moreno (Emilio Figueroa), Hank Worden (Mose Harper), Lana Wood (Debbie as child), Walter Coy (Aaron Edwards), Pippa Scott (Lucy Edwards), Pat Wayne (Lt. Greenhill), Beulah Archuletta (Look), Jack Pennick (private), Peter Mamokos (Futterman), Bill Steele (Nesby), Cliff Lyons (Col. Greenhill), Mae Marsh (woman at fort), Ruth Clifford (deranged woman at fort), Dan Borzage (accordianist), Chuck Roberson (man at wedding)

THE WINGS OF EAGLES (1957)
Production: Metro-Goldwyn-Mayer
Producer: Charles Schnee
Director: John Ford
Screenwriters: Frank Fenton and William Wister Haines, based on the life and writing of Comdr. Frank W. Wead, USN
Cinematographer: Paul C. Vogel
Editor: Gene Ruggiero
Art Directors: William A. Horning and Malcolm Brown
Music: Jeff Alexander
Cast: John Wayne (Frank W. "Spig" Wead), Maureen O'Hara (Minne Wead), Dan Dailey (Carson), Ward Bond (John Dodge), Ken Curtis (John Dale Price), Edmund Lowe (Adm. Moffet), Kenneth Tobey

(Herbert Allen Hazard), James Todd (Jack Travis), Barry Kelly (Capt. Jock Clark), Sig Ruman (manager), Henry O'Neill (Capt. Spear), Willis Bouchey (Barton), Dorothy Jordan (Brentmann), Peter Ortiz (Lt. Charles Dexter), Louis Jean Heydt (Dr. John Keye), Tige Andrews (Arizona Pincus), Dan Borzage (Pete), William Tracy (air force officer), Jack Pennick (Joe), Bill Henry (naval aide), Charles Trowbridge (Adm. Crown), Mae Marsh (Nurse Crumley), Olive Carey (Bridey O'Faolain), Chuck Roberson (officer), Major Sam Harris (patient), Cliff Lyons

THE RISING OF THE MOON (1957)
Production: Four Province Productions/Warner Bros.
Producer: Michael Killanin
Director: John Ford
Screenwriter: Frank S. Nugent, from the story "The Majesty of the Law" by Frank O'Conner and the plays "A Minute's Wait" by Michael J. McHugh and "The Rising of the Moon" by Lady Gregory
Cinematographer: Robert Krasker
Editor: Michael Gordon
Art Director: Ray Simm
Music: Eamonn O'Gallagher
Cast: Noel Purcell (Dan O'Flaherty), Cyril Cusack (Inspector Michael Dillon), Jack McGowran (Mickey J.), Jimmy O'Dea (porter), Tony Quinn (railroad station chief), Paul Farrell (chauffeur), Dennis O'Dea (police sergeant), Eileen Crowe (his wife), Maurice Good (P. C. O'Grady), Frank Lawton (major), J. G. Devlin (guard), Michael Trubshawe (Col. Frobisher), Anita Sharp Bolster (Mrs. Frobisher), Maureen Porter (barmaid), Maureen O'Connell (May Ann McMahon), May Craig (May's aunt)

THE GROWLER STORY (1957)
Production: U.S. Navy
Producer: Mark Armistead
Director: John Ford
Cinematography: Pacific Fleet Combat Camera Group
Editor: Jack Murray
Cast: Ward Bond (Quincannon), Ken Curtis (Capt. Howard W. Gilmore)

GIDEON OF SCOTLAND YARD (1958)
Production: Columbia British Productions
Producer: Michael Killanin
Director: John Ford

Screenwriter: T. E. B. Clarke, from the novel by J. J. Marric (John
  Creasey)
Cinematographer: Frederick A. Young
Editor: Raymond Poulton
Art Director: Ken Adam
Music: Douglas Gamley
Cast: Jack Hawkins (Inspector George Gideon), Dianne Foster (Joanna
  Delafield), Anna Massey (Sally Gideon), Anna Lee (Mrs. Kate Gideon),
  Cyril Cusack (Herbert "Birdie" Sparrow), Andrew Ray (P. C. Simon
  Farnaby-Green), James Hayter (Robert Mason), Ronald Howard (Paul
  Delafield), Howard Marion-Crawford (chief of Scotland Yard),
  Laurence Naismith (Arthur Sayer), Derek Bond (Det. Sgt. Eric Kirby),
  Griselda Harvey (Mrs. Kirby), Frank Lawton (Det. Sgt. Liggett), John
  Loder (Ponsford), Billie Whitelaw (Christine)

THE LAST HURRAH (1958)
Production: Columbia
Producer: John Ford
Director: John Ford
Screenwriter: Frank S. Nugent, from the novel by Edwin O'Connor
Cinematographer: Charles Lawton Jr.
Editor: Jack Murray
Art Director: Robert Peterson
Cast: Spencer Tracy (Frank Skeffington), Jeffrey Hunter (Adam
  Caulfield), Dianne Foster (Maeve Caulfield), Pat O'Brien (John
  Gorman), Basil Rathbone (Norman Cass Sr.), Donald Crisp (the
  cardinal), James Gleason (Cuke Gillen), Edward Brophy (Ditto
  Boland), John Carradine (Amos Force), Willis Bouchey (Roger
  Sugrue), Basil Ruysdael (Bishop Gardner), Ricardo Cortez (Sam
  Weinberg), Wallace Ford (Charles J. Hennessey), Frank McHugh
  (Festus Garvey), Anna Lee (Gert Minihan), Jane Darwell (Delia
  Boylan), Frank Albertson (Jack Mangan), Charles FitzSimmons (Kevin
  McCluskey), Carleton Young (Mr. Winslow), Bob Sweeney (Johnny
  Degnan), Edmund Lowe (Johnny Byrne), William Leslie (Dan
  Herlihy), Ken Curtis (Monseigneur Killian), O. Z. Whitehead
  (Norman Cass Jr.), Dan Borzage (Pete), Jack Pennick (policeman),
  Ruth Clifford (nurse), Harry Tenbrook, Bill Henry, Frank Baker

KOREA: BATTLEGROUND FOR LIBERTY (1959)
Production: U.S. Dept. of Defense
Producers: John Ford and Capt. George O'Brien, USN Ret.

Director: Rear Adm. John Ford, USNR
Cast: George O'Brien (Sgt. Cliff Walker), Kim-Chi Mi, Choi My Ryonk

THE HORSE SOLDIERS (1959)
Production: Mirisch Company/United Artists
Producers: John Lee Mahin and Martin Rackin
Director: John Ford
Screenwriters: John Lee Mahin and Martin Rackin, from the novel by
   Harold Sinclair
Cinematographer: William H. Clothier
Editor: Jack Murray
Art Director: Frank Hotaling
Music: David Buttolph
Cast: John Wayne (Col. John Marlowe), William Holden (Major Hank
   Kendall), Constance Towers (Hannah Hunter), Althea Gibson
   (Lukey), Hoot Gibson (Brown), Anna Lee (Mrs. Buford), Russell
   Simpson (Sheriff Capt. Henry Goodboy), Stan Jones (Gen. U.S.
   Grant), Carleton Young (Col. Jonathan Miles), Basil Ruysdael
   (commandant, Jefferson Military Academy), Willis Bouchey (Col. Phil
   Secord), Ken Curtis (Wilkie), O. Z. Whitehead (Hoppy Hopkins),
   Judson Pratt (Sgt. Major Kirby), Denver Pyle (Jagger Jo), Strother
   Martin (Virgil), Hank Worden (Deacon), Walter Reed (union officer),
   Jack Pennick (Sgt. Major Mitchell), Major Sam Harris (passenger), Bill
   Henry, William Leslie, Dan Borzage

SERGEANT RUTLEDGE (1960)
Production: Ford Productions/Warner Bros.
Producers: Patrick Ford and Willis Goldbeck
Director: John Ford
Screenwriters: Willis Goldbeck and James Warner Bellah
Cinematographer: Bert Glennon
Editor: Jack Murray
Art Director: Eddie Imazu
Music: Howard Jackson
Cast: Jeffrey Hunter (Lt. Tom Cantrell), Constance Towers (Mary
   Beecher), Woody Strode (Sgt. Braxton Rutledge), Billie Burke (Mrs.
   Cordelia Fosgate), Juano Hernandez (Sgt. Matthew Luke Skidmore),
   Willis Bouchey (Col. Otis Fosgate), Carleton Young (Capt. Shattuck),
   Judson Pratt (Lt. Mulqueen), Bill Henry (Capt. Dwyer), Walter Reed
   (Capt. MacAfree), Chuck Hayward (Capt. Dickinson), Mae Marsh
   (Nellie), Fred Libby (Chandler Hubble), Cliff Lyons (Sam Beecher),

Jack Pennick (sergeant), Hank Worden (Laredo), Chuck Roberson (juror), Shug Fisher (Mr. Owens)

TWO RODE TOGETHER (1961)
Production: Ford-Sheptner Productions/Columbia
Producer: Stan Sheptner
Director: John Ford
Screenwriter: Frank S. Nugent, from the novel *Comanche Captives* by
   Will Cook
Cinematographer: Charles Lawton Jr.
Editor: Jack Murray
Art Director: Robert Peterson
Music: George Duning
Cast: James Stewart (Guthrie McCabe), Richard Widmark (Lt. Jim
   Gary), Shirley Jones (Marty Purcell), Linda Cristal (Elena de la
   Madriaga), Andy Devine (Sgt. Darius P. Posey), John McIntire
   (Major Frazer), Paul Birch (Edward Purcell), Willis Bouchey
   (Harry J. Wringle), Henry Brandon (Quanah Parker), Harry Carey
   Jr. (Ortho Clegg), Ken Curtis (Greely Clegg), Olive Carey
   (Abby Frazer), Chet Douglas (Ward Corbey), Annelle Hayes (Belle
   Aragon), David Kent (Running Wolf), Anna Lee (Mrs. Malaprop),
   Jeanette Nolan (Mrs. McCandless), John Qualen (Ole Knudsen),
   Ford Rainey (Henry Clegg), Woody Strode (Stone Calf), O. Z.
   Whitehead (Lt. Chase), Cliff Lyons (William McCandless),
   Mae Marsh (Hannah Clegg), Frank Baker (Capt. Malaprop), Ted
   Knight (Lt. Upton), Jack Pennick (sergeant), Chuck Roberson
   (Comanche), Dan Borzage (post doctor), Ruth Clifford, Bill Henry,
   Major Sam Harris

THE MAN WHO SHOT LIBERTY VALANCE (1962)
Production: Ford Productions/Paramount
Producer: Willis Goldbeck
Director: John Ford
Screenwriters: Willis Goldbeck and James Warner Bellah, from the story
   by Dorothy M. Johnson
Cinematographer: William H. Clothier
Editor: Otho Lovering
Art Directors: Hal Pereira and Eddie Imazu
Music: Cyril J. Mockridge
Cast: John Wayne (Tom Doniphon), James Stewart (Ransom Stoddard),
   Vera Miles (Hallie Stoddard), Lee Marvin (Liberty Valance), Edmond

O'Brien (Dutton Peabody), Andy Devine (Link Appleyard), Ken
Murray (Doc Willoughby), John Carradine (Starbuckle), Jeanette
Nolan (Nora Ericson), John Qualen (Peter Ericson), Willis Bouchey
(Jason Tully), Carleton Young (Maxwell Scott), Woody Strode
(Pompey), Denver Pyle (Amos Carruthers), Strother Martin (Floyd),
Lee Van Cleef (Reese), Robert F. Simon (Handy Strong), O. Z.
Whitehead (Ben Carruthers), Paul Birch (Mayor Winder), Joseph
Hoover (Hasbrouck), Jack Pennick (barman), Anna Lee (passenger),
Frank Baker, Major Sam Harris

HOW THE WEST WAS WON (1962)
Production: Cinerama/Metro-Goldwyn-Mayer
Producer: Bernard Smith
Directors: John Ford ("The Civil War"), George Marshall ("The
   Railroad"), Henry Hathaway ("The Rivers," "The Plains," "The
   Outlaws")
Screenwriter: James R. Webb, suggested by the series in *Life* magazine
Art Directors: George W. Davis, William Ferrari, and Addison Hehr
Music: Alfred Newman and Ken Darby

   "THE CIVIL WAR" EPISODE:
   Cinematographer: Joseph LaShelle
   Cast: George Peppard (Zeb Rawlings), Carroll Baker (Eve Prescott
     Rawlings), Russ Tamblyn (Confederate deserter), Claude Johnson
     (Jeremiah Rawlings), Andy Devine (Cpl. Peterson), Willis
     Bouchey (surgeon), Henry (Harry) Morgan (Gen. U.S. Grant),
     John Wayne (Gen. Sherman), Raymond Massey (Abraham
     Lincoln)

DONOVAN'S REEF (1963)
Production: Ford Productions/Paramount
Producer: John Ford
Director: John Ford
Screenwriters: Frank S. Nugent and James Edward Grant, from the story
   by Edmond Beloin
Cinematographer: William H. Clothier
Editor: Otho Lovering
Art Directors: Hal Pereira and Eddie Imazu
Music: Cyril J. Mockridge
Cast: John Wayne (Michael Patrick "Guns" Donovan), Lee Marvin
   (Thomas Aloysius "Boats" Gilhooley), Elizabeth Allen (Amelia Sarah
   Dedham), Jack Warden (Dr. William Dedham), Cesar Romero

(Marquis André de Lage), Dorothy Lamour (Miss Lafleur), Jacqueline Malouf (Lelani Dedham), Mike Mazurki (Sgt. Menkowicz), Marcel Dalio (Fr. Cluzeot), Jon Fong (Mr. Eu), Cheryline Lee (Sally Dedham), Tim Stafford (Luki Dedham), Frank Baker (Capt. Martin), Edgar Buchanan (Boston notary), Pat Wayne (navy lieutenant), Chuck Roberson (Festus), Mae Marsh, Major Sam Harris (members of family council), Dick Foran and Cliff Lyons (officers), Dan Ford (child)

CHEYENNE AUTUMN (1964)
Production: Ford-Smith Productions/Warner Bros.
Producer: Bernard Smith
Director: John Ford
Screenwriter: James R. Webb, from the book by Mari Sandoz
Cinematographer: William H. Clothier
Editor: Otho Lovering
Art Director: Richard Day
Music: Alex North
Cast: Richard Widmark (Capt. Thomas Archer), Carroll Baker (Deborah Wright), James Stewart (Wyatt Earp), Edward G. Robinson (Secretary of the Interior Carl Schurz), Karl Malden (Capt. Wessels), Sal Mineo (Red Shirt), Dolores Del Rio (Spanish woman), Ricardo Montalban (Little Wolf), Gilbert Roland (Dull Knife), Arthur Kennedy (Doc Holliday), Patrick Wayne (2nd Lt. Scott), Elizabeth Allen (Guinevere Plantagenet), John Carradine (Major Jeff Blair), Victor Jory (Tall Tree), Mike Mazurki (Top Sgt. Stanislaw Wichowsky), George O'Brien (Major Braden), Sean McClory (Dr. O'Carberry), Judson Pratt (Major "Dog" Kelly), Carmen D'Antonio (Pawnee woman), Ken Curtis (Joe), Shug Fisher (Skinny), Chuck Roberson (platoon sergeant), Harry Carey Jr. (Trooper Plumtree), Walter Reed (Lt. Peterson), Willis Bouchey (colonel), Carleton Young (aide to Carl Schurz), Denver Pyle (Sen. Henry), John Qualen (Svenson), Dan Borzage (trooper); narrated by Spencer Tracy and Richard Widmark

YOUNG CASSIDY (1965)
Production: Sextant Films/Metro-Goldwyn-Mayer
Producers: Robert D. Graff and Robert Emmett Ginna
Directors: Jack Cardiff and John Ford (Ford began the film and shot several scenes, but then fell ill and was replaced by Cardiff)
Screenwriter: John Whiting, from the autobiography *Mirror in My House* by Sean O'Casey
Cinematographer: Ted Scaife

Editor: Anne V. Coates
Art Director: Michael Stringer
Music: Sean O'Riada
Cast: Rod Taylor (Sean Cassidy), Maggie Smith (Nora), Julie Christie (Daisy Battles), Flora Robson (Mrs. Cassidy), Sian Phillips (Ella), Michael Redgrave (William Butler Yeats), Dame Edith Evans (Lady Gregory), Jack McGowran (Archie), T. P. McKenna (Tom), Julie Ross (Sara), Robin Sumner (Michael), Philip O'Flynn (Mick Mullen), Pauline Delaney (Bessie Ballynoy), members of the Abbey Theatre

SEVEN WOMEN (1965)
Production: Ford-Smith Productions/Metro-Goldwyn-Mayer
Producer: Bernard Smith
Director: John Ford
Screenwriters: Janet Green and John McCormick, from the story "Chinese Finale" by Norah Lofts
Cinematographer: Joseph LaShelle
Editor: Otho Lovering
Art Directors: George W. Davis and Eddie Imazu
Music: Elmer Bernstein
Cast: Anne Bancroft (Dr. D. R. Cartwright), Margaret Leighton (Agatha Andrews), Flora Robson (Miss Binns), Sue Lyon (Emma Clark), Mildred Dunnock (Jane Argent), Betty Field (Florrie Pether), Anna Lee (Mrs. Russell), Eddie Albert (Charles Pether), Mike Mazurki (Tunga Khan), Woody Strode (lean warrior), Jane Chang (Miss Ling), Hans William Lee (Kim)

VIETNAM! VIETNAM! (1972)
Production: United States Information Agency
Executive Producer: John Ford
Producer: Bruce Herschensohn
Director: Sherman Beck
Editor: Leon Selditz
Narrated by Charlton Heston

Select Bibliography

WESTERNS AND AMERICAN CULTURE

Aquila, Richard, ed. *Wanted Dead or Alive: The American West in Popular Culture.* Urbana and Chicago: University of Chicago Press, 1996.

Bergon, Frank, and Zeese Papanikolas, eds. *Looking Far West: The Search for the American West in History, Myth, and Literature.* New York: New American Library, 1978.

Durham, Philip, and Everett L. Jones, eds. *The Western Story: Fact, Fiction, and Myth.* New York: Harcourt Brace Jovanovich, 1975.

Fiedler, Leslie. *The Return of the Vanishing American.* New York: Stein and Day, 1960.

Fischer, Christiane, ed. *Let Them Speak for Themselves: Women in the American West.* New York: E. P. Dutton, 1977.

Hitt, Jim. *The American West from Fiction (1823–1976) into Film (1909–1986).* Jefferson, N.C.: McFarland, 1990.

Rossi, Paul, and David C. Hunt. *The Art of the Old West.* New York: Knopf, 1971.

Slotkin, Richard. *Gunfighter Nation: The Myth of the Frontier in Twentieth-Century America.* New York: Atheneum, 1992.

Smith, Henry Nash. *Virgin Land: The American West as Symbol and Myth.* New York: Vintage, 1950.

Taft, Robert. *Artists and Illustrators of the Old West, 1850–1900.* New York: Charles Scribner's Sons, 1953.

Taylor, George Rogers, ed. *The Turner Thesis: Concerning the Role of the Frontier in American History.* Boston: D. C. Heath, 1956.

Tompkins, Jane. *West of Everything: The Inner Life of the Western.* New York: Oxford University Press, 1992.

Turner, Frederick Jackson. *Frontier and Section,* ed. Ray Allen Billington. Englewood Cliffs, N.J.: Prentice-Hall, 1961.

Tuska, Jon, and Nick Pierarski. *The Frontier Experience: A Reader's Guide to the Life and Literature of the American West.* Jefferson, N.C.: McFarland, 1984.

WESTERN FILM

Bataille, Gretchen M., and Charles L. P. Silet, eds. *The Pretend Indians: Images of Native Americans in the Movies*. Ames: Iowa State University Press, 1980.

Bazin, André. "The Evolution of the Western." In *What is Cinema?* vol. 2, pp. 149–57. Berkeley: University of California Press, 1971. Reprinted in *Movies and Methods*, ed. Bill Nichols, pp. 150–7. Berkeley: University of California Press, 1976.

"The Western, or the American Film *par excellence*." In *What is Cinema?* vol. 2, pp. 140–8. Berkeley: University of California Press, 1971.

Buscombe, Ed, ed. *The BFI Companion to the Western*. New York: Atheneum, 1990.

Buscombe, Ed, and Robert E. Pearson, eds. *Back in the Saddle Again: New Essays on the Western*. London: British Film Institute, 1998.

Cameron, Ian, and Douglas Pye, eds. *The Book of Westerns*. New York: Continuum Press, 1996.

Cawelti, John G. *The Six-Gun Mystique*, rev. ed. Bowling Green, Ohio: Popular Press, 1985.

Coyne, Michael. *The Crowded Prairie: American National Identity in the Hollywood Western*. London: I. B. Taurus, 1998.

Fenin, George N., and William K. Everson. *The Western: From Silents to the Seventies*. New York: Bonanza Books, 1973.

Frayling, Christopher. "The American Western and American Society." *Cinema, Politics and Society in America*, ed. Philip Davies and Brian Neve, pp. 136–62. New York: St. Martin's Press, 1981.

French, Philip. *Westerns*. New York: Viking, 1974.

Gallagher, Tag. "Shoot-Out at the Genre Corral: Problems in the Evolution of the Western." *Film Genre Reader 2*, ed. Barry Keith Grant, pp. 246–60. Austin: University of Texas Press, 1995.

Hardy, Phil. *The Western: The Complete Film Sourcebook*. New York: Morrow, 1983.

Kitses, Jim. *Horizons West*. Bloomington: Indiana University Press, 1970.

Kitses, Jim, and Gregg Rickman, eds. *The Western Reader*. New York: Limelight Press, 1998.

Langman, Larry. *A Guide to Silent Westerns*. Westport, Conn.: Greenwood Press, 1992.

Lenihan, John H. *Showdown: Confronting Modern America in the Western Film*. Chicago: University of Chicago Press, 1980.

McDonald, Archie P. *Shooting Stars: Heroes and Heroines of Western Film*. Bloomington: Indiana University Press, 1987.

Mitchell, Lee Clark. *Westerns: Making the Man in Fiction and Film*. Chicago: University of Chicago Press, 1996.

Nachbar, Jack. *Western Films: An Annotated Critical Bibliography*. New York: Garland, 1975.

Nachbar, Jack, et al. *Western Films 2: An Annotated Critical Bibliography from 1974 to 1987*. New York: Garland, 1988.

Nachbar, Jack, ed. *Focus on the Western*. Englewood Cliffs, N.J.: Prentice-Hall, 1974.

O'Connor, John E. *The Hollywood Indian: Stereotypes of Native Americans in Films*. Trenton: New Jersey State Museum, 1980.

Parish, James R. *Great Western Stars*. New York: Grosset & Dunlop, 1976.

Pilkington, William T., and Don Graham, eds. *Western Movies*. Albuquerque: University of New Mexico Press, 1979.

Rainey, Buck. *Saddle Aces of the Cinema*. San Diego: A. S. Barnes, 1980.

Rothel, David. *The Singing Cowboys*. South Brunswick, N.J., and New York: A. S. Barnes, 1978.

Sarf, Wayne Michael. *God Bless You, Buffalo Bill: A Layman's Guide to History and the Western Film*. Rutherford, N.J.: Fairleigh Dickinson University Press, 1983.

Schatz, Thomas. *Hollywood Genres: Formulas, Filmmaking and the Studio System*. New York: Random House, 1981.

"The Western." In *Handbook of American Film Genres*, ed. Wes D. Gehring, pp. 25–46. New York: Greenwood Press, 1988.

Stedman, Raymond William. *Shadows of the Indian*. Norman: University of Oklahoma Press, 1986.

Tuska, Jon. *The American West in Film: Critical Approaches to the Western*. New York: Greenwood Press, 1985.

Warshow, Robert. "Movie Chronicle: The Westerner." In *The Immediate Experience*, pp. 35– 54. New York: Atheneum, 1971.

Wright, Will. *Six Guns and Society: A Structural Study of the Western*. Berkeley: University of California Press, 1976.

JOHN FORD

Aleiss, Angela. "A Race Divided: The Indian Westerns of John Ford." *American Indian Culture and Research Journal* 18 (1994): 167–86.

Anderson, Lindsay. *About John Ford*. London: Plexus, 1981.

Baxter, John. *The Cinema of John Ford*. New York: A. S. Barnes, 1971.

Bogdanovich, Peter. *John Ford*. Berkeley: University of California Press, 1968.

Budd, Michael. "Genre, Director and Stars in John Ford's Westerns: Fonda, Wayne, Stewart and Widmark." *Wide Angle* 2, no. 4 (1978): 52–61.

"A Home in the Wilderness: Visual Imagery in John Ford's Westerns." *Cinema Journal* 16, no. 1 (Fall 1996): 62–75.

Carey, Harry Jr. *Company of Heroes: My Life as an Actor in the John Ford Stock Company*. Metuchen, N.J.: Scarecrow Press, 1984.

Darby, William. *John Ford's Westerns: A Thematic Analysis, with a Filmography*. Jefferson, N.C.: McFarland, 1996.

Davis, Ronald L. *John Ford: Hollywood's Old Master*. Norman: University of Oklahoma Press, 1995.

Dempsey, Michael. "John Ford: A Reassessment." *Film Quarterly* 28, no. 4 (Summer 1975): 2–15.

Ellis, Kirk. "On the Warpath: John Ford and the Indians." *Journal of Popular Film and Television* 8, no. 2 (1980): 34–41.

Eyman, Scott. *Print the Legend: The Life and Times of John Ford*. New York: Simon and Schuster, 1999.

Ford, Dan. *Pappy: The Life of John Ford*. Englewood Cliffs, N.J.: Prentice-Hall, 1979.

Gallagher, Tag. *John Ford: The Man and His Films*. Berkeley: University of California Press, 1986.

Kaminsky, Stuart M. "The Genre Director: Character Types in the Films of John Ford." Chap. 11 in *American Film Genres: Approaches to a Critical Theory of Popular Film*. Dayton, Ohio: Pflaum, 1974.

Leutrat, Jean-Louis, and Suzanne Liandrat-Guigues. "John Ford and Monument Valley," in *Back in the Saddle Again: New Essays on the Western*, ed. Edward Buscombe and Roberta A. Pearson, pp. 160–9. London: British Film Institute, 1998.

Levy, Bill. *John Ford: A Bio-bibliography*. Westport, Conn.: Greenwood Press, 1998.

Luhr, William, and Peter Lehman. *Authorship and Narrative in the Cinema*. New York: Capricorn, 1977.

Maltby, Richard. "A Better Sense of History: John Ford and the Indians." *The Book of Westerns*, ed. Ian Cameron and Douglas Pye, pp. 34–49. New York: Continuum, 1996.

Marshall, George J. "Ford on Ford." *Films in Review* (June/July, 1964): 321–32.

McBride, Joseph, and Michael Wilmington. *John Ford*. New York: Da Capo, 1975.

McCarthy, Todd. "John Ford and Monument Valley." *American Film* 3, no. 7 (1978): 10–16.

Nolly, Ken. "Printing the Legend in the Age of MX: Reconsidering Ford's Military Trilogy." *Literature/Film Quarterly* 14, no. 2 (1986): 82–8.

"The Representation of Conquest: John Ford and the Hollywood Indian, 1939–1964." *Hollywood's Indian: The Portrayal of the Native American in Film*, ed. Peter C. Rollins and John E. O'Connor, pp. 73–90. Lexington: University of Kentucky Press, 1998.

Pechter, William S. "A Persistence of Vision." *Twenty-Four Times a Second: Films and Film-Makers*, pp. 226–41. New York: Harper & Row, 1971.

Place, J. A. *The Non-Western Films of John Ford*. New York: Citadel Press, 1979.

The Western Films of John Ford. Secaucus, N.J.: Citadel Press, 1975.

Sarris, Andrew. *The John Ford Movie Mystery*. London: Secker & Warburg/British Film Institute, 1976.

Sinclair, Andrew. *John Ford: A Biography*. New York: Dial Press, 1979.

Siska, William C. "Realism and Romance in the Films of John Ford." *Wide Angle* 2, no. 4 (1978): 8–14.

Stowell, Peter. *John Ford*. Boston: Twayne, 1986.

Studlar, Gaylyn, and Matthew Bernstein, eds. *John Ford Made Westerns: Filming the Legend in the Sound Era*. Bloomington and Indianapolis: Indiana University Press, 2001.

White, Armond. "Stepping Forward, Looking Back." *Film Comment* 36, no. 2 (March/April 2000): 32–9.

Wollen, Peter. *Signs and Meaning in the Cinema*, rev. ed. Bloomington and London: Indiana University Press/British Film Institute, 1972.

Wood, Robin. " 'Shall We Gather at the River?': The Late Films of John Ford." *Film Comment* 7, no. 3 (Fall 1971): 8–17.

"John Ford." *Cinema: A Critical Dictionary*, Vol. 1, ed. Richard Roud, pp. 371–87. New York: Viking, 1980.

STAGECOACH

Action 6, no. 5 (September–October 1971). Special Issue on Ford and *Stagecoach*. Reprinted in *Directors in Action*, ed. Bob Thomas, pp. 139–73. Indianapolis and New York: Bobbs-Merrill, 1973.

Anobile, Richard J. *John Ford's Stagecoach*. New York: Avon Books, 1975.

Browne, Nick. "The Spectator-in-the-Text: The Rhetoric of *Stagecoach*." *Film Quarterly* 21, no. 2 (Winter 1975–1976): 26–38.

Buscombe, Ed. *Stagecoach*. London: British Film Institute, 1992.

Clandfield, David. "The Onomastic Code of *Stagecoach*." *Literature/Film Quarterly* 5, no. 2 (Spring 1979): 174–80. Reprinted as *"Stagecoach"* in *Western Movies*, ed. William T. Pilkington and Don Graham, pp. 31–9. Albuquerque: University of New Mexico Press, 1979.

Ford, John, and Dudley Nichols. *Stagecoach*. New York: Simon and Schuster, 1971.

Nichols, Dudley. *Stagecoach*, in *Twenty Best Film Plays*, ed. John Gassner and Dudley Nichols. New York: Crown, 1943.

Skerry, Philip J. "Space and Place in John Ford's *Stagecoach* and *My Darling Clementine*." *New Orleans Review* 14, no. 2 (1987): 87–91.

Solomon, Stanley J. *Beyond Formula: American Film Genres*. New York: Harcourt Brace Jovanovich, 1976.

Index

Air Force, 52, 75n
All Quiet on the Western Front, 94
Altman, Rick, 84, 86, 87, 97, 100, 106–7
Anderson, Lindsay, 17, 75n8
Anderson, Marian, 103, 111n34
Anderson, Sherwood, 96
Argosy Pictures, 44
auteurism, 13, 44, 52–3, 56, 75–6n11, 84–5, 105–6
Authors League of America (ALA), 54
authorship, 13, 18, 48–81

B Westerns, 2, 4, 21, 24, 28–31, 42, 119, 155n5. *See also* Westerns
Balio, Tino, 34
Bancroft, George, 181, 182
Barthes, Roland, 16
Bataan, 46n19
Battle of Elderbush Gulch, The, 46n20, 131n15
Baxter, John, 17
Baxter, Warner, 31
Bazin, André, 2, 18, 22
Beard, Charles, 69
Beau Geste (1939), 34
Berg, Charles Ramirez, 144
Bernstein, Matthew, 157n32
Biberman, Herbert, 55
Big Jim McLain, 5
Big Trail, The, 5, 23
Binger, Ray, 180, 183
Birth of a Nation, The, 117, 118, 123

Bogart, Humphrey, 25, 91
Bogdanovich, Peter, 6, 15, 17, 45n
Bond, Ward, 57
Bordwell, David, 106
Born Reckless, 52
Breen, Joseph, 66, 157n32
Bringing Up Baby, 52, 60
Browne, Nick, 17–18, 168, 172–3
Burnham, Michelle, 116–17
Buscombe, Ed, 1, 11, 17, 18–19n4, 35, 44n1, 78n34 , 87, 92, 162–4

Cagney, James, 25, 31–2, 91
Canutt, Yakima, 3, 29, 49
Canyon Passage, 58
Capra, Frank, 45n7, 52, 58, 68, 74n6, 75n11, 98
Captain Blood, 24–5
captivity narratives, 116–17
Carefree, 52, 60
Carradine, John, 71, 181
Carringer, Robert, 49, 74
Cavell, Stanley, 158, 176n1
Charge of the Light Brigade, The, 24–5, 33
Cheyenne Autumn, 114, 128
Chief Big Tree, 114
Churchill, Berton, 28–9, 71, 73, 78n38, 181
Cimarron, 23, 91
Citizen Kane, 3, 49
Clair, René, 52
Colbert, Claudette, 85, 96

combat films, 43–4
Coolidge, Calvin, 63
Cooper, Gary, 4
Cooper, Merian C., 6, 23, 24, 44, 77n32
Cooper, James Fenimore, 116, 145–7, 148, 150, 154, 156n28
Corliss, Richard, 53, 76n12
Cortez, Ricardo, 114, 130n1
Coyne, Michael, 78n38
Crowther, Bosley, 53
Cukor, George, 52
Curtiz, Michael, 25, 32, 52

Dagle, Joan, 137
Dances with Wolves, 130n6
Dark Command, 2
Darwell, Jane, 157n34
Davis, Ronald L., 8
Dead End, 29
de Havilland, Olivia, 24–5
de Maupassant, Guy, 6, 27, 45
DeMille, Cecil B., 2, 31, 52, 117, 119, 120, 122, 128
Destry Rides Again, 149
Devine, Andy, 181
Dietrich, Marlene, 149, 167
disaster films, 3, 27
Dodge City, 2, 21, 24, 25, 29, 30–2, 34, 36–7, 42, 91
Donovan's Reef, 128
Dramatists Guild, 54
Drums Along the Mohawk (novel), 83, 96–7, 105, 108n5
Drums Along the Mohawk, 4, 8, 21, 34, 35, 42, 82, 83–4, 85–7, 94–101, 104

Edmonds, Walter D., 83, 96–7, 105, 108n5
Emerson, Ralph Waldo, 176n1
Everson, William K., 32–3
Eyman, Scott, 57, 76n13, 77n32

Fenin, George N., 32–3
Fiedler, Leslie, 156n28
Five Came Back, 3
Flynn, Errol, 2, 24–5, 29, 31–2, 34
Fonda, Henry, 35–6, 43, 44, 85, 96
Ford, Dan, 7
Ford, Francis, 28

Fort Apache, 14, 44, 80n53, 155–6n13, 157n34
Foster, Stephen, 9
Foucault, Michel, 115, 117, 119–20, 127, 129
Four Men and a Prayer, 94
Frontier Marshal, 21, 29
Fugitive, The, 52

Gallagher, Tag, 13, 160–2, 165–6, 167–8, 173, 176
gangster films, 32, 35
genre, 97–8, 106
Glennon, Bert, 180, 183
Goldwyn, Sam, 24, 98
Gone with the Wind, 9, 46–7n33, 105, 107, 149, 154n33
Goulding, Harry, 7
Grand Hotel, 3, 27, 46n18, 179
Grant, Barry Keith, 145
Grapes of Wrath, The, 3, 35, 43, 133, 160
Griffith, D. W., 117, 123, 131n15
Green Berets, The, 5
Gruenberg, Louis, 71
Gunga Din, 34

Hageman, Richard, 9, 71, 80n53
Hale, Alan, 78n39
Harling, Frank, 71
Hart, James D., 116
Hart, William S., 33, 35
Harte, Bret, 3, 27
Hawks, Howard, 5, 52, 60
Haycox, Ernest, 6, 14, 23, 26–7, 45n6 & n16, 49–50, 58, 60, 61, 74n4, 77n26, 119
Hell's Angels, 94
Hepburn, Katharine, 167
Herrmann, Bernard, 49
Hickock, Wild Bill, 16
Higashi, Sumiko, 128
High Sierra, 35
Hitchcock, Alfred, 2, 45n7, 74, 75–6n11, 173, 177n9
Hitler, Adolph, 70
Holt, Jack, 28
Holt, Tim, 28
Hombre, 2
horror films, 118

How Green Was My Valley, 160
Hurricane, The, 3, 6, 24, 27, 52, 60, 87, 92–4, 98, 128

Informer, The, 6, 52, 54, 85, 87, 92–4
International Alliance of Theatrical Stage Employees (IATSE), 55
Iron Horse, The, 6, 51, 119
It's a Wonderful Life, 58

Jacobs, Lewis, 75n10
Jefferson, Thomas, 134–5, 139
Jesse James, 21, 24, 30–2, 34–6, 42, 91
Jessel, George, 55
Johnson, Noble, 114
Judge Priest, 52, 78n39, 94, 114

Kapsis, Robert, 76n11
Kazan, Elia, 52
Keaton, Buster, 164
Kentucky Pride, 13
King, Henry, 32
King Kong (1933), 6

Lady Vanishes, The, 27
Lake, Stuart, 44
Lang, Fritz, 16, 36, 52, 56
Last of the Mohicans (novel), 116
Last Hurrah, The, 114
Leatherstocking Tales, The, 145–6, 154, 156n28
Lehman, Ernest, 74
Leipold, John, 71
Let Freedom Ring, 85
Little Big Man, 130n6
Lives of a Bengal Lancer, 33
Long Voyage Home, The, 52
Lord, Robert, 24–5
Lost Horizon, 27
Lost Patrol, The, 6, 27–8, 46n19, 52, 94
Lovering, Otho, 181
Lubitsch, Ernst, 98

Maland, Charles J., 6–7, 10, 18
Man of Conquest, 21, 31
Man Called Horse, A, 130n6
Man from Laramie, The, 16
Man in the Saddle, 58
Man Who Shot Liberty Valance, The, 4, 16–17, 21, 98, 150, 160

Mann, Anthony, 16, 52
March, Frederic, 56
Mary of Scotland, 52, 167
Mayer, Frank, 181
Mazurki, Mike, 114
McBride, Joseph, 4, 15, 17, 27, 37, 41
McCarey, Leo, 52
McPherson, Colvin, 106–7
Meek, Donald, 181, 182
Meet John Doe, 68
melodrama, 3, 158, 159–60, 176
Men without Women, 52
Merriam, Frank, 56
MGM, 24
Mineo, Sal, 114
Mitchell, Thomas, 9, 27, 29, 71–3, 80n57, 93, 181, 182
Monogram Pictures, 80n57
Montalban, Ricardo, 114
Monument Valley, 4, 7–8, 9, 11, 16, 25, 29, 37, 38, 91, 114–15, 135, 181
Mourning Becomes Electra, 52
Movie-goer, The, 1–2
Mr. Deeds Goes to Town, 68
Muni, Paul, 24
Munson, Ona, 149
My Darling Clementine, 4, 44, 114, 143, 144, 150

Native Land, 76n17
Nichols, Dudley, 6–7, 23, 25–9, 41, 44, 46n18, 48–81, 85, 157n32, 161, 165, 179–80, 182
Now, Voyager, 158
Nugent, Frank S., 23, 31–2, 48, 74, 85, 105–6, 108–9n9

O'Hara, Maureen, 167
Oklahoma Kid, The, 21, 25, 31, 35, 91
Olson, Culbert, 56
Olympia, 57
omnibus films, 3, 27

Paramount Pictures, 24, 80n53
Parrington, V. L., 69–70, 79n49, 80n50
Pells, Richard, 51, 56
Pennick, Jack, 79n46
Percy, Walker, 1
Perez, Gilberto, 101–2, 104, 107

Philadelphia Story, The, 158
Pilgrimage, 52
Pinky, 52
Pioneer Pictures, 23
Place, Janey, 11, 13
Plainsman, The, 24
Platt, Louise, 71, 167, 181, 182
Plough and the Stars, The, 52
Plunkett, Walter, 49
Poague, Leland, 8–9, 18
Popular Front, 48–81
populism, 74–5n6
Power, Tyrone, 35
Production Code of America (PCA),
    66, 85
Psycho (1960), 2

Raiders of the Lost Ark, 3
Rancho Notorious, 16
Red River, 5, 15
Renoir, Jean, 52
Republic Pictures, 4, 7, 29
Return of the Cisco Kid, The, 31
Return of Frank James, The, 32,
    35–6
Reynolds, Walter, 181
Richards, Jeffrey, 74n6
Riefenstahl, Leni, 57
Rio Grande, 44
Riskin, Robert, 52, 75n10
Ritt, Martin, 2
RKO Pictures, 27
road movies, 3
Road to Glory, The, 94
Robin Hood, 25
Rogers, Lee, 106
Rogers, Will, 79n47
romantic comedy, 159–60, 176
Roosevelt, Franklin Delano, 51, 57,
    61–3, 70, 79n42, 80n52
Rothman, William, 10, 13, 18
Rowlandson, Mary, 116
Rules of the Game, 160
Run of the Arrow, 130n6

Sahara, 46n19
Said, Edward, 127–8
Sandburg, Carl, 96
Sand Pebbles, The, 117
Sandrich, Mark, 60

Sante Fe, 25
Sarris, Andrew, 4, 15, 17, 52–3, 75n8,
    76n12, 78n38
Scarlet Street, 52
Schatz, Thomas, 2, 3, 18
Schwartz, Nancy, 55
Scott, Ned, 183
Screen Playwrights (SP), 55, 76n17
Screen Writers Guild (SWG), 53–6,
    61–2, 67, 69–70, 76n17
Searchers, The, 11, 17, 47n45, 106, 114,
    117–19, 128–9
Seas Beneath, 52
Selznick, David O., 6, 23, 77n32, 107
Selznick International Pictures (SIP),
    23–4
Sergeant Rutledge, 114, 128
Seven Women, 114, 128
Shadow of a Doubt, 177n9
Shanghai Express, 27
Sheehan, Winfield, 51
Sherlock Jr., 164
She Wore a Yellow Ribbon, 4, 44, 80n53,
    114
Shootist, The, 5
Shuken, Leo, 71
Siegel, Don, 5
Sinclair, Andrew, 124
Sirk, Douglas, 75n11
Slotkin, Richard, 33, 34–6, 41, 47n38,
    102, 118–19, 154, 155n5
Smith, Henry Nash, 137, 145–6, 150
Spencer, Dorothy, 30
Spielberg, Steven, 3
"Stage to Lordsburg" (story), 6, 23,
    25–7, 49–50, 58–61, 74n4. *See also*
    Haycox, Ernest
Stand Up and Fight, 21
Stanwyck, Barbara, 167
Starship Troopers, 117
Steamboat Round the Bend, 52, 79n47,
    114
Steinbeck, John, 43
Stella Dallas, 175
Stepin Fetchit, 114
Stern, Philip Van Doren, 58
Stowell, Peter, 10, 99
Strand, Paul, 76n19
Strode, Woody, 114
Studlar, Gaylyn, 10, 18

Sturges, Preston, 52
Submarine Patrol, 87, 92–4, 110n24
Summerville, Slim, 182
Sun Shines Bright, The, 114

Taylor, Robert, 31
Telotte, J. P., 15, 18
Temple, Shirley, 33
Texas Rangers, The, 24
They Died with Their Boots On, 25, 46n19
They Made Me a Criminal, 35
Third Man, The, 1
3 Bad Men, 6
3 Godfathers (1948), 13, 14, 157n34
Tin Star, The, 75n9
Toland, Gregg, 49, 71–3
Tompkins, Jane, 118, 129
Trevor, Claire, 2, 23, 29, 39, 71, 77n32, 80n57, 89, 167, 180–1, 182, 183
Triumph of the Will, 57
Trooper Hook, 130n6
Trotti, Lamar, 52
Turner, Frederick Jackson, 10–11, 91, 104, 132, 133, 135–9, 147, 151, 154
20th Century–Fox, 23, 24, 43, 44, 51, 77n32, 95–6, 104–5
Two Rode Together, 114, 128, 130n6
Tyler, Tom, 182

Union Pacific, 2, 21, 24, 31–2, 34, 37, 58, 117–30
United Artists, 6, 18–19n4, 25, 95, 98, 104–5

Valentino, Rudolph, 130n1
Vanishing American, The, 7

Virginia City, 25
Virginian, The (novel), 151

Wagon Master, 3, 17, 80n53, 106
Wallace, Henry A., 56
Wallis, Hal, 24, 25
Walsh, Raoul, 5
Wanger, Walter, 4, 6, 23, 25, 29–30, 56, 61, 66, 77n32, 85, 92, 97, 98, 167, 179, 182
war films, 43–4, 94
Warner Bros., 24, 32
Warner, Jack, 25
Wayne, John, 2, 4–5, 23, 28, 29, 38–9, 57, 71, 77n32, 80n57, 89, 167, 181, 182
Weaver, Mary, 95
Wee Willie Winkie, 33, 94
Welles, Orson, 3, 49
Wellman, William, 45n7
westerns, 2, 4, 6, 11–12, 21–2, 24, 28–36, 41–2, 115–20, 127–8, 129–30, 136, 145, 147, 155n5, 183
Wilder, Billy, 52
Williams, Raymond, 49
Williams, John, 116
Wilmington, Michael, 4, 15, 17, 27, 37, 41
Winchell, Walter, 111n34
Wister, Owen, 151
Wood, Robin, 47n38, 133, 153, 154n38

Young Mr. Lincoln, 8, 18, 35, 43, 83, 84, 85, 87, 94–9, 101, 103–5, 156n14, 160

Zanuck, Darryl F., 24, 43, 44, 85, 96, 97